Sol y Mar

Ana Eli Yansa

Copyright © 2011 **Ileana Filomeno**
All rights reserved.

ISBN: 0615538304
ISBN-13: 9780615538303

Table of Contents

Acknowledgment v

Reconocimiento vii

Solimar's Symphony 1

Marisol's Misery 15

Solimar S. Santana Sleeps 31

Marisol's Melancholia 47

Solimar Meets Saúl 49

Marisol Meets Marisol 63

Saúl Meets Solimar 67

Everybody Meets Roberto 79

Sol y Mar 93

Home Meets Hell's Angel 119

Existence Begins Where Life Ends 129

Life takes on Life 147

Nocturnal Life 181

The Enchanted Island 189

La Isla not so Bonita 203

Mar y Sol 231

Dedication 253

Nurturing 281

Author's Note 300

Glossary 301

Acknowledgment

This novel should have been published many years ago. It is to say that I should have trusted the talent that God deposited in me since I was but a young woman who could see situations in various dimensions and translate them into a written word. Therefore, I begin by thanking Him first, acknowledging that I never abandoned the idea of one day publicly conveying the message of gratitude I feel for the cosmic force that moves me forward. As a Christian, I call him Jesus. As a Latina, I call him Papa Dios; as a human I call him God to further acknowledge the wide umbrella he has opened to shield humanity from the storms.

I thank my mother, Francisca Rios, if for nothing else but to see her name in print although God knows that a woman of valor, faith, strength, weaknesses and character cannot be pigeon holed, nor are there words sufficient that can describe the fortitude, joy and guidance she has plentifully lavished upon me, although at this writing, she still doesn't know of my endeavor. You see, it is a surprise, or rather a gift.

I thank my daughter, Amanda Eve, for her laughter, which is mine – for the twinkle in her eye, which also belongs to me and her willingness to fight for herself and still stop long enough to help others along the way. I thank her for letting me be her mother and I acknowledge her father's contribution in also helping her become a woman of strength and kindness.

I thank my mentor, editor and friend, Hector Valle, who has guided me through this maze through his talents, patience and personal belief in my person. I hope to one day collaborate with him.

I thank those who have walked side by side with me in my various spiritual journeys. Those that have prayed with me, gone to war for me and instructed me on how to maintain faith and lightheartedness, even in the darkest hours.

I thank those that have supported my natural journey; always wondering what I was up to, never judging or questioning my mission. Those would be my true friends.

I thank my muse, who shall remain nameless, who appears to me whenever she chooses and forces my attention on the most poignant and sometimes heart wrenching things you could imagine, forcing upon me a sensitivity that I would not otherwise possess, rescuing me from walking among, or becoming one of the living dead.

Lastly, I want to thank the Eagle that soars over our heads, although it is little more than a bird of prey, utilized as an insignia of greatness, it is so not great at all. It is a vulture albeit one with power, strength and beautiful plumage. What the Eagle has revealed to me has been more than enough. Enough to keep my eyes on the prize; enough to keep my eyes upon the horizon with hope and prayer for all of mankind; enough to motivate me to bring to you Sol y Mar; enough to know that eagles, like humans perish, but the Sun and Sea are forever God's reminder that He, in fact, exists and how so erroneously we identify with irrelevant symbols that mark our journey.

Reconocimiento

Esta novela debería haberse publicado muchos años atrás. Debo decir que debería haber confiado en el talento que Dios depositó en mí desde que yo no era más que una jovencita que podía ver situaciones en varias dimensiones y traducirlas a palabra escrita. Por eso, empiezo a agradecerle primero a Él, reconociendo que nunca abandoné la idea de transmitir públicamente el mensaje de gratitud que siento por la fuerza cósmica que me mueve adelante. Como cristiana, le llamo Jesús. Como latina, le llamo Papá Dios. Como humana, le llamo Dios para reconocer además los amplios paraguas que Él ha abierto para proteger a la humanidad de las tormentas.

Doy las gracias a mi madre, Francisca Ríos, aunque sea sólo por ver su nombre impreso. Dios sabe que una mujer con su valor, fe y fuerza, con sus debilidades también y su carácter, no puede ser encasillado, y no hay suficientes palabras para describir la fortaleza, la alegría y los consejos que me transmitió tan generosamente, aunque, a pesar de este escrito, ella no conoce mi esfuerzo. Como veis, es una sorpresa o acaso un regalo.

Doy las gracias a mi hija, Amanda Eve, por su risa, que es la mía, por el centelleo de sus ojos, que también son míos, y por su disposición para luchar por sí misma y aún así detenerse lo suficiente como para poder ayudar a los demás. Le doy gracias por permitirme ser su madre y reconozco la contribución de su padre en ayudarla también a convertirse en una mujer fuerte, llena de valentía y sobre todo, humilde y buena.

Doy gracias a mi mentor, editor y amigo, Héctor Valle, que me ha guiado a través de este laberinto con sus talentos, su paciencia y su creencia personal en mí. Espero poder colaborar algún día junto con él.

Doy las gracias a aquéllos que han andado junto a mí en mis varios viajes espirituales. Aquéllos que han rezado conmigo, que han ido a la guerra por mí y me han instruido en cómo mantener la fe y el corazón ligero, incluso en las horas oscuras.

Doy las gracias a aquéllos que han apoyado mi viaje natural, siempre preguntándose en qué andaba yo, sin juzgar ni cuestionar nunca mi misión; Ésos son mis amigos verdaderos.

Doy las gracias a mi musa, que permanecerá sin nombre, que se me aparece cada vez que le place y centra mi atención en las cosas más dolorosas y desgarradoras que podáis imaginar, obligándome a una sensibilidad que de otro modo yo no poseería, rescatándome de caminar entre los muertos en vida o de convertirme en uno de ellos.

Por último, quiero dar las gracias al Águila que planea sobre nuestras cabezas, aunque no sea poco más que un ave de presa. Aún siendo utilizado como insignia de grandeza, no es en absoluto tan grande. Es un ave con poder, fuerza y un bello plumaje. Lo que el Águila me ha revelado es más que suficiente para mí. Suficiente para mantener mis ojos en la recompensa; suficiente para mantener mis ojos fijos sobre el horizonte, con esperanza y oración para toda la humanidad; suficiente para motivarme para traeros Sol y Mar; suficiente para saber que las Águilas, como los seres humanos, perecen, pero el sol y el mar son el recordatorio de que Dios, de hecho, existe, y de cuán erróneamente nos identificamos con símbolos tan opuestos a la fe para cambiar nuestra existencia hacia algo mejor.

Solimar's Symphony

    Names have much to do with people's personalities; it seems to be a constant badgering into your soul every time someone refers to you, addresses you or otherwise disrespects you. People with beautiful names tend to walk with a little more pride; people with common names behave, well, commonly. Solimar was reflecting on these thoughts as she emerged from the ocean, forcefully breaking through the bit of its vastness she occupied to catch a breath of air and bask in the sun. From a distance a man sitting on the rocks, caught a glimpse of her, and watched as she powerfully broke through the waves gloriously revealing her splendor and strength. He quickly replaced his shades that had been, up until then, resting on the top of his head, hoping to get a clearer view through the tinted prescription lenses. His heart skipped as he flicked his cigarette into the ocean. He had fully expected to realize his childhood dream and actually see a mermaid. He still believed in them, in their cry, their incomprehensible beauty, their maritime legend and the absolute possibility that yes, they very well could exist. Why not? But then he noticed her extraordinarily long tanned legs and smirked while thinking 'at least I can talk to this one' and begun to take that uncertain walk towards the phenomenon he so very wanted to meet in person. He was about a quarter of a mile away, having gauged her position through a telescope stationed on the rocks for tourists. He didn't care that he had to walk in the sun that was beating down on humanity with no reprieve and even less consideration; he was determined to meet that which came forth from the ocean, whatever it was, fins or not. Unbeknownst to him, he started that long arduous walk towards destiny hoping to meet a woman whose name is Solimar. Solimar meaning Sun and Sea and she ardently worshipped both.

In the interim, Solimar was somewhat lost in thought; she loved that her dad had a fantastic last name, which is the only thing the bastard had ever given to her. As Solimar stood on the beach, the humid sea breeze enveloped her body, caressing her, but in actuality, it was doing so much more than that, it was refreshing her tired mind and weary soul. She licked the sea salt from her lips, trembled slightly then tilted her head trying to dispel the waterlog that threatened her hearing. It had been a long time since she had seen her father; not since she was but a tyke still in diapers, barely maintaining her balance. It was one of the reasons she was so interested in the history of her surname. She wanted to somehow, in any way, connect with her roots. Solimar had spent much time researching her genealogy to little or no avail. She stood there, appearing as if a sand sculpture, save for the digging of her toes into the receding tide, enjoying the racing of the sand on her feet, and closed her eyes as she attentively listened to the waves gently crashing upon the reefs, something a sculpture could never appreciate. Had she had the presence of mind or inclination to look around her, she might have noticed the strident and determined steps of the man advancing upon her, sandals in hand, leaving a trail of footprints leading up to her, but she did not. She was too caught up in not wanting to dwell on filial affiliations or the lack thereof, which was the impetus for her refuge to the beach, among a more pressing matter, but with the inevitable pull in her heart and the fact that her mind would not allow her to rest from her quest, she simply acquiesced and gave permission to her mind to drift back to that day at the church library, researching on their free internet service while listening to her favorite music. Happy as she could be for the moment, she had been interrupted by a woman lurking nearby. This woman tried to behave in a manner that would readily distinguish her as a Christian, but Solimar knew an imposter when she saw one. Solimar sensed that this woman was too heavenly bound for her own earthly good ... in other words, self-righteous to the max to be effective in any way, shape or form. She looked over Solimar's shoulder, much like people do on the subway when they are too cheap to buy their own newspaper, basically being nothing else but intrusive. Solimar tried to ignore her but finally pulled the headphones from her ears and hid her annoyance. She simply asked "Can I help you?" but meaning to say; 'Will you please get the hell away from me?!' The woman, upon realizing that Solimar was researching and simultaneously listening to the music of Carlos Santana, actually the infamous "Black Magic Woman" to be exact, leaned over quite respectfully and whispered to Solimar "That is satanic music. Look it up. Even his name has Satan in it, both in English and in Spanish."

Solimar did not comprehend, but did understand well enough that this was always a part of the education of Solimar Santana. People seemed to always take the liberty of 'informing' her about 'facts'. These 'facts' delivered in a manner that amounted to be more of a condescension, rather than informative, always left Solimar with a bad taste in her fresh mouth. '*Entrometida, estupida* nosey ass!' she thought to herself, but at that moment, Soli, in her desperate attempt to not be the person she really thought people saw her as, and in a further effort to become a person more acceptable to society, by society's supposed standards, did not confront the woman's ignorance, but instead said in a measured tone, "I'm sorry, I didn't know, and yes, of course, I will look it up while I'm online. Thank you." The church lady winked and walked away triumphantly believing that she had fulfilled her evangelical duties for the day.

A week later, after the frantic search for the meaning of names, Solimar approached the unnamed woman who dared to comment on what she was listening to on her IPod and said "I gave a lot of consideration to what you pointed out to me last week, and I would like to know if you can explain it to me at length together with the pastor." Elated at the idea of having an audience with the pastor, the woman said "But of course my dear! Did you make an appointment with him?" Solimar casually responded, "He is waiting for us in the rectory." Stirred by much enthusiasm and her burning desire to exercise her rank as an elder, further gaining the pastor's approval, the church lady responded "My dear, oh dear girl, there is no rectory here, we are not Catholics, we are Christians. Let's go to his office and hurry up. Our pastor is an extremely busy man, you know, trying to keep the flock healthy and all." Solimar thought 'what's the fucking difference between Catholics and Christians?' and gave the woman a weak smile; a smile recognized by most others as not being a smile at all, but something of a vague warning. This woman had just corrected her yet again and Solimar was incorrigible, having traveled from church to church trying to find answers that nobody seemed to have. Upon entry, the pastor said "C'mon in ladies, I only have a few minutes, but Solimar said our meeting wouldn't be long. What troubles you today?" Solimar hurriedly explained the situation as the pastor and his avid follower condescendingly nodded their heads in agreement. Solimar, as eloquently as she could muster said "I realize that I am brand new to this church and perhaps you are not aware that I come from a Catholic background and …" She was stopped in mid-sentence when the pastor abruptly interrupted her not yet completed explanation as to her curiosity and defense. "Don't worry about that dear heart, you've already accepted Christ and you needn't worry about a blessed thing. All your prior sins have been forgiven!" The duo chuckled knowingly as Soli's blood begun to rapidly brew, ready to meet the boiling point. "No, but you guys don't understand. I just wanted to show you my research on the Santana name. Like for instance, my name Solimar literally means sun and sea. Okay? Are you following me? Santana is a compilation of Santa and Ana. Santa meaning saint and Ana being the name of the woman who gave birth to Mary, like in Mary the mother of our Lord, the lady that nobody around here seems to honor! Look, its right here in black and white written by theologians. You know, Apocrypha, the hidden books?" Solimar shook her head at their expressions, noting that they appeared as helpless as deer captured in the headlights of an oncoming tractor trailer. "Jesus Christ! Even the Muslims believe in Mary and her mother! What is wrong with you people?! These people didn't just drop in from heaven and started procreating without sex – hello - unless you're now going to tell me that nobody in the Messiah's lineage ever fucked!"

The pastor, noticing that Solimar was furiously raking her hair off of her face and becoming visibly upset, tried to be calming and said "You are right to be curious and conduct all the research you like, but I don't understand how this has anything to do with anything. From your account and my understanding, Sister Claire was only trying to educate you on matters that perhaps, as a young Christian, you may not yet be aware of, and by doing so, she was putting you on the right path. If you, in fact, have been listening to satanic music, which incidentally, uh, what is the name of that chap again?" Sister Claire happily piped in and said "Carlos Santana" causing the ordained minister to completely lose his train of thought and said "yeah, I remember, you know back when I was young and didn't know the Lord, I used to listen to his music too along with Led Zeppelin, Eddie Kendricks and a whole bunch of others that threw us all into a revolution ....." Realizing that he was revealing his 'former' fleshly weaknesses, he turned his attention to the subject at hand and said "Solimar, Sister Claire has the right to warn you in the event that you didn't know. I don't see anything wrong here." The two became thoroughly confused at Solimar's stance and the pastor asked, "Solimar, what does all this have to do with your conversation of last week? I'm not quite following, please clarify it for me." Solimar elaborated by saying "I don't see Satan in the name or in the music. I see that God elected the beauty of the name, not whatever negativity you people see. *Santa Ana* was and is the mother of Mary, the grandmother of Jesus, our Christ, or so the legend goes. Like isn't it all a legend anyway?" Where is Satan in all of this? Where, where, where, prove it to me so I can learn something already!"

The minister quickly glanced at Sister Claire and discreetly motioned towards the water cooler. Sister Claire, knowing her place, scurried off to fetch him a glass of water and offered Solimar a glass, as well. Solimar leaned back into her chair and said "No, thank you. I get my water supply from the church where they actually take the time to bless it. I don't patronize Poland Springs nor do I serve the Devil in the event you were wondering about it." Claire aggregated to the situation and as a result, stepped into the worse embarrassing moment of her life by stating "You belong with us now; holy water does not exist child because all water is holy in God's eyes. That is just an annual legalistic ritual that them Catholics do with all of their pomp and circumstance. Jesus loves you and so do we and that is all you need to know; now come on, drink up and forget about all of this nonsense." With that clear affirmation, Solimar stood up, towering over the church lady and retorted "Yeah, and if Jesus is all that, he probably loves my name too. By the way, my name happens to be Solimar Santana, not "child" you fucking self-righteous, ignorant bitch who thinks you have the right to pan out advice without knowing who you're talking to first." Sister Claire immediately feigned faint and the pastor just as quickly ransacked his desk searching for the bouquet of smelling salts that contained a good quantity of ammonia and eucalyptus encased in a cautiously prepared sack adorned with miniature plastic flowers. He always kept it handy to revive the ladies when they had the "Holy Ghost" upon them.

Solimar giggled and said "You know what? You two are simply pathetic. Don't worry pastor, you don't have to ask me to leave, I know where the door is and this Santana will not be visiting this boring ass place no more. Incidentally, last Sunday, I left my tithe, which should cover my expenses and unsolicited education in Bullshit Theology 101. Actually you guys are still at the remedial level." Solimar paused while the keeper of the flock was tapping Claire gently on her face, her wig shifting, threatening to fall from her head as he kept on waving the bouquet of smelling salts under her nostrils, wishing that one of the other 'sisters' could be readily located nearby. Solimar giggled once again and deliberately taunting them asked "When did Sister Claire last tithe? When did she last give her ten percent of anything other than her unsolicited advice?" Sister Claire's envious green eyes flew open with anger and righteous indignation, but held her tongue realizing that it would suit her much better at this juncture to continue on with her self-induced fainting spell. Pastor knew Sister Claire was way behind in her tithing and had meant to have a talk with her about it. "Solimar, you have it all wrong! Please let us talk and work things out with a modicum of civility!" Solimar stated "Sorry, Pas, I don't poop where I eat, but I see that doing that is acceptable around here. I rather go to McDonalds, get a kid's happy meal and call it a day on any particular Sunday." She walked out of the church, never to be seen again, leaving the pastor and the church lady ashamed and barely able to face one another.

Having relived that unpleasant scenario, Solimar was whisked back into reality with the next wave that this time kissed her feet. She squeezed the salty water from her hair, toweled off and tried to dispel that incident from her mind as she walked towards her beach chair. Happy to be in Miami Beach, she shielded her eyes from the sun and looked as far as she could into the horizon, turning her attention away from the 'spooky ones' and remembering a vacation long ago when she would rise before all others, including the sun, and run to the shoreline to pray the rosary before starting another glorious day. With her rosary in hand, wrapped in the arms of the sun, sitting at the feet of the sea, she felt empowered, but now she could barely whisper a Glory Be, which is nothing but a four line prayer, the last line being Amen. She vaguely wondered 'Where did God fall off? Did it happen with Adam and Eve or was it something that

I did?' The two biblical stumpers took hold of her questioning soul and she sadly surmised, bowing her head slightly, that maybe, just maybe, her misfortune really did have something to do with her name, or worse yet, her persona. She shrugged her slender shoulders. Hell, she liked her name well enough, but had an issue with the "S" in between. Leave it to Puerto Ricans to royally screw a good thing up. Oh well. Nobody would ever need to know, or find out what the secret "S" stood for. For all of her God-given beauty, aquamarine eyes perfectly set onto a caramel-colored canvas, delicately framed by high cheek bones, a body that still had not quit even after all of the abuse and an unmanageable mane of tangled jet black hair with wisps of gray that hung past her hips, she intuitively knew that a tidal wave was well on its way and she could do nothing for herself but allow it to sweep her away. Something inside was quietly shattering, shifting rather quickly, but not quickly enough to be merciful, like the San Andreas Fault in California ... just a matter of time before one good tremor, and it breaks off and floats away, but up until now, it only seemed to be nothing more than an imposing threat.

Bueno .... Well. Having resigned to whatever was coming her way, she delicately strutted her God-bestowed glory to the area she had selected to take in the sun. She adjusted the beach chair to face the high noon rays, threw on her oversized, tortoise-shell sunglasses and reached for her partner, a Newport menthol cigarette. She desperately fumbled around her beach bag looking for a calling card. She pulled out her thermos filled with freshly prepared Sangria and upon finding the calling card sitting in the bottom of the beach bag, amid strewn tobacco, settled in to call her dearest friend who had been deported to Panamá on the stupidest charge ever imaginable: being married to an asshole.

"Hola Bella." Solimar had not quite dialed yet, therefore was forced to find out where the hello had come from. She slid her glasses down the bridge of her nose, using not her index, but her middle finger, looked up and there stood what she would have thought was God in her past, but knew for sure, here comes the devil's advocate, if not the Devil incarnate. She quickly summed him up at about 6'2, 200 lbs, perfectly proportioned, but who in the hell could deny those engaging eyes. He had thick, black hair hanging rather low over his right eye and he was totally clean. Clean shaven, clean apparel, clean everything. The white polo shirt he sported bore thin red stripes at the shoulders and matching casual ankle length pants invited her to rip them off of him to see what else he had going on. He was ready to be eaten, totally fresh! His teeth were makeshift kernels of white corn and his skin glistened like polished bronze. No band on the left ring finger; not even the hint of a tan line which would have signified that he had just slipped it off and into his pocket. This was an observation that Solimar had acquired as a result of having been fooled more than once during her misspent youth. However, Soli still responded defensively, thinking to herself 'here goes the bullshit'. She shouted back, "Holler Bello, I speak *Ingles*, am *Americana* and no I'm not looking to help you stay in this country, not even for any sum of money you have in those dockers, so ciao Bello!"

The man smiled and said "Okay, *linda*, I just wanted to point out to you that your right breast is catching a tan and that perhaps a woman with a rosary in her hand and a cigarette in the other, wouldn't like that *bery mucho*." And then, as if to further grate on her nerves he spoke in a mock accent. "It is no bery good lookin' for you Bella, know what I say?" Soli ripped the shades from her face and peeked down. There in full view was her right tit hanging out of her skimpy bikini top; her rosary somehow entangled around the handle of the thermos, as she had no real intention of reciting it, and her cigarette now a turret on a decrepit sand castle. She quickly pulled the towel over her and watched him walk away shaking his head, perplexed and bewildered by her unwarranted outburst. His encounter with the woman he had longed to meet left much to be desired. Mortified, Soli grabbed up her things and made a mad dash to the hotel, which was only twenty feet away, if that. When she got into the lobby, still wrapped in her towel, she realized that the rosary beads no longer hung from her thermos cup. "Shit, damn, fuck and *puta madre*, I have to go back." 'Oh hell no' combated the voice inside; 'I might see God/Devil man again. Damn it! How many rosaries don't I have?' She shook her head realizing that she could indeed afford to lose one. She proceeded to the ninth floor, without a second thought. She undressed and prepared for a hot, steamy shower, but as she was ready to turn on the faucet to create a sauna effect, the sounds of the street pulled her towards her balcony. Nothing beats the rhythm of Miami Beach. The world met her in her solace, and as she begun her little dance, sweat and patches of sand clinging to her body, falling into the most delicious trance as she listened and desired to be a part of the life and festivities going on right outside of her window, the phone rang scaring the living daylights out of her. All she could think of was that she was happy she wasn't preparing to masturbate! Slightly annoyed, she picked up and heard a squeal on the other end. Solimar broke into a smile and breathed "Mari." They instantly broke into girlish laughter, though well into their forties. They blessed themselves that one was named Solimar and the other Marisol. Same name, juxtaposed, different women with the same name. "What are you up to woman?" Marisol asked, still giggling like a schoolgirl while Solimar decided that it would be best not to tell her exactly what she was up to. "Missing you *estupida*, I was just getting ready to call you when God showed up and told me my right tit was hanging out of my bikini!"

"God showed up?" Marisol asked believing that Solimar could have actually had an epiphany or maybe too much

Sangria with dinner, which was impossible since Solimar had a hollow leg and could drink just about anyone under the table, especially when it came to Sangria. Soli waited a minute to let Marisol digest her absolute stupidity and then laughed until tears rolled down her face. "*Que te pasa* Soli, it's not that funny. He could show up anytime He wants to you know?" Solimar agitated said "Woman, what would God be doing chasing my skinny ass on Miami Beach? He is probably East of Eden somewhere rearranging things for us to get back there and not fuck things up next time around!"

"So it was a man that told you that your bodacious little *teta* was hanging out?" Marisol's curiosity always made Solimar wonder why this woman was studying psychology; she should well know the damn answers!

"Yes, he was a fucking Adonis who incidentally looked a little like me, so that would make him a blue-eyed devil." They both broke out into peals of laughter, but gradually, without either one of them wanting to let go of it, the laughter subsided, leaving them in a vacuum that was painfully transforming into their mutual reality.

"Soli?"

"Que Mari?"

"Come to Panamá."

"For what Mari?"

"Come for me."

"Shit, damn and fuck, don't you know I have to get my black ass back to New York?"

"Why can't you just runaway from it all?"

"Ah bills for starters; I couldn't even afford to take this vacation, if it hadn't been for Ricardo paying for all of this after you passed your midterm, I wouldn't be here! But you know Mari, I just had to jump on a plane and go anywhere after the bullshit that went down with you, but you're not around no more; work sucks to death, life in church is the pits and I can't go back there now even if I wanted to because I told off some church lady in front of *el pastor*! I can't be myself anywhere, so I came here!"

"Solimar! Slow down! Ricardo didn't pay for that vacation; that bastard used my credit card. He wanted me out of the way since he knew I had a week off, but that is neither here nor there! I'm glad you used it because if you hadn't I'd still have to pay for it anyway. You need to trade in that extra ticket any way you can and come here! I know you've got connections. You left to escape and you are half way here. You can be yourself here with me. Besides, you are the only piece of the States that I have left to hold on to and I miss it there."

"Mar, let me think this over because you're truly tempting me here and I cannot afford a wrong move at this stage of my life."

"*Esta bien*, Sol, just let me know, *quieres*?"

"Mari, don't do the Spanglish thing, it doesn't suit you …. You pretty much, well somewhat, master both languages. I speak Spanglish because it is my native tongue."

"Okay *Amiga*, I won't, but just so you know, if the shit doesn't work itself out with the extra ticket, I have the money to bring your black ass over here. Thank God they let me empty out one bank account because it was in the school's credit union under my parents' name with me as a beneficiary or something like that and luckily Ricardo's name wasn't in on that one and most of those deposits were wired from Panamá and I made not one single withdrawal, you know, just in case, *si por las moscas*, so that money wasn't confiscated when I was convicted and deported… all you have to do is say the word. You don't even have to go back home, just come straight here."

"Marisol. I'm tired of running, but yes, I do want to see you. I have a picture of us on this stupid hotel room's nightstand; you're my friend, but we are separated now; what on earth can we do?"

"What picture Soli?"

"The one we took on Halloween, remember at SOBs, when I dressed up as a hooker and you dressed up like a gypsy?" Mari sincerely responded, taking on Solimar's habitual use of profanity as a way of getting her point across "How can I ever fucking forget that night? We almost ended up incarcerated for indecent exposure, thanks to you and your great idea, but you can still come to Panamá and we can just hang out, but no more *puta* outfits."

"*Oye Chica!* You're such a pain!"

"And you Soli are not the bitch that you try so hard to be so stop it." Once again they giggled as teenaged girls would when phones were landline princess telephones and chatted about the weather and the Adonis Soli left at the beach, rosary beads and all, and the love that took Marisol's life, livelihood and hopes from her, followed by the typical Puerto Rican goodbye, an hour later, trying to still say *Adios* after forty minutes of substantial conversation.

Marisol's Misery

Marisol clicked off the call, but the tears in her eyes had already welled. She couldn't find the charger belonging to the phone, although she noted that the battery signal was relatively low. She placed the receiver in the pocket of her bathrobe, poured herself a glass of white wine, popped an Excedrin PM and settled into her tiny balcony, which was more like a fire escape without the slats. The fully furnished apartment she rented consisted of a double bed, a thirteen inch black and white TV complete with aluminum foil wrapped rabbit ears for antennae, a small settee, an even smaller desk, a wobbly, dirty Queen Anne chair and two cheap tin snack tables to dine on. The air conditioner was louder than it was effective. She'd be cooking on a hot plate or microwave until further notice and the refrigerator was only large enough to stack a few TV dinners, chicken pot pies and the occasional bottle of wine, depending on her inventory. She had to share the common bathroom outside of her door and clean up after herself after each use. These were the non-negotiable house rules; take it or leave it. The place was run down, had not seen paint in years and the hot water was lukewarm on a good day. The day she arrived, even prior to unpacking, Marisol called a cab to bring her to a local shop called "Cortina and Things." She purchased a set of bed sheets, a couple of pillows and a mattress cover, recalling Solimar's horrible experience with bedbugs that took her three months to get rid of. During that time, Solimar literally slept in her bathtub, piling it high with quilts, leaving Marisol appalled that she didn't take her up on her offer to come sleep over her place during the extermination process. Marisol tried hard not to think of why Solimar had refused to stay with her. That was just another sad memory; one to be forgotten as quickly as possible. Besides all of that, she shuddered to imagine the atrocities that may have occurred upon those sheets that covered the bed that she would now call her own. She dutifully tried to return the sheets and bedspread to the landlord's wife who gave her a bored look and said "Suit yourself, *Nena,* but if you expect me to throw these away, you better leave behind the new ones that you got from that fancy store, *comprendes*?" Marisol understood it indeed. She was far, very far away from a land she so desperately wanted to call home. It had been three weeks since that terrible day when she was escorted onto an airplane, without a chance to go back to her luxurious apartment, well luxurious by comparison to this place, and gather her belongings. Marisol was already missing Ricardo's panache and extraordinary taste for the good life. He made sure that they were going to live the American Dream and live it effective immediately. Instead of living on campus for a year, which was what Marisol had intended until she completed her studies, Ricardo secured an apartment for them in a quiet, tree-lined street in an area called Edgewater, New Jersey. Living there caused Marisol a forty-five minute commute by bus each way, on the days when traffic was light, and she was unhappy about that, but had gone along with her husband's inconsiderate plans. The apartment came furnished, but without Marisol's knowledge or consent, Ricardo made a deal with the landlord to place all of the old furnishings in storage and allow him to refurnish it himself. To Marisol's surprise, after completing a week long internship that required her to stay overnight observing psychiatric patients, she came home to find an immaculate, freshly painted and newly furnished apartment. Her living room thrived with colorful abstract art, a couple of leather butternut squash colored sofas, one being a pull-out and a Plasma TV installed upon the wall that invited the most discriminating guest to relax and enjoy.

Marisol's Misery

Her tiny kitchen seemed all the larger having been painted stark white with mocha colored accents and a theme that made it feel more like a café than a *cocina*. When she walked into her bedroom, she found her husband, Ricardo, languishing in bed, wrapped in a luxurious sky blue robe that matched the celestial colored fabrics he had chosen for their new bedding and ultra modern bedroom set, replete with a mirrored ceiling. Marisol was speechless and Ricardo tenderly held her and softly said "Welcome home gorgeous. I hope you like it." Although grateful, she asked "how can we afford all of this, we haven't even found real jobs yet?" Ricardo cuddled her and said "I already have a job, I start tonight. I'll be working as a security guard and will be making $40,000 a year with a promise of a raise in three months to $50,000 if everything works out and they will be paying me cash so we don't have to worry about taxes because, as you know gorgeous, I can't work on the books under your Visa. The only thing bad about it is that I'll be working nights, so you'll be on your own a lot." Marisol was not disturbed by this, knowing that she had to sacrifice whatever they had to in order to get ahead in life. She never bothered to ask how he paid for all of this or if he had put it on credit; that thought never fully crossed her mind as Ricardo was already all over her body, kissing, tickling and telling her how very much he had missed her. Marisol, having been given two days off said "Listen, let me go bathe and then we can spend time enjoying ourselves in our new *casita*." Ricardo leaned back and said "Go ahead, but make it quick because I start work tonight." Marisol who was tired, excited and hungry all at once, peeked into the kitchen to see that her husband had already skillfully prepared a *picadillo*, a simple dish that primarily consists of ground meat, onions, diced potatoes and exotic spices to be served over steaming white rice or, her favorite, *arepas*, flat bread made out of white corn meal. The subtle fragrance of this hearty dish enticed her further to get this evening started. It had been weeks since she had made love to her husband, and she was feeling guilty about it, loving him all the more for being so understanding and accommodating to her every need. By the time Marisol got back from her shower, wearing a loosely fitting cotton nightie, Ricardo was dressed, all ready to go and said "I forgot to tell you, I have orientation tonight, so they need me there two hours earlier. One of the guys just called while you were in the shower and offered to pick me up so I don't want to leave him waiting outside or be late for my first night on the job. Save me some *picadillo*; don't eat it all, okay?" Having said that he gave her a quick peck on the cheek and walked out the door, stepping into a brand new car that Marisol had no idea had been leased in her name. This was a glimpse of the life Marisol had been condemned to live - a life of lies, thievery, fraud and a one-sided marriage; a glimpse that Marisol was unable to see at that time for she was blindly in love; so much that she was unable to see the forest for the trees.

    Marisol shook the memory away from her. Her receding memory of that particular disillusion was that of eating her dinner straight from the pot, as opposed to the candlelight dinner she had planned on as she bathed that early evening preparing to be loved by her husband. Further recalling that mid-way into their relatively short-lived marriage, she had discovered that Ricardo had maxed out all of her credit cards, never once having applied for any of his own, she realized that he didn't have to and blamed herself, accepting the harsh reality that upon their marriage she had trustingly named him on each line of credit as an authorized user, giving him access to over $100,000 in credit, not to mention the American Express card, which had no limit.

    After the police raid, arrest and subsequent deportation, Marisol placed Solimar in charge of administering her credit cards, negotiating pay-offs and giving her Power of Attorney over her belongings. Soli was mad as all hell, but mainly because her confidant was not just gone, but a goner, and there was nothing she could do to help her friend other than to do what was asked of her. She placed her things in the nearby storage warehouse and fought with both credit card companies and Mari's old landlord as he adamantly demanded that his old furniture be restored to his apartment at no expense to him. Solimar blatantly told him to go fuck himself and that ended that argument. She took the important things home with her. For Solimar, the important things consisted of Mari's books, lingerie, summer clothing, picture albums and anything small that she could throw into a few boxes. She had to now try and figure out how to ship boxes over there without them getting ransacked or worse, stolen. She had absolutely no idea what to do with the shipment of furniture. 'We ain't dealing with the US Postal system here,' Solimar thought to herself, 'and I don't think La Flor de Mayo Express Shipping Fucking Company goes to Panamá.'

Still, Marisol had hopes of at least recuperating her furniture to resume her life in Panama, having literally been evicted from the land of her now broken dreams. She had very little money to start over with and her credit was just about non-existent. Reflecting on this blessed mess of *pura mierda*, or to put it mildly, pure shit, Mari pulled out her rosary beads and chuckled. 'Who am I kidding? Both Soli and I have been spiritually dead for years and there isn't any way to get us jump started now!' She carefully placed the delicate string of silver beads with the hanging cross back into its protective little black pouch and sighed. She couldn't even cry, not even with the sliver that carefully, yet persistently pierced her soul, feeling more like someone was stabbing her heart. Nobody knew that she was right back where she had started. She was home, but she was an utter failure. Well, maybe by now someone might have an idea, but Marisol had still not checked in with anyone she knew, least of all her parents. The sheer humiliation she had endured was quite beyond her power of understanding of what had just happened to her. She allowed the emotional pain to wash over her like a powerful, but warm tidal wave, similar to that which Solimar envisioned earlier, and as it pounded her chest, throwing her heart into the grips of agony, racking her full five foot frame from head to toe - much like sister-friend, Solimar, Marisol acquiesced, resigning herself to the unknown. Solimar had and continued to anticipate a tidal wave; Marisol was living its relentless thrashing and was drowning. 'How could that man jeopardize everything, and the fucker is still there and I am here?!' The pain became replaced quickly by anger, but not enough to get her moving. Marisol was emotionally and spiritually paralyzed.

    The deportation process had been deft and swift. Mari, while handing in her thesis, ironically enough entitled, "The Paradox: Narcissism, Self Depravation and Its Effects on a Holy Institution" was startled to hear her name announced through the paging system, asking her to please report to the Dean's Office. She left her paper with the professor and ran down the stairs, afraid that perhaps there was bad news from Panamá or that maybe Ricardo had gotten into an accident, which he often did, being highly accident prone or looking for an opportunity to sue. She was met with INS officers patiently waiting in the Dean's Office, one who matter of factly asked if she was Marisol Espinoza-Betancourt. Upon her confirmation, they said "Come with us Ma'am. You are under arrest; if you cooperate, we won't have to take you in handcuffs; just follow us and everything will be explained to you when we get downtown." Marisol maintained her composure and did not resist. She later learned that she was being charged with possession of illegal substances with the intent of distribution. Mari was given a court-appointed attorney who obviously had no interest in defending a 'foreign drug dealer,' and the argument he made for her was vague at best, using her educational expenses as the end to those means. It was in the courtroom that she learned that her New Jersey residence had been under surveillance because neighbors had reported to her landlord an unusual amount of visitors during the day time hours while Marisol was at school and subsequently working her mediocre part-time job as a waitress near campus, which incidentally, Columbia University was not very removed from an area highly infested by drugs and immigrants, a location strategic to Ricardo's investments and enterprising endeavors. Her mind raced trying to piece together the puzzle. As the judge spoke, Marisol was desperately trying to formulate a defense for herself. It ran through her mind that by the time she'd got home each night, her husband was at his supposed night shift job working security, or so he said, but there were no paystubs to prove his employment. They only saw one another two nights per week, sometimes only on Sundays, Ricardo always claiming that he had to make the overtime pay as much as possible to pay off their mounting bills. However, Ricardo remained quite the attentive husband, always leaving Marisol's dinner slowly sweating in a Bain de Marie, better known to them as a *Baño de Maria* wherein the foods are maintained warm to perfection in a double boiler set upon a low flame as opposed to microwaving food cooked hours before, potentially robbing its nutrients and toughening the meats. Mari, in love with her extremely attractive, always impeccably dressed and charming husband, who more than well cared for her, never saw it coming, and was unable to present a defense that would not hurt him in the process. Son of a bitch; all transactions had been made out of their nicely appointed rented basement apartment between the hours of 8:00 a.m. and 6:00 p.m. and his clients, who highly respected his position, were an abundance of undocumented immigrants that didn't want to get caught up in a bind themselves and high school students that were more than grateful to have a local supplier that every so often threw them a bone or two on the house.

Ricardo, in his greed for money, power and lust, mistakenly established what he thought was a discreet relationship with a beautiful young lady named Natalia. Natalia resided in the same three-family house from which the Betancourts rented, owned by her father. Natalia and Marisol often left their respective apartments at approximately 7:15 each weekday morning. Ricardo made it a point to dutifully walk his wife to the door and kiss her good-bye, keeping his eyes on the stairs that led to the street, catching a glimpse of Natalia's high-heeled steps and mini skirts that flawlessly revealed her preference for thongs instead of conventional panties. Ricardo also made it a point to be around when Natalia arrived from school and befriended her during the time that he was renovating the apartment. He invited her to help him shop under the guise that he wanted to surprise his wife and could use a woman's opinion. Natalia spent quite a bit of time helping Ricardo redecorate his apartment while Marisol spent day and night working her internship in a psychiatric ward, with minimal breaks to call home. Nobody saw anything wrong with Natalia and Ricardo's friendship, and even her father was supportive of the fact that Natalia was helping out for a change, instead of hanging out with her loser friends. On the fourth day, after putting the finishing touches on the bedroom to their mutual satisfaction, Natalia sat at the built-in bar off the small kitchen and Ricardo, ever the host, played bartender from the other side. Ricardo casually lit up a cigarette, took a long drag and slowly blew the inhaled smoke directly into Natalia's unblemished face. Ricardo had noted Natalias' height and rather boyish body, while his wife's body was short stacked with dangerous curves that he preferred to avoid. Not knowing that the cigarettes were laced, Natalia asked if she could have one as well as a glass of white wine. He handed her the Marlboro cigarette which he had expertly tampered with, having emptied it then refilling it with a mixture of tobacco and cocaine. He poured her a glass of crisp Chardonnay that he now stored in the wine cooler he had purchased for $200.00, which held his party stash of a dozen bottles, thinking it more chic then just refrigerating each bottle. Natalia smoked her 'cigarette' and drank her wine, feeling a nice sensation coursing through her, alerting her senses and arousing her sexuality. Ricardo then took the liberty of revealing his well-protected stash of marijuana and openly started rolling joints and preparing blunts, while she watched and learned. "You know, Ricky, my friends from school are always looking to score. There is a guy from the Heights that comes around once in a while and the kids go crazy buying as much as they can because he doesn't come around that often." Ricardo detecting a business opportunity said "Well, I can always supply you and you can sell them to your friends. I'll give you a split and we can both make a little pocket money." Natalia, now feeling mighty good from the effects of the cocaine in the cigarette, the wine and the puff of marijuana Ricardo offered her to sample while he was rolling, responded "Yeah, why not? Sounds like that's what's up to me!"

Ricardo walked from around the bar, took her free hand and carefully placed it on his crotch, gently rubbing it until it caused friction, more excited with the idea of making money than he was about fucking this bimbo, but he needed to release himself as well, and thought it best to convince her that they were truly a team. Natalia did not resist, giving Ricardo the go ahead to further explore her body. He unbuttoned her skimpy top and snapped open the closure to her bra, which was easy enough as the clasp was nestled between her breasts. "C'mon gorgeous, let's seal the deal and break-in the new sheets." He guided Natalia to the bedroom, watched her undress, not particularly interested in the strip-tease act she was putting on, but very interested in her young and healthy physique which was rather lanky, but very desirable, at least in his eyes. He thoroughly loved that she had a boyish, pixie-like haircut with many streaks in it that oddly complimented her unnaturally tanned skin. He immediately tried to engage her in oral sex and she took no offense. Natalia enjoyed giving head, but when Ricardo was about to climax, she pulled back and said "it is my turn now." She propped herself on her knees offering up the only orifice she had ever used and said "I'm a virgin so please give it to me from behind." This couldn't please Ricardo more as he had tried to get his wife to give him anal sex on many occasions, but she had refused because the one time she did try to please him, it hurt her as Ricardo had not taken the time or measures to prepare her properly and caused her to bleed. He pounded and fingered Natalia's firm assets until they were both satiated. They made their disgustingly unholy pact and spent the afternoon frolicking in Marisol's bed getting high, Ricardo now introducing her to pure cocaine, giving her the option to smoke it from a pipe or snort it up her aquiline nose. Natalia falling head over heels and rapidly losing her inhibitions, indulged in the drug enhanced sexual buffet Ricardo had to offer. At his instance, she spread her legs so that he could apply a bit of the enchanting white crystalline powder to numb her fiercely protected treasure and she begged him to keep licking it off as if offering a bowl of water to a thirsty dog lapping breathlessly until she was crazy with desire to feel him inside of her. Virgin or not, Natalia willingly submitted to Ricardo's perversion, excited by the fact that he did not try to deflower her as others had tried in the past, causing her to trust him even more. As he toyed with her, all afternoon long, he promised that once a week she could bring her friends over for a little play and get high time in the house, watch porn, eat and do whatever they wanted, so long as she continued selling and above all kept her mouth shut. Natalia had her conditions also. No penetration in the vagina because she needed to be married a virgin, if not she would lose her inheritance and be the shame of her family. Ricardo had struck the deal of his life and said "Don't worry gorgeous, I will not do anything to get you in trouble. We're partners now so just be cool, lay low and do what I say and everything is going to be fine."

    Their clandestine affair continued for a few months and the business took off without a hitch. Ricardo collected on a daily basis from Natalia, as he did from his regular clients. He paid Natalia more in pleasure than in money, giving her just enough to keep her hungry and working steadily and satisfying her yen for an occasional shopping spree at the mall located in the adjoining county. He reserved Thursdays for the kids to come over and have their little fun, all the while pumping them for information, trying to figure out their parents' economic status and joining in on their jubilee. Ricardo allowed them to freely have sex on his marital bed for those who wanted privacy. He permitted them to have sex on the couch, the pull-out sofa, kitchen floor and even on the bear skin rug, which he had never used with his wife, stating that it would be too costly to clean. He never allowed them to go home without eating, having had gotten them high off cocaine, marijuana, sex and life in general. Ricardo cooked sumptuous meals for his little band of merry makers, leaving leftovers for Marisol warming in the old-fashioned steam bath, leading Mari to feel that the meal was lovingly prepared just for her.

Ricardo was on top of his corrupt world and Marisol, his docile wife, was the perfect smokescreen to cloak his derisive and deviant behavior. To the world, he was Marisol's husband, the security guard who was helping his wife complete her education with the agreement that when she got established, she would in turn pay for his education to help him realize his dream of becoming an interior decorator, a field that he pursued to fulfill his narcissistic personality leaving no room for anything other than to be surrounded by material beauty, seeking praise and validation at all times, hiding his true self from the world, while projecting his false reflection.

It was Natalia's devotion to him and her growing dependency on his supply of cocaine that caused her to warn him that her father, his landlord, had called the police, but she wasn't exactly sure why. She was sure her dad had no idea of what went on in Ricardo's apartment, as he had never mentioned anything to her about it. Ricardo, by then, had grown quite tired of Marisol, occasionally complaining that she was always running around, leaving the household duties to him. Marisol, trying to juggle school, work and a commute that took three hours a day from her, was too exhausted to make love, not that Ricardo ever really wanted to unless he wanted a quick oral fix. Besides, he had Natalia to use as his personal sperm receptacle. Marisol would come home, quickly shower, grab a bite to eat, study a little and go to bed where she would try and catch up on the last of the string of nightly *novelas*, which was her only escape from her brutal reality, being mentally and physically exhausted, often times falling asleep before her favorite show was over and forgetting to set the VCR for the next day's episode. Although Ricardo was not there for the most part, Marisol had stopped trying to lure her husband when they were together because he had made several comments that she should join a gym. Marisol had gained some weight and was feeling badly about it thanks to Ricardo's delicious home-cooked, carbohydrate-packed meals and his playful reference that she was now starting to look like a baby cow, changing her name to "Moo Moo." Ricardo was genuinely fed up with Marisol, but was not ready to give up the stability and cover that she innocently provided for his little kingdom of kids, drugs and money. He was patiently biding his time for the paperwork to go through, officially making him a legal resident as opposed to being the husband of a woman who held nothing of substance but a Student Visa, a hope and a dream of one day becoming an American citizen. Ricardo was deeply contemplating his position, acknowledging to himself that Marisol was still the best ticket in town, while planning bigger and better things for his future that did not include her. Within the confines of his forgotten soul, he envied his wife, her achievements and her manner of being, but above all, he resented her love for him, a love he was incapable of returning to anyone but himself.

He heard the familiar tap on the door indicating that Natalia was on the other side. It was Thursday and Ricardo immediately dismissing the venom that poisoned his existence, and eagerly anticipating his weekly orgy, opened the door to find that Natalia was all alone. Bearing a solemn demeanor, she advised him that they needed to talk right away. Natalia advised Ricardo what she had overheard her father tell the police. Ricardo did not question her, but instead said "Well, gorgeous, if that is the case, I can't take any chances. If what you are saying is true, I gotta go." Natalia wanted to take off with Ricardo, but she couldn't. She had been in the process of a pre-screening telephone interview with a well known lingerie and swimsuit designer to potentially model their upcoming string-bikini line. This was the chance of a lifetime but she told Ricardo that she would give up her dream for him. Ricardo sinisterly thought to himself 'Another dumb bitch that wants to ride on my coattails…' He convinced her that he'd be back for her, which wasn't the hardest thing in the world to convince a twenty year old who was still in high school and smoked grass and snorted cocaine on a daily basis. Ricardo gave Natalia a hurried kiss, handed her a couple of bags to hold her over and rushed her out the door and out of his life. He hastily packed up a few things, mainly his recently purchased designer clothes and a few accessories. Decision made, on his way out, he remembered that Marisol had a collection of jewelry that was easily worth fifty grand on the black market and he returned to quickly grab them, taking the entire jewelry box and hiding it underneath the passenger's seat of his car. He had enough money to burn, securely hidden in the seats of his car, not to mention the duffle bagful he had in the house, which cash he distributed inside of the pockets of the clothing that he had packed and decided that Canada might be the place to go to even though he had no contact there.

By the time the raid on the apartment happened, Ricardo Betancourt was long gone, but of course, there was one thing he did leave behind - bags upon bags of marijuana and cocaine, which he had no time nor care to flush, and although it wasn't much to be bothered with, it was just enough to prove that this merchandise wasn't being used for medicinal or recreational purposes yet it was more than enough to incriminate the holder of the lease, Marisol Espinoza-Betancourt. He had stashed them in her very closet, on the shelf too high for her to reach, having asked permission first if he could store his winter clothing there. The landlord immediately cooperated and gave all the information he had regarding the lovely couple downstairs. Oddly enough, he failed to mention that his daughter was a frequent visitor to the apartment and good friends with Marisol's husband.

Immigration and Naturalization Services was at Columbia University within the hour and Ricardo had long since hauled ass, driving ever so carefully across the Canadian border. By the time Soli got the call, Mari had already been sentenced to deportation and her only plea was to get in touch with her friend, Solimar Santana, in order that her possessions could be looked after. They allowed her the phone call, under strict supervision. Soli calmly, heart racing and tearless told Marisol that she would immediately take care of everything. This was another phone call that ended in a silent, tearful goodbye, except this time, not the Puerto Rican festive hour-long *'Adios Amiga, hasta mañana'* kind. They had no idea when or if they would ever see each other again. Solimar realized that the exchange revealing that their whole world had collapsed occurred in one minute and thirty-nine seconds.

While in the van to the airport, Mari pleaded with the INS officer, "*Por favor*, not in handcuffs, I'm really not a fucking criminal." The officer, taken by her gentle yet adamant plea, released her from her shackles, and said, "Let's pretend that I'm your boyfriend and we are going on vacation. Maybe you can get some shut-eye on the plane and no need for you to worry; my job is to watch over you." She smiled weakly at the suggestion, but eagerly nodded her consent, as the restraints were already digging into her wrists. The officer's heart shattered. After all, both his paternal and maternal grandparents were born in Panamá although they had long since migrated to the States, but he never considered that he would see the land of his forefathers for the very first time under these conditions, having planned to vacation in Panamá for his honeymoon. Mari had a habit of speaking everything through her large, rounded brown eyes, and the officer turned his gaze away from her, in love with her one deeply dimpled cheek. He didn't even want her to know his name. He could fall in love with a woman like her and that wouldn't work. He was already engaged to be married to an average type woman that was more than sufficient for him and moreover, he was raised to be an honorable man regardless of his internal emotional struggles. They arrived without incident. The only thing that moved Marisol to tears was the announcement on the plane as they landed, "*Bienvenidos a Panamá!*" and the thunderous clapping that followed, acknowledging the pilot's smooth landing, safely welcoming her back to a land she had walked away from in search of the much coveted American Dream.

Marisol's Misery

Marisol's reverie was jarred by the screams of a woman and she suddenly woke up from her pill-induced coma to the sound of a heated argument directly below her. This balcony faced no beach, no street, just a good old stinking alleyway. "*Sueltame!* Let go of me!" The woman screamed loudly, but the man did not loosen his grip on whomever he was holding. Mari could only tell it was a woman by the shrill of her voice. Marisol cringed when she heard the impact as he cracked the woman across the face with all of his frustration, knocking her senseless, and as she fell back reeling, he cried, *"Puta!"* Mari immediately hid and turned off the light. She did not know what to do, but wanted to help, when suddenly something ferociously ugly woke up within her, and she said to herself in good American slang "Fuck that bitch; I've been slapped before; I ain't getting involved in this shit." She turned the light back on, poured a bowl of cold cereal, realized she had no milk and said fuck it again drowning the cereal in the last of her white wine. Mari's misery had come alive and was manifesting itself in reverse, turning against her, yet something in that man's intonation as he brutally and heartlessly called the woman "Puta!" – Something in the something that she could not place her finger on, reminded her of a time when she too had been similarly treated. Marisol tossed the bowl of half-eaten, wine-drenched cereal into the sink, closed the window and went to bed with the ghosts of her seasons passed.

Solimar S. Santana Sleeps

Solimar's naked, freshly showered body seemed to walk itself effortlessly around the suite. Soli had no thought as she followed her body, and actually tippy toed naked onto the balcony, inhaling the humidity, prancing around the suite with no intention of even putting on a panty. Although she was not an exhibitionist, she really did enjoy her nudity in the privacy of her own space. She didn't want to touch herself again – yuck – its just no fun! Well, not today anyway. In her state of loneliness, her mind kept drifting in different directions and the tormenting thoughts started to dominate her. Pouring herself yet another glass of Sangria, sans the fruits, she set to the task of detangling her hair and thought that it would be a good a time as any to focus and listen to the recording of the "Marriage and Singles Seminar." She had come across this information in the weekly bulletin of St. Teresa's, her local church, and decided that having nothing better to do, would take a ride to the church in New Jersey where they were hosting this seminar and "Christian networking" better known as a holy hook-up.

She had taken her seat in the pews designated for "Singles," but didn't stay long although she tried to stick it out as long as she could. Halfway through listening to the recording of this counseling session, she remembered the precise moment when she first saw Marisol and Ricardo, the very first couple to take advantage of the priest's blessing during that dreaded event. They appeared normal, but something struck a chord in Solimar's heart; something about them didn't seem quite right and actually seemed rather odd. She couldn't put her finger on it, but Solimar felt a discomfort in their presence. It was almost as if he was subtly trying to outshine her. It all seemed like a façade and Solimar wondered why this woman kept her head bowed down the entire time. Solimar thought to herself 'let me slip the hell on out of here.' Signaling the usher, she paid him the five bucks for the recording and left him her mailing address. Solimar headed for the bar down the street for a little brunch and a little something to drink to get her head off this situation, picking up a Sunday paper along the way. She wasn't all that happy that she had never been married, but on the other hand, she fiercely treasured and protected her freedom. Solimar sat her pretty little bottom on the corner barstool facing the door, rolling her veil and shawl into a ball and stuffing it into her handbag. Still modest, Solimar dressed in a light, lavender colored dress that revealed nothing other than her need to fit in and be just an ordinary, lovely lady. Her strappy five inch heels, of course, killed the effect that she was trying to create.

    The bar/restaurant was desolate; she being the very first customer of the day. Solimar opened the newspaper and patiently waited to be served, being in no hurried rush to get back home to do absolutely nothing. She preferred to do nothing right there in a place where nobody knew her and to boot, what seemed like a pretty nice little area where living was easy, unlike the hustle and bustle of the Big Apple. Having ordered an ample brunch for herself, half of which she intended to take home for Monday night's dinner and a full pitcher of Sangria, she cozily settled in to catch up on current events, something she hadn't done in quite some time because she just plain did not feel like acquainting herself with the bullshit and horrors that were going on in the world around her. She changed into the flip-flops that she habitually carried in her purse and sat back to read. A full half hour did not pass before the lady with the husband at the church walked in alone. She sat at a small table far from the bar, opting to give her back to the door, refusing many of the window seats. She shyly asked for a menu while Solimar quietly observed her. The woman was very well-dressed; wearing a deep rose-colored twin pullover set and a simple yet flattering floral skirt and pumps to match. Her hair was neatly coiffed, unlike Solimar's crazy mane and everything outwardly seemed correct, but the nagging feeling in Solimar kept saying 'everything is absolutely fucking wrong here.' The woman wore a strand of pearls.

Solimar could not remember what motivated her, but she impulsively walked over to the lady; the clapping sound of her dollar store flip-flops breaking the silence; Solimar making a mental note to patronize the juke box next. The woman looked up at her a bit startled and Soli bluntly said "Hola, why don't you come join me and we will eat together, like, why eat alone Chica?" Marisol studied this stranger for a brief moment, deciding what to really do, hating to eat alone, and with minimal hesitation followed her gut instinct that told her that Solimar was harmless. She smiled and said "Why not?" Extending her perfectly manicured hand she said, "*Yo me llamo Marisol y tu?*" Solimar, already a bit tipsy from her intake said "*De veras*? Marisol? You've gotta be shitting me!" Marisol, a bit taken aback and mildly offended by this bold statement said "Excuse me?" Solimar laughed and said "Chica, my name is Solimar!" Marisol joined in and lost herself in Solimar's crystal, yet hearty laughter as they walked together up to the bar and Soli said "Chica, I've ordered a lunch fit for a motherfucking queen, actually two queens, so eat up and drink, it's on me already!" Marisol immediately began to protest. "No, no, no, I will pay half of the bill. It is not fair." Solimar looked at her and kindly said "Why look gift blessings in the mouth? I don't really think you got all that blessed at Our Lady of Grace today in that stupid ass seminar or whatever they call it!" Marisol picked up the pitcher, poured herself a glass of Sangria and suspiciously asked "How do you know about that?" Solimar still giggling over the coincidental names said "I was there, part of the singles group, and I ran out of there like a bat out of hell! I saw you and Mr. Rico Suave Bolla at the altar and I said to myself 'this is too damn much for me' and I left and came here." Intrigued and impressed by Solimar's candor, Marisol pressed on. "Why did you leave, like what happened, *que paso*?"

"Marisol. Mar, can I call you Mar?"

"Yes, you may, but only if I can call you Sol."

"Okay, *vale*, you can call me Sol or Soli. I assume that was your husband or your man, but I can't pin it; something didn't sit right in my belly. It was like looking at a complete puzzle, but some of the pieces had been stripped down to the cardboard, so I fully couldn't make it out. I got the impression that something wasn't right between you guys and something said to me 'if the priest is gonna bless that mess, I don't need no blessing.'" Marisol was forthright and asked her "*Eres bruja?*" Not knowing if Solimar truly understood Spanish, having noted Solimar's butchering of the language, repeated her question "Are you a witch?" Solimar replied "Hell no! Well, not that I know of anyway. I just see what I see, feel what I feel, spit out what I sense and know what I know. Why are you here alone, I mean, after church and getting blessed and all that good stuff?" Marisol simply said "My husband, ummm Rico Suave Bolla, said he had to go to work." Solimar, forever inquisitive asked "So why didn't you go home and prepare his pretty-boy ass a blessed kick-ass meal and gave him a real good roll in the hay before sending him off?" Marisol paused and nervously started piling her plate with the food spread before them, which incidentally, took up a quarter of the bar. "Well, he said he needed time to take a nap, go over some papers, change clothes and you know I respect that, even married people need their privacy sometimes." Solimar choked on her half sip of Sangria and said "You know what? Why don't we change the subject?"

The conversation was starting to reawaken Solimar's feelings for Alejandro, whom she thought she would marry, but didn't and now was grateful that she hadn't because she would have found herself locked-up calling friends to bail her out of jail if Alejandro ever said to her that he needed "privacy." Solimar deliberately kept Marisol's company long after the meal was done. She waited until Marisol looked at her expensive wristwatch, no doubt a gift from her husband, and said "Listen, I have to prepare for class tomorrow and now it is my turn to take a nap thanks to all of the Sangria that I had, my head is a little woo-woo. Can we exchange numbers? Next time will definitely be on me." Solimar handed her a business card and wrote her private contact information on the back of it. Marisol had no business card to exchange, but jotted down her number on the back of a bar napkin. She gave Solimar a friendly peck on the cheek and said "Thanks, I really needed a girl's day out; I haven't made many friends. Well, I have my classmates and co-workers, but it isn't the same. This really did me good; it almost reminded me of my carefree days back in Panamá when I was a student, even though I still am. *Gracias, Amiga*, I really do appreciate it." Solimar touched by her gratitude said "Hey, I'll keep in touch, especially now that you ate up tomorrow's dinner and offered to pay for our next meal, I will definitely be calling." They laughed, gave each other a cordial hug and Solimar watched yet another woman walk out to encounter the worst loneliness ever: being married, but miserably alone.

Recalling the union from that day forward, Sol and Mar had become inseparable; Solimar regularly taking the train uptown to meet Marisol after work, often having dinner at the restaurant where Marisol waitressed, waiting for her shift to be over. Solimar's thoughts were now racing all over the place, fueled by the red wine she had purchased to make a new batch of Sangria, drinking it straight from the bottle as the recorded sermon played on. 'Why did I insist on booking the same hotel suite that I had shared with Alejandro so long ago?' she questioned herself. 'You can't recreate things when the thing you're trying to recreate is a person. Alejandro, Alejandro, why didn't we make it? We were so happy, but damn it, your arrogance kept me walking on eggshells.'

Soli quickly decided to shift her thoughts before she had to confront, once again, the fact that this son of a fucking bitch broke her heart when she learned that he had been flirting with one of her few girlfriends. A friend she no longer spoke to as a result because there was reasonable doubt, in her mind, that they might have actually taken it to the next level, although both denied any involvement one with the other and probably forever will. Her jumbled thoughts turned again to Marisol. 'I can't believe Mari is not here with me. This was supposed to be our vacation. We were so excited shopping and getting ourselves together to come have a little fun in the sun. Shit! We had even planned to visit that nice Cuban shrine in Miami dedicated to their patron saint! Damn it! What the hell is the name of it? Ermita de la Caridad or something like that! Solimar became more intense as she remembered that the son of a motherfucking *hijo de puta* Ricardo had stolen her friend's jewelry. 'When, where and how will I tell her that her inheritance has been robbed?'

The marriage litany played on. 'Alejandro dumped me, but I must be still in love to do some dumb shit like this. It's over. It's over. All of it is over, even my friend is gone!' Solimar could no longer focus. It was too much for her to handle all at once. She couldn't breathe. She felt like she was drowning in her own sorrow. It was that moment that she thought of the tidal wave she had envisioned on the beach. She felt tightness in her chest. The anxiety was overwhelming her. She tried to breathe, slow deep breaths. She threw her head back and then stretched down to put her head between her knees. She took shallow breaths when she heard the drone of the priest babbling on about blessed relationships and being 'evenly yoked'. "What the fuck do you know about relationships you pontificating pedophile?" she growled. Soli walked with determination over to the table where she had stationed the cassette player and roughly took the stupid tape out of it and with a bobby pin started to unravel it. After pulling out the entire ribbon, she dumped it in the garbage and managed to go to bed where she was met with a moment's peace before a fine film of sweat covered her golden, sun-glazed body. The torture again overtook her will to sleep peacefully and the demons begun their snickering as they watched her struggle. Slowly, one at a time, they gathered around her luxurious hotel room bed. Some climbed into bed to touch and poke her while others whispered nothing into both of her ears, but they all watched in glee and ecstasy; their already distorted faces becoming even moreso in joyful anticipation of the destruction that they may collectively effectuate. Somehow she was reminded by this motley crew that she was nothing but a worthless human, having been placed inside a well put together persona. They adopted the name Solitita instead of Soli or Solimar, taunting her with the loving nickname her mother had given her when she was still alive and Solimar was but an infant.

"Drink a little bit more Solitita, take a sleeping pill, drink yourself into oblivion Solitita, nothing will happen to you ... you are with us now! How could you talk to that church lady like that you bad girl? You ought to be ashamed of yourself. She was right you know, but we are proud of you for standing up for yourself and letting her have it right there in front of that old preacher man that doesn't even know what stigmata is. And oh, your God, you went to that Marriage and Singles Conference and walked out! What gives you, of all people, the right to counsel Marisol; you've never been married yourself! But the kicker is, you lost respect even for God which makes you satanic, you blue-eyed witch. You're so bad that even your father left your mother because you weren't even meant to be born. He never wanted you period. Accept the reason why he left and that is why Alejandro never came back after you left him. You didn't leave him, he left you, like everybody does and everybody will! You are destined to be alone!" On and on went the insults and accusations, and the kicking and the biting of the tongue begun as they pulled out the fight in her.

"Jump, Solitita, *brinca!* Nothing will happen to you, you'll land on the sand!" Soli, literally feeling the pokes, the bites, yet still asleep, began her nocturnal walk. Open eyed, she stared but registered nothing, yet followed the voices that were nothing more than disembodied whispers and relentless taunting. No faces, no bodies, nothing but worthless sounds that resonated and took up residence in her mind. There were many, and each had its own name. Shame, for starters. Depression, a close second. Curse and Suicide, the leaders of the pack, just to name a few. As she was heading towards the balcony to effectuate her jump, her Guardian Angel quickly touched down in one fell swoop and gently guided her away from the sliding door and towards the front door, with the sweep of the tip of her feathery wing. *'What man intends for evil, God intends for good!'* Solitita obediently opened the door, stepped out and bam! The forceful sound of the heavy door slamming behind her woke her from her deep, disturbed slumber. Shocked awake, she tried to collect her bearings. "How in the hell did I get out here?" That unanswered question culminated in the realization that she was now stark naked outside of her hotel room. As she fumbled to get back in, she realized that she could not for her electronic hotel room key could not possibly fit in a pocket she did not have. Soli stood frozen, completely naked, once again splendid yet wide-eyed and terrified. Covering her breasts with one arm and using her other to shield her vulnerability, she dodged into the alcove that contains the ice machine and snacks until a worker, hopefully a maid and not a bellhop or maintenance worker, would come by and she could ask for help. She knew that one day she would laugh about this, but that day surely wasn't today. As she tried to hide behind any machine, she heard the approaching sound of a masculine voice. The person, the man, had to be on a cell phone because there was no corresponding conversation. Yes! She would ask him to call the lobby and send someone right away, but she would have to act swiftly and with the heart of a lion, but God Almighty, how would she get his attention without attracting his attention?

"Ciao, Mami, love you, *hasta mañana, te quiero mucho.*" He ended his conversation and his footsteps grew nearer. 'Great, he's talking to his woman so I don't have to worry too much here, even though you never know.' A naked woman in the snack room trumps a girlfriend on the phone any day. Before she could think of a way to hail him, Soli's faceless hope stepped into the alcove; ice bucket in hand, just as Soli had prepared to step into the corridor. Soli having decided to act swiftly and courageously, stepped out of the corner she was hiding in, parting her hair so that it would cascade over her breasts like a wanna be Lady Godiva, her right hand covering her private area like a wanna be Eve caught in sin and extending her left hand authoritatively blurted out, "May I use your cell phone? I've been locked out of my room and need immediate assistance." The man's jaw dropped. He burst into laughter and said "you can use anything you want, including me."

"That won't be necessary, just your phone if you don't mind!" retorted Soli. Recognizing her tone and distinctive, raspy voice, he politely asked "Bella, *eres tu?*" Soli's nightmare came alive, except she was not in bed fighting it off. Out of all the damn people, there he was: Adonis also known as God/Devil, The Devil's Advocate and the Blue-Eyed Bastard and right now, an Angel in disguise. "Are you okay, did something happen to you, did someone try to hurt you?" The look of concern was surpassed by the depth of the color of those eyes; those incredibly God-given eyes. Soli regained her composure thinking 'what the hell I have the same ones!' "*Nada*, but this is no time for idle conversation, *quieres*?" He said "take the phone, I'll be right back." He quickly disappeared leaving Soli to remember the phone number to the hotel's lobby. By the time she started dialing, God/Devil was back with his hotel bathrobe. He gently said, "*Perdon*, allow me." Soli still in a stupor obeyed his command, turned around, lifted her unruly hair and allowed him to dress her.

"*Gracias.*"

"*De nada* Bella. May I invite you to my room while we wait for management?" Sure. He took her by the hand and walked her two flights up to the 11th floor. On the way, she asked, "If your room is on the 11th floor, why were you getting ice on nine?"

"The machine here is broken, and they are currently repairing the machine on the tenth floor."

"Why didn't you just go up to 12?"

"Why go up when you can go down and rescue a damsel in distress, and a naked one at that?" Solimar rolled her eyes. They walked into his suite and Soli went straight for the couch. She literally curled up into the fetal position, her eyes tightly closed before even finding her position. The voices in her head had somewhat subsided, but still they lingered and she was combating them off although exhausted. Saúl mixed his drink, a good old Cuba Libre, Bacardi and Coke, twist of lime and plenty of ice in a tall glass. He watched Solimar from the small bar that divided the kitchen from the living area, shaking his head. He couldn't keep his gaze off of her when he noticed that she was actually softly giggling in her sleep. He walked over to her ready to shake her awake, but remembered a time when he tried to wake up his newborn brother because he was laughing and their mother gently instructed him not to ever wake up a baby when they are laughing in their sleep because this is when their Guardian Angel is talking to or playing with them. He believed his mom and as he considered waking her anyway because this was no baby, but one hell of a babe, he thought it better not to take that chance and alarm or interrupt her angelic conversation. Instinctively, he began to fix her a little something to eat. He ransacked the fridge and figured that the Cuban sandwich he had purchased at the deli earlier that day might do her just fine. He took the sandwich out of its plastic container, fired up the frying pan full blast and hoped that this would work. He watched that the bread did not burn, and turned it on the other side. The kitchen was not his forte, but he gave it the old college try, very much wanting to give this girl that emerged from the sea, something to eat, foolishly wondering if mermaids had the mystical power to turn fins into legs.

Confident that the sandwich was sufficiently warm, he carefully balanced it on the spatula, flipped it on to a plate and proudly prepared to present it to her. Ever so carefully he whispered "Bella, you want to share a little something to eat?" She opened her red rimmed eyes and said "*Si*, I'm starving. I forgot to order in, I fell asleep." She stretched and yawned as he lovingly offered his plate, pickles, cole slaw, potato chips and all. They both automatically moved towards the balcony, where Soli shyly smiled at him as he turned on the dim light and proudly announced "I made this for you." Soli nodded her thank you and they both took a bite. At first chew, they simultaneously spat. "*Oye Mijo,* what are you trying to do here, give me botulism?" Saúl laughed uncontrollably. The sliced pork and ham were not only dry; they were colder than a stepmother's tit. The bread was hot indeed, but the Swiss cheese was only semi-melted and the pickle inside the sandwich was soggy. To see this man laugh so heartily made Soli laugh as well. When they were through, Soli said, I have some eggs downstairs, want an omelet?" Saúl hurriedly said "Oh no, Bella, I don't trust either one of us right now. Let me order something up from room service." He handed her the menu. A short while later, room service appeared with their meal and a replacement of Solimar's key.

"You look ever so familiar to me" stated Soli while munching on her grilled chicken caesar salad. "Well, it isn't often you get to look in the mirror without looking. We have the same color eyes, same skin tone and the combination isn't very common." Solimar contemplating his response asked "Where are you from?"

"I guess you still think I'm an immigrant looking for a wife?" Soli choked on a crouton, having forgotten her rudeness when they met at the beach. Saúl thoroughly enjoyed her mild embarrassment just as much as he had already enjoyed her previous one. Solimar reached for her glass of water, trying to clear her throat to apologize, but before she could, Saúl simply said

"I'm on vacation, assuming just like you. I, too, am American born, of Puerto Rican and Cuban descent, if that interests you."

"Sheesh. Nice combo. I'm pure Puerto Rican."

"I can tell."

"Como?"

"Your temperament; the pronounced Nuyorican accent; maybe even the color of your skin. Cubans tend to be either light or dark, not so very much in between." Having settled that issue, they leisurely enjoyed their midnight snack, Soli lounging in Saúl's robe wearing it as if it belonged to her, and they entertained themselves talking nonsense for a while. After some time, Solimar realized that Saúl was nodding off. 'Gee, I guess I'm boring him.' She gently nudged him, but not a minute before cleaning up the table and putting out the plates for hospitality to pick up. Solimar, if nothing else, knew how to be grateful. He opened his eyes and said, "Bella, I was not asleep, I was only watching you through my eyelids."

"Bello, we haven't even been formally introduced; however, I must get to my room like right now because it is 2:15 in the a.m."

"Si, *mi amor*, let me walk you."

'*Mi amor*?!' Code red, code red, get the fuck out Soli, you don't need this shit! "No, no, *esta bien*, it is fine, I can let myself out. I have the key now. I will be alright."

"Well okay Bella. Whatever you say boss lady, but you must leave the robe behind. I'm out of here first thing in the morning and don't want to pay for something I haven't even worn once. I, very much like you, prefer to walk around in the buff." Soli knew in her mind that if she would let him walk her, she might let him have his way with her. She gave him a nod of understanding, quietly unbelted and let the heavy terry cloth robe naturally slide off of her slender shoulders and onto the floor. She bent over, picked it up, walked over to the couch and neatly folded it, leaving it right there. Saúl was mesmerized; noting that her beauty was ever the more pronounced now that she was somewhat relaxed. "Thanks, brother; you really were a Godsend to me tonight. How could I ever repay you?" A thousand and one possibilities ran through his mind and other parts of his anatomy. With that statement of sincere gratitude, she picked up the key, gave him a kiss on his forehead and walked to the door while blowing yet another kiss and whispering "Sleep with the Angels." Saúl never in a million years expected that move and was left holding his dick in one hand and wiping the drool from his mouth with the other. The soft brush of her succulent nipple as she kissed his forehead tantalized the skin of his cheek that it had grazed. Soli had found the stairwell, thanks to him, and was in her room in the flash of a bolt of lightening.

The morning found Solimar up and about quite early. As she sipped her coffee, she contemplated Marisol's proposal. 'Should I just fucking run for my life? No. I have to look over what is left of her property and mine.' She picked up the phone and dialed Mari to brainstorm and perhaps come up with other options. There was no answer. Soli had no idea whatsoever if there was a time difference, so she just assumed that Mari was still sleeping. Just then, her phone rang. Good! "Mari?"

"Hola Bella" came through a gentle, but musky voice. 'Oh shit, he sounds even better on the phone.' Soli enjoyed the imaginary tingle of the touch in various places of her body that had gone neglected for quite some time. "How did you get my room number?"

"Miss, did you already forget about last night?" Solimar wanted to forget about last night, but was unable to thanks to this reminder. "What's up?"

"That would be a trick question that I rather not answer, Mamita." His response made her nipples ache. "Alright smarty pants that lives staying on my ass 24/7, what may I do for you?" Saúl, naked and still in bed, pulled the phone away from his ear and let out a chuckle, but he couldn't help but say "I haven't begun to ride your ass, but you will know when I do." Solimar hadn't had a good roll in the hay in months and wanted to volley back and forth with him, but instead said, "Well, what can I do for you Mister Bello?" Saúl responded with a big grin on his face.

"Well, let's see Miss Bella. The last thing you said before you left was something to the effect of how could you ever repay me. So seeing that I am a gentleman, and have the decency not to put you in the compromising position you left me in, I decided to ask if you would like to go for a dip."

"Where, when?"

"The pool, the ocean, we can dip to the bar, whatever!"

"I thought you were like leaving today."

"I changed my plans to stay on just one more day. I am rather selfish, you see, and with that invitation of repaying a debt, I thought I might as well cash in before tipping out." Furiously pacing the room and having arrived at the half true conclusion that this beautiful man was a confident, cocky bastard, Solimar asked "*como?*"

"Woman, have you looked in the mirror lately? I'd be the envy of this resort to be seen parading up and down with you!" Solimar, not quite ready to give in, decided to ante up the game, a giant, wicked smile crossing her face. "Well, that would be fine, but what's not to say that I, too, would enjoy a little head? I mean head game." Saúl smiled in anticipation. "What do you mean?"

"If being the envy of the resort is the goal here, perhaps we can make an entrance, then separate after a while and see who picks up more numbers."

"Oh so you want to play?"

"*Por que no*, Bello, like why not? Or is it that you don't know how to play the game?" Saúl, without missing a beat said "Sure Bella, I like that idea, it gives me a very comfortable hard-on."

"Puta! You are on!"

"Puta! You're on! But please have the common decency of putting some clothes on this time, huh? That would be an unfair advantage." Solimar got a laugh out of last night's escapade after all and said "Gimme a half hour so I can refresh myself."

"I'll pick you up."

"Gee, what a gentleman; two whole flights."

Soli hung up, excitement coursing through her veins. Competition always fueled her and the thought of a man again, even just to play with, made her feel inexplicably excited although not very hopeful. She jumped back in bed and started to play with herself abiding by the unwritten handbook rules for single women. Single Ladies Rule Number One: Never go into the meat market hungry. Rule Number One, Subparagraph "A": There is nothing more radiant than a woman freshly loved. 'I have the right to love myself and this will have to do…. for now.' Solimar's eyes rolled to the back of her head and she moaned as her back arched in ecstasy.

Marisol's Melancolia

Mari woke up with a headache from hell. The bottle of wine was gone and the pill bottle open. 'Where on earth *esta* Sol?' No doubt she was somewhere on the beach sun bathing her left tit this time. Knowing her friend, there would be no sense in having an uneven tan although she certainly didn't need one. Marisol had no idea that her friend had reached out to her while she was knocked the hell out. Mari prepared to take on the day. She looked in the mirror and realized that her hair was a matted mess. 'Okay, Marisol, let's get a grip.' She too somehow woke up disrobed, except not on exhibition. She gathered her toiletries, placed them into a basket and went for the communal bathroom. The thought made her skin crawl, and she had been avoiding bathing as much as possible. Chanel and shared bathrooms don't work very well together. She locked herself in and realized that she no longer had the luxury of leisurely showering, baths or even the use of the toilet; already someone was knocking on the door. She turned the shower on, ignoring the persistent knocking and thought 'screw it, this is my time.' She shampooed her hair with the cheap products she picked up, lathered up, rinsed, dried off, robed up and kept it moving. As she exited the bathroom, after cleaning up after herself, a man impatiently waiting, tapping his foot rudely greeted her "*Oye puta*, what took you so long?" Marisol turned and with a highly arched eyebrow said, "I know you ain't talking to me."

"Yeah, puta, I'm talking to you." Suddenly the voice coincided in her memory with last night's altercation. *"Puta es tu madre* you fucking *maricon!*" The man stared at her menacingly and she put down her little basket taking from it her razor and said "Come on *chucha madre*, I will gladly shave your dick off with this disposable razor and have the grim reaper at your door in a heartbeat and if you want more, don't be fooled by the cross hanging on my neck; God is probably East of Eden anyway and I can meet Him West of Eden if He wants me to...I will kill your ass with no remorse!" Taken aback, he said "Calm down Ma, I was just fucking with you." Marisol steadied herself and looking at him directly in his eyes, disposable razor in hand said "I ain't your Ma. Go fuck with the bitch that gave you birth you fucking dog or the woman you slapped last night, but not with me. Not with me! Maiming someone like you would taste better than eating a slice of Red Velvet Cake and I know you don't know squat about that."

"Suave, Mama, suave, I got you, I got you."

"You ain't got shit, not even enough heart to be a piss poor ass man." Marisol turned on her cheap *chinelas* and opened the door that led to her hellish sanctuary. Once inside she smiled faintly and thought to herself, 'Why couldn't I have controlled my household the way I just controlled this piece of shit?' She took the last apple from the bowl atop the microwave in her makeshift kitchen. She didn't bother to wash or peel it, but cut bit by bit into it and ate each slice off of the knife's blade.

Marisol decided not to pressure Solimar, but firmly decided to wait to hear from her for only one more day to find out whether or not she had considered coming to Panamá. This was survival and although she loved her friend to pieces, there was no time for Solimar's antics. Nine will get you ten that Solimar was frolicking on the beach with Adonis, but she did deserve it, after all she had done for Marisol. 'One more day' thought Mari. One more day of staying in this self-imposed prison of misery and then she surmised that she'd just have to get the fuck out of there, go to the family, go to the church and confess her non-sins, and start all over again. One more day and another hellish night to endure, but she was determined to do so.

Solimar Meets Saúl

Solimar had just finished 'preparing' for her date when she heard the gentle tap on her door. She did not quite understand why he didn't just open the door and let himself in; after all he had already seen her naked, why then stand on ceremony? "Come in Bello Bello" called out Soli from her suite's bedroom. "Bella, I can do many things, but I can't walk through doors." Soli giggled then wiggled her flat ass to the door. Still standing inside, she straightened up, smoothed the pony tail that she had piled high upon her head and affectionately greeted him with a kiss on the cheek. She wore a bikini and had wrapped herself in a sarong the color of their eyes adorned with many coins, a thin chain circling her 24 inch waist, several ankle bracelets circling above her sandaled feet. "You look adorable Bella; I think already that you might best me at my own game." Soli laughed and responded kindly …. "That is going to be difficult; there isn't a woman here that can resist such a refined and beautifully made creature as you are." Saúl hesitantly inquired. "I know this might seem odd to ask, but may I ask you a personal question? Solimar could not imagine what would be more personal than that which had transpired in the last 24 hours, but said "Go on."

"What is your name? *Como tu te llamas?*" Soli pursed her lips and flippantly answered with a wink "Bella. Do you have *un problema* calling me Bella?" Saúl shook his head no; after all he had named her that himself. With that declaration, subtly signaling that she preferred to remain anonymous, he kissed her forehead, offered his arm and escorted her to the pool's bar. As they walked, Saúl became amused, but even moreso enchanted by the faint sound of tiny cymbals with every step she took. Solimar was indeed an amazingly beautiful woman, but was but one step away from tacky, with all of her drapings, bracelets and dangling earrings. Even her pony tail holder had miniature bells. Saúl, although outwardly conservative, didn't mind, but kidded her and said "Bella, what's up with all the bells and whistles?" Solimar seriously looked at him, raised her left arm adorned with nine thin copper bracelets, raked the bit of hair off his eyes and said "I just wanted you to hear me coming." Saúl bit down hard on his lower lip knowing that she did not know what she had just said and smiled as he responded "Lady, I heard you coming when I saw you emerging from the ocean. I heard you clearly then and I really hear you now. My ears are well trained to decipher the cry of the sirens."

Seated at the bar, having ordered a pitcher of Bloody Mary and real Cuban sandwiches, Solimar, intrigued by this man who compared her to a mermaid childishly asked "Do you honestly believe in *sirenas*?" Saúl smiled broadly and said "I'm sitting with one right now. All I have to do is wrap that skirt or whatever you call it real tight right down to your ankles so you can't move, take off that bikini top, loosen your hair, sit you on a rock and take pictures!" Saúl smiled a rather devilish grin and then said "Maybe that's what I'll do so you can "repay" me." Solimar, as cautious yet gullible as always, asked "Do you believe in Santa Claus?" Saúl replied "Do you?"

"Well, the jury is still out on that one, but I would like to; I kind of think that it is neat for a guy to believe in things that don't exist; I mean, people gotta believe in something, right?"

"Well then consider yourself a believer, Bella. What would you like for Christmas? Tell me anything at all and I will make sure to get in touch with Santa and if I can't get him because he is too busy with the little ones, I'll bring it to you myself." Solimar took a long sip from her drink and said "you know I really don't have the answer to that question. I can't recall ever having been asked what I would like for Christmas, not even when I was small." She licked the end of her straw, winked at him and said "I'll have to think about that one for a while." It was Saúl's turn to take a long sip of his drink; his stomach churning with desire and his heart responding compassionately to her honesty and the sensuality that she exuded. Saúl simply said "You have a choice. In all actuality, you have many choices, but right now what would you like to do first? Think about what you want for Christmas, while I make suggestions, or have fun playing the game you proposed?" Solimar, tempted, but not ready to get caught up in a hopeless bind announced "Its playtime!" Saúl hid his disappointment and said "What the hell? We already know the object of the game. Take two hours and see how many numbers you can pick up and I will do the same."

"But wait. What is the prize?"

"I think dinner for two at the Four Seasons would suffice."

"*Estupido*, that is in New York!"

"Well, yes, a reason, win or lose, to see you again sometime, maybe this Christmas." Soli contemplated his proposition, took a swig and said "We will reconvene in a couple of hours; synchronize your watch, and now hit the ground running, let's go, *vamonos*, we've got work to do!" They kissed each other on the cheek and separated to work the room. As Soli departed, she felt like although fun, she really did not want to trawl for numbers she had no intentions on dialing and decided to walk the beach instead. She spent her time tanning on the beach, looking for the lost rosary beads and just in general having a good time by herself; not thinking about much of anything. True to Marisol's thoughts, Solimar actually released her left breast from its restraint, while nobody was looking of course, and took in a bit of sun. It felt heavenly and she begun to feel an unfamiliar feeling; the sensation of being secured. She applied herself to the process of not thinking and dedicated her time to absorbing the sights and sounds of her favorite place, *la playa*.

The two hours quickly passed when she realized that she had all but ten minutes before having to go back into the game that she herself had created. Soli started to run up to her room to jot down a bunch of fictitious numbers when it occurred to her that she didn't have to do that. She turned to head back to the tiki bar when she heard the now famous call of "Bella" and once again turned, this time to see him running to catch up to her. His powerful body ran along the surf shirtless. Soli's heart leaped, yet she stayed firmly in place, pleasantly surprised that he came for her rather than waiting at the bar. As he jogged towards her, she noticed that without stopping he actually was dropping his shorts and all hell broke loose in her mind. 'He truly is a god or something damn near close to it.' He ran naked on the beach towards her and she pointed towards the sea. He did, in fact, receive her signal and covered himself in the waves, his powerful body emulating that of a dolphin's. Soli tore off her sarong and ran towards the ocean in her string bikini. Inspired by his bravado, she tore off her top and swam to him with the strength of an athlete, entering his opened arms, wrapping her legs around his waist.

"*Nena*, are you okay?"

"I'm okay, are you?"

"No, Bella that was the most miserable two fucking hours of my life!" Bella threw back her head, laughed and said "Don't be so hard on yourself; I spent my two hours of fame literally scouting the beach, looking for my lost beads and tanning my other tit to match the one that was hanging out yesterday. I didn't pick up anybody because I don't want to be with anybody." Saúl answered simply "Neither do I, unless you let me want to be with you." He kissed her all over her face and she buried her head in his neck whispering "Now how the fuck are we going to get out of this one? You are totally naked and my tits are hanging out, like usual."

"The same way you got your ass downstairs yesterday. We just have to be bold, but please stay with me for a while longer; people are leaving and I am not ready to let go of you." They kissed deeply, each trying to get inside of the other.

"Bello?"

"*Si Bella mia?*"

"I really had fun today, the most fun I've had in ages, and to be honest, I was gonna write down a bunch of numbers when I realized that I didn't have to do that either." Soli smiled at him and asked "So how many numbers did you get?"

"None." Solimar could not believe that he did not get one bite judging from the bait he was working with. "Mami, I watched you from the bar the whole time. I took over some dude's binoculars and watched you the whole time. I never once let you out of my sight. Hell, the guy even said 'Hey, you could keep the lenses, but it'll cost you.'"

"Did you pay him?"

"Hell yeah I paid him. Well, I put his tab on mine and gave them back when I saw you struggling to make your way back to the bar. You looked so cute, walking around all big and bad. Did you find your beads?"

"Nope."

"Well, that is alright. I'm sure you have a fistful of them. *Vamos*, let's go home." He possessively led her by her hand as if she already belonged to him and not minding, she allowed him to take control. As they stepped from the ocean appearing like twin naked sea gods claiming land, Solimar was able to retrieve her top and quickly covered her breast, but her bronze Adonis had lost his shorts to the tide. Giggling, she quickly wrapped him in her sarong. He looked rather silly, but on second thought, Solimar concluded that he looked like an island warrior and she liked that. They made their way back to Saúl's room after, of course, having to appear at the front desk to retrieve a duplicate key and Solimar basked in the irony of it all. "Bello?"

"*Si querida*, what is it?"

"Remember when I tried to walk off with your robe yesterday?"

"*Si.*" Solimar, biting the tip of her index finger said "Well, I think that would be my sarong that is wrapped around your hot naked ass." Realizing that they were steps from his door, Saúl mischievously smiled and asked her "Do you want it right now?"

"Ssshhhhh, I'll get it later."

"Oh yeah, you can bank on that *preciosa*." Solimar held the door open long enough to allow her peek to linger over his body, noting a tiny patch of hair on the small of his back. Saúl turned and seductively asked "*Deseas algo mas*? Solimar, caught off guard, gasped and said "Ahhhhh, no, no, *nada*; just come downstairs. I'll be making us a bite to eat." Solimar, enthralled, waited for the elevator and rode it down two flights, amid a crowd of properly dressed guests and she still dripping wet in her bikini with no sarong.

Soli inwardly smiled as she prepared their omelet filled with some unknown cheese she had purchased. Although not a vegetarian, Solimar never hesitated to spend a little extra on exotic fruits, cheeses and organic vegetables. She sliced a sun-ripened tomato and poured just a hint of balsamic vinegar on it. 'You are damn right I have a fistful.' She served his cheese omelet accompanied by toasted French bread and a thick slice of cantaloupe, fine slices of kiwi together with a handful of Bing cherries and seedless grapes. She prepared a pitcher of Sangria and got ready to get her swerve on when Mari popped into her mind. "Excuse me. I need to make a phone call."

"Si Bella, take your time, I'm fine right here." Soli went into her bedroom and dialed again. The phone rang incessantly, but Mari had not even set up a voice mail. Damn. Solimar went to join Saúl and have their breakfast style dinner when it dawned on Soli that he would be leaving tomorrow.

"Bello."

"*Que*?"

"You are leaving tomorrow, right?"

"Yes, I just switched flights to spend the day with you and it was well worth it."

"I hope you don't mind my asking, but can you tell me where you live?" Saúl leaned back, wiped his mouth gently on the paper towel she had provided and contemplated her complexity which caused him to wonder why she would want to know his place of residence and not his name, not knowing where she was going with this and not caring either. His tanned skin glistened from the shower he took in Soli's suite while she cooked and the baby oil he himself pampered his body with. The white V-neck tee shirt he had retrieved from his suite along with his robe and body fitting boxer shorts only served to offset his smile and Solimar silently trembled awaiting his response. "Bella. *Yo vivo en* Isla Verde, Puerto Rico, where I was born. My parents retired years ago and then made an investment with their friends who had by then relocated to Panamá, so I am stopping through there before heading back to my home."

"Panamá? Did you just say Panamá?"

"Oh goodness, this omelet is quite delicious, did you sprinkle adobo on it or something?"

"Hear me out here! My friend just got deported to Panamá. That is the phone call I was trying to make. Wait! Let me get the address." Soli came running out of the room and showed him a tear and wine stained piece of paper with an address and phone number on it, in hopes that tomorrow he could get to her friend. Saúl said, "I think I know where that is. Rio Abajo is a bit tricky, but doable..."

"If I don't get through to her by the time you leave tomorrow, could you go to her for me? I've been trying to reach her and there is no answer. I'm getting nervous. She hasn't called and it is not like her. She wants me to go to her, but really I cannot."

"*Por que no?*"

"You ask me why not? Come on, I have to get back home. It's called work, back to reality, back to my life."

"Well, if your friend is in trouble, isn't that more important?"

"And who the fuck is going to feed me, *el Espiritu Santo*?

"Ummmmm, I think he already did his job with *La Santisima Virgen Maria*. What if I feed you instead?"

"What do you mean?"

"Bella, or whatever your real name is, I will have you on a flight with me in no time, all expenses paid and we will find your friend and you and I will have time to better acquaint ourselves and you come out the winner in this whole deal because you get to see another part of the world and they will get to see a real live *princesa* although I prefer to think of you as a *sirena*." Soli's heart raced and her palms began to sweat. "I can't do this. I'm down to my last fifty bucks."

"Well you do drive a hard bargain, but you won't ever best me at my game Babe. What if I put a thousand bucks in your Carolina Herrera handbag over there? Would that help make your decision?"

"It's a Kate Spade."

"It should be a Carolina Herrera … you know, support your own?" She downed her Sangria, poured another and said to him simply, "I cannot accept your generous invitation; however, if you give me your flight information, I will book myself. My friend, Marisol, has offered to pay my way, so she can just write out a check to my credit card when we get there or give me the cash if she has it on her. Thank God that I did bring my passport. Will you help me get to this address?"

"It will be the first thing we do as soon as we land, but I want to warn you about something. Rio Abajo is about nine or ten kilometers from the airport and maybe to you it will seem like what you are not expecting."

"What the hell is a kilometer?" Saúl smiled and said "Bellisima, it is not far, but it is an area filled with West Indians, all that came and settled, looking for work when the Canal was being built. It is an impoverished place, but filled with good, proud people…. There is a foundation there called the Silver People Heritage, or something like that. I know that this is too much information for you right now, but please just trust me. We will find your friend and all will be well."

After finishing his omelet, polishing off his fruit salad and downing the last of the Sangria, Solimar sent Saúl packing to get the flight information. He came back shortly and handed her an envelope filled with cash. Solimar, although touched, said "Please don't do this. I'm not that kind of woman." He reached for her and said "Listen, I know this is hard on you, let me help make it easier. I already know that you are very proud and you will feel safer with the extra dollars in your

Kate Spade handbag over there. Take it as a gift, no strings attached, you owe me nothing." Soli couldn't resist, her heart bursting with thankfulness, gave him a hug and ran to the phone and immediately called the airline and yes there were three coach seats available on the plane, and seven available in the first class cabin, but she definitely could not afford to fly first class next to him so she reserved a seat in coach, and that was more than fine with her. Solimar was a humble soul, mistaken for arrogant due to her beauty. When she returned, confirmed reservations in hand, Saúl explained to Soli that they would be going into a part of town that was a bit downtrodden and potentially dangerous. He instructed her to "tone it down a bit," not wear any jewelry and to trust that they would find her girlfriend and get her out of there. "Where will we go after that?" Soli asked, wide eyed and concerned. She'd had experienced enough ghetto in her life and couldn't even consider that Mari would settle into a place such as the one being described to her. She definitely would not be staying there, not if she could help it. "You guys can come to my parents' house, there is room." Soli did not quite like this idea of a man showing up at his parents' home with not just one, but two women. "Let me try to see if I can book my time share; I'm part of their exchange program. I don't even know if there is a location in Panamá, but I think that would afford Mari and me the privacy that we need."

"Look Bella, you do whatever you want, but I didn't find you in Miami to lose you to La Republica de Panamá." His tone was a bit irate and he begun to rake his fingers through his hair. Soli did the same. She didn't want to blow this, but damn! She still couldn't wrap her head around what she was doing. Should she look a gift horse in the mouth or was she really just getting herself into a situation that she would be unable to handle? She shyly commented "*Machista, si*?"

"A bit, but in the event that you have not figured it out, this machista is quickly falling for you and I don't even know your name."

"*Yo me llamo Solimar.*" He let the name roll off his tongue savoring it syllable by syllable. "Sol y Mar...Ummmm, Sun and Sea or would that be "SeaSun" in English? Tell me that your parents didn't go to hell and back to name you, but if you don't mind, I'd like to call you Solita!" Solimar, recalling the nickname her mother so lovingly gave to her said "Please don't, that is too close to what my mom used to call me; she used to call me Solitita, but you can call me Soli or Sol if you like." Saúl stared at her, piercing her with his aquatic eyes, inviting her to drown in them, wanting to know her, wondering what was behind this imp of a black magic woman that made him hang on her every word, her every move and the tinkering of bells that always seemed to follow her. Saúl was accustomed to beautiful women, having briefly dated a former Miss Puerto Rico. He wasn't the type of man to love them then leave them. He just didn't love them, but this one had him baffled and he found himself doing the unimaginable, kneeling at her feet. Soli, who was perched upon a barstool, looked down and wondered what he was doing. He started by kissing her knees while massaging her calves and her ankles. As he approached her toes, ready to suck each one individually, Solimar begun to quiver and quake. "Stop it!" Solimar was visibly upset. He looked up at her and simply said, "I'm only paying homage to probably several goddesses at once, not just you. Forgive me if I have offended you or overstepped my boundaries." Having been slightly injured by her abrupt rejection, Saúl got up on his feet and said "I guess you better start packing, I'm all packed and ready to go since I was scheduled to leave today, remember?" Soli looked into his eyes, feeling heady from the kisses and confused. She said "I don't even know your name."

"Bello." He replied flatly. Soli weakly smiled all the while realizing that she had met her match. She said "Go, *mi amor*, I will pack and see if I can book my time share although that is probably not very likely." Saúl leaned in and gently kissed the tip of her refined nose understanding that she was reluctantly tossing caution to the wind and placing herself in his hands.

Soli was filled with desire, but restrained herself. "I'll be by for you at 5:00 so we can have a decent breakfast before heading towards the airport; airplane food sucks and besides, I rather eat with you instead of us having breakfast apart. I can't believe you booked coach, but that's fine. Sleep with the Angels, Soli." He winked at her and she returned the wink. By midnight, after having packed everything including the hotel's complimentary toiletries, Soli had this feeling of dread in her heart. She still had been unable to reach Mari. Soli piled her hair up high, making a messy bun out of it, rubbed her face and dialed Saúl's room. "*Que es mi Bella?*" came through his soothing voice. Soli didn't even bother to ask how he knew it was her. "Want some company?"

"I was actually in the process of petitioning God to help a brother out with some good company particularly that of a blue-eyed sorceress with long hair and a shitty-ass attitude."

"Prayer answered. I'll be right up." Soli didn't bother getting dressed. She threw on her hotel robe and walked up the stairs in her flip-flops assuming that he might like to start where she had interrupted him. Instead, he was standing at the door completely nude and she dropped her robe even before the door slammed shut behind her. Saúl picked her up and walked to his bedroom, laid her down and tucked her in. He spooned her and she just let the tears flow. Solimar was frightened. Saúl was touched by her softness, the mild coconut scent of her skin and the silent, but steady flow of lukewarm tears, amazed by the size of each drop. He tucked her under his chin, wrapped his leg and arm around her, cradling her head in the crook of his right arm. He rocked her and begun to hum a little Spanish lullaby. Soli chimed in with the words and the lullaby turned into a tickling session that ended up in a full-fledge pillow fight in the raw. Exhausted at 3:00 a.m., Soli asked "do you think we can grab two hours worth of sleep here?"

"Yes, Ma'am you most certainly can. You can sleep on the lounge chair in the balcony."

"What?! Puta, I have my own fluffy bed downstairs!"

"Solimar, can't I just watch you from here? In the event that you haven't noticed, I'm hard as hell and am trying not to touch you, but it's getting really kind of difficult. We've been fucking around naked just about all day long!" Soli tried to decipher all of this and decided to go with the flow. "Aren't you gonna get some sleep?"

"No Solimar. If I grab some shut eye, we won't make the flight. Go take your nap already. I'll put on some coffee and I'm just going to watch over you from here."

"Yeah, you're gonna watch me through your eyelids." Soli sashayed her little flat behind over to the balcony, slammed down the pillow and allowed the moonlight to clothe her nakedness. Saúl, who was not attracted to model types, preferring a well-proportioned woman, smiled to himself while thinking 'this girl is shaped like a hanger, has no ass, a bit of tits and a waist that I probably could never expand even if I fed her beer and chips day and night, but damn if I don't want her.' The more he admired her, the sicker he became with desire for her, a knot forming in his stomach and his groin aching relentlessly. As he went to close the glass sliding door, Solimar whimpered and he saw another giant tear roll down her cheek. That was it for him. "Come to me Solimar, *ven*." Soli walked as if drugged and fell into his arms. "Can I make love to you?"

"*Si*." Neither recalls who asked or who consented, they just made love and clung to one another for dear life. They slept soundly wrapped in each other, twisted like a pretzel, when Saúl jumped up startled and yelled "Fuck! We missed the plane Soli!" Soli rubbed the sleep from her eyes and said "Calm down, we will get the next one."

"There is only one flight from here to there. *Puta Madre*, now what?" Soli cried. "It's all my fault, *mi culpa*." At this Saúl softened, drew her close and rocking her said "Sol, baby, I'm not mad at you. Nothing bad happened. We just fucked up or were too busy fucking around."

"You don't understand Bello; I have to get to Marisol." Saúl's face lit up with a mischievous smile and slid his index finger down her nose before kissing it. "Solimar y Marisol. How cute, the two of you. Don't worry Babe; we are getting to Panamá today. Just go downstairs and fix yourself, you look a beautiful wreck. We are out of here today!"

Solimar offered herself to him once again and although they were both painfully tender from a few hours prior, they managed with the help of a little baby oil. They took each other in until they exploded together amidst hungry kisses and private wishes. He softly disentangled himself from her, and as he did, they both let out a small howl from the delicious discomfort of their disengagement. Saúl sent her downstairs to get ready with a mild pat to her behind. Soli had no energy to question, no energy to fight, no energy even to fully bathe. She did the best she could at the sink and threw on her denim skirt, which she had pressed the previous night together with a white tank top and hurried on little silver sandals as she rushed against the clock. She went with no makeup. Her hair was a tangled mess, and she didn't bother trying to detangle it as due to its length would have taken too much time. She decided to braid it and tried to make it look presentable. She felt like a truck had run her over, both physically and emotionally. Still, no prayer in her, but this time staring at her somewhat broken and somewhat happy image in the mirror, she managed to softly say out loud "Glory be to the Father, to the Son and to the Holy Spirit ... as it was in the beginning it is now and ever shall be world without end, Amen." She genuflected, crossing herself various times and with that she walked out the door, pulling her luggage behind her and taking her first steps towards an uncertainly safe haven.

Marisol Meets Marisol

Mari woke up from another drunken, pill-induced stupor. She couldn't find the freaking phone. 'Damn it! I'm in no condition, but I have to get out of here!' She placed one delicate leg in front of the other and dragged herself to the make-shift *cocina* to brew a small pot of coffee. A knock on the door startled her, as nobody, but nobody knew she was there, save for Solimar and her nasty landlord, but her weekly rent payment wasn't due just yet. She opened the door cautiously, with the security chain still latched, to encounter none other than Mr. Puta who was cleanly shaved, presentably dressed, holding out her toiletry basket. "You left this yesterday out here when you threatened to kill me, Marisol." Marisol startled that he knew her name and against her better judgment, smiled at his feeble attempt to be civil. Having no choice, but to unlock the chain to get her basket, she opened the door and said "Thank you, Puta; I really do appreciate your concern."

"Can I come in?"

"*Puta, chucha madre no!*"

"Please?"

"What part of motherfucking no, don't you get man?"

"Please. Pretty please. *Por favor.* I got something important to say to you." Mari stood aside and allowed him in. As he made his awkward entrance, memories that she tried to oppress suddenly flooded her and she was once again overwhelmed by recollections best forgotten.

Roberto sat on the broken chair. The legs of the chair gave way and he fell down, and despite the fact that it was not funny at all, Marisol doubled over with laughter. When she realized that Roberto didn't think that it was a laughing matter, she quieted down and offered him a cup of coffee. "Wanna cup?"

"Of what?" He asked stifling his embarrassment. "*Estupido de mierda*, you piece of shit, what the hell else do people drink in the morning other than coffee?" Roberto smiled, gold tooth and all, and said "Well, judging from all the bottles ...." Mari's compassion and personal embarrassment kicked in forcing her to ask politely "Would you like a drink instead?" Roberto nodded eagerly realizing that she honestly meant it and was not making fun of him. Already he had started his tremors and was in need of a shot. Mari caught this and went straight for the bottle of rum she had not yet opened and prepared for him a rum, heavy on the orange juice, popped open a bottle of multivitamins and gave him one. Roberto giggled and said "Hey girl, I didn't come here to get high."

"It's a vitamin, *idiota*. Why did I bother to let you in?"

"Mari, don't you remember me?" Marisol remained frozen in time as he recited *"ad infinitum per veritatem."* Marisol hypnotized repeated "Towards the infinite through the truth."

"Yes, Marisol. That is the motto of our alma mater. What we were taught to live by; I'm glad you haven't forgotten it. Remember me now?"

"I don't want to remember you Rober, you slapped me for no good cause, remember that shit?"

"I slapped you for a very good cause Marisol. You kept your eyes on those books and never on the world. You never saw anything other than that which was only right in front of you, but you never saw me."

"Did you complete your law degree Roberto?"

"Yes, I did. Did you finish your degree in medicine?"

"Well, it was not medicine, per se, it was social work then I switched to psychology, but no, I took a long break then opted out to a student exchange program, which took me several years to get into and once I did, it winded me deported right back here; long story for another day."

Marisol was mystified by the fact that Roberto had once again happened upon her life, but this time, in the moment of her greatest despair, recalling clearly their short-lived soirees, the heated passion that sadly ended in the infraction of a man hurting a woman for reasons that she will never understand. "I came to get you out of here. I heard that tonight a couple of gangs will be settling their differences in the alleyway and it could get real ugly. Wouldn't want anyone climbing up the fire escape and breaking into your spot trying to get away, you know?" Marisol, unnerved simply said "*Gracias.*"

"I have a place you can spend the night at. It is a hole in the wall, but you will be safe."

Marisol cut up her eyes and stated "It can't be worse than this hell hole." He looked around the room and said "It might be about the same."

"You expect me to go sleep with you?"

"I don't have a problem with that, but if you don't want to, well, I'll bring you back around 3:00 or 4:00 in the morning; by then the only thing that'll be left is spilled blood and guts."

Marisol shuttered at this thought. How could her life possibly get any worse? She said "Come back for me this afternoon. I will go with you. How much will I owe you for this favor?"

"In case you haven't noticed, I'm a bona fide drunk. Just keep the booze flowing and we'll be good. Maybe we will hang by the Canal all day long or perhaps the river if it pleases you better and we can catch up on how life has treated us throughout the years." Mari was a bit surprised at him, or even that he was actually the man she threatened to castrate a day before.

"You are a well-spoken drunk."

"I used to be a lawyer, but shit happens."

"*Esta bien*, I'll see you at 3:00 or so."

Roberto pushed forth the empty glass, quietly asking for another.

Marisol said "*Hombre*, its only 8:00 o'clock in the freaking morning."

"Well, as the Americans say, its noon somewhere in the world." She complied, albeit a bit afraid, but gave him his drink which he swallowed in one quick gulp and disappeared with not even a courteous goodbye. Marisol secretly hoped that he did not get drunk before coming by for her later, but realized that she had little or no options.

Mari searched high and low for her charger and found it underneath her bed. As she tried to call Soli, she realized that the phone's battery had discharged completely and rather than wait, Mari hurriedly threw on a pair of jeans and ran to the local *bodega*, purchased a phone card and used the public phone outside of the store. When she requested to be connected to Solimar Santana's room, she was informed that Miss Santana had checked out that very morning. Mari slammed down the phone. Frustrated and helpless, she went back to her apartment and got ready to be picked up by Roberto. Hell, she was not ready to face the music yet, and that bitch of a girlfriend had not come through. Solimar was on her way back to New York. Little did Marisol know was that Solimar S. Santana was preparing to board a private jet, thanks to the one only known to her as Bello.

Saúl Meets Solimar

"Mami, you smell so good, what perfume is it that you're wearing?" Solimar, somewhat annoyed said "Eau de Pussy. I haven't even showered." Saúl laughed and said, "I guess there was something to the movie, The Scent of a Woman." Soli rolled her eyes. She was desperate with anticipation and excitement. They awaited their "private jet" on the tarmac, passports in hand. Solimar was growing more and more concerned as the moments passed. It was not customary for her to run off with a man just on his word or her need. That is when she realized that she still did not know his name. "Listen here, I'm traveling with a man I call Bello, what is your name please." Saúl broke it down in syllables as he preferred the two syllable Spanish version of his name as opposed to the monosyllabic English version. "*Sa...úl, mi amor.*" Solimar shook her head, expecting something a bit more exotic. "I prefer Bello."

"Call me what you want, but just call me."

Within moments, the pilot showed up and asked for their passports. Saúl stepped back to allow Soli to reveal hers first. There it was in big bold letters: **Solimar S. Santana.** Saúl's heart pounded. He quickly put forth his passport as Soli boarded the plane. She turned to see him and waved him to hurry, her slender fingers dancing in mid air like a tattered flag beckoning a heart to return home, a heart that relocated elsewhere. Saúl boarded with a tight smile on his lips, not wanting in any way to disappoint his girl. Soli's excitement was contagious, but he knew he had to get to the bottom of this. "*Que pasa Puta*, you look like you just seen a ghost?" Soli excitedly asked. "*Nada*. I just have a bit of a headache. Try and get some sleep Soli. I'll do the same."

"I can't sleep, you're crazy?! I'm going to Panamá! I want to see everything and I mean everything, including the clouds!"

"Well, see them by your lonesome. Panamá is just an isthmus located in the middle of nowhere connecting North and South America bordered by Costa Rica, Colombia, the Caribbean Sea and the Pacific Ocean. Solimar asked "What in hell is an isthmus?" With that he reclined his chair, turned away from her and allowed the invisible tears to flow. "Something like a fucked up island."

In his heart, in his soul, in his mind came the simple words "*Santa Maria, Madre de Dios.*" He reached for the Blessed Mother's intercession then reached into his pocket and handed Solimar her lost rosary. "Pray for us Soli. I have forgotten how." Astounded, Soli took the beads from him. "What the hell? When did you find this?"

"I found them in the sand the day I met you. I went back for you, but you had already left and I picked it up. I was holding it hostage as an excuse to see you again."

"What do you mean?" He kept his back to her as he did not want her to see the distraught look on his face or have to respond to an inquisitive stare. "Sol, if I hadn't bumped into you that night, I would have hunted you down and returned your beads, if only just to see you once again; I had already changed my flight for that purpose. I used the ice machine thing as an excuse to walk every floor of the hotel hoping to find you and was ready to camp out in the lobby until I did. I even aggravated the hell out of the concierge, describing you and trying to get him to reveal your name and room number that day."

Soli didn't know whether to laugh or cry, when the pilot announced "Please fasten your seatbelts. We are clear to take off. We expect to land in Panama City at 1:30 p.m. The weather is clear and I expect our flight to go smoothly. Relax and enjoy your ride." As they took to the skies, Soli raised the armrest between them and snuggled behind his back. She playfully tickled him until he turned around and turned into her. They kissed for what seemed like hours, fondled one another respectfully, and the devils surrounding them laughed the perpetual laugh like only devils do. They were in love beyond love and Saúl's tears flowed freely with every kiss. Soli did not question the tears. Her heart was crushed already.

Their Guardian Angels convened and immediately called a conference and filed an emergent application for extra wings and wisdom on how to proceed. Pacing back and forth, strategizing, they agreed that they had to temporarily pour angelic blessings, which are not so easily dispensed, but with God's permission, they were carefully spilled from the spiritual realm and the Warriors that had been summoned appeared and were instructed to watch over these two while the reinforcement arrived. The two slept peacefully in one another's arms. The Warriors, knowing that this was but a temporary measure, came into unanimous agreement that declaring war was the necessary remedy. The Angels agreed with the Warriors' strategy and awaited Heaven's consent. A battle was indeed formally declared in the heavenlies on behalf of these two poor, innocent, yet seemingly disgraced souls. Hell was about to meet fury and that is never fun. There would be casualties, but hell and Satan were about to be served. Usually it is the other way around. Satan lives at Heaven's gate constantly badgering God, pointing out what God already knows in advance. In the case of Solimar and Marisol, he would have a field day about their backsliding ways and seemingly loss of faith in Him. The Guardians with their insight and protective love of their charges anticipated that they would be granted permission to bring on the war first in order to avoid an untimely death, as Death itself was approaching the arena, the stench of sulfur infiltrating the atmosphere. The Guardians called for emissaries, but instead St. Michael showed up, having already dispatched the messengers, mid-flight, who had been on their way to this heavenly meeting. The Guardians and Warriors bowed their heads, covering their heads and faces in reverence and carefully listened to Michael's instructions communicated in a furious flutter of wings and tongues of vivid fire. They quietly retreated as the Archangel disappeared into the stratosphere, leaving a twinkling, yet blinding white light behind him ... a reflection of the sword conferred upon him by no other than the Almighty who sits on the heavenly throne when Michael was knighted, having replaced Lucifer, the fallen one.

Soli missed out on the flight experience, as did Saúl. They slept the sleep of the just, forehead pressing upon forehead, and did not even feel the touch down. They were literally flying on wings of Angels. Their "personal" pilot gently woke them up. They still had their seatbelts loosely fastened around them from takeoff. They really didn't need them, having a legion of angels monitoring even the breaths they took in. Soli woke up in a daze, a bit disappointed to have missed the spectacular view, but excited to be minutes away from her friend she hurriedly exclaimed "*Yala, vamos*, let's hit it Bello."

"Soli relax your nerves, we still have to clear customs."

"Puta! Fuck and damn all this shit to hell!" Soli pouted and Saúl licked the tip of her nose. "Puta Bella, we are in Panama City!" Soli broke out into an ear to ear smile. 'This man is calling me a whore and I love it' she thought to herself before spitting it out anyway. "Puta your daddy!"

Saúl's heart continued to break while his smile continued to broaden. Twenty minutes later they were walking through the terminal on their way to the taxi stand when Soli asked "how was it that the process went so smoothly?"

"I'm a diplomat Solimar. I work out of the *embajada* here and when I'm not working here, I am working out of the consulate in Puerto Rico. Solimar's jaw dropped. *"Que sorpresa!* Ain't you a little box of surprises! I feel really safe now!"

What both Saúl and Solimar did not anticipate was the next surprise they were about to encounter that would forever change their lives. Saúl had not counted on the fact that the limo driver would be holding up a sign publicly announcing his name. His personal chauffer had the day off having already exchanged it to meet with Saúl the day before. His replacement saw no harm in raising a sign, considering that he had never met Saúl before and had no idea what he looked like, never once considering that a *diplomatico* would recognize a limousine adorned with the Panamanian flag and matching plates. Saúl tried to hurry her past the sign, but no sign would escape the eyes of Solimar Santana, especially one bearing the cause of her fascination with her heritage and last name. There for her and the world to see was her ultimate welcome to Panamá: **SANTANA.**

"Santana?" Your last fucking name is Santana?" Solimar's mind was incapable of capturing the ramifications of that bit of information. Saúl said "Listen, we have to get over to Marisol's. We will figure this out later."

"You knew motherfucker?"

"I know nothing and don't talk to me that way unless you want me to start treating you like a little bitch." Soli bit her tongue and proceeded with caution, remembering not to ask a question you did not want answered or already knew the answer to. She climbed into the limo and they silently rode over to the part of town that no one any longer wanted to be in, including them. Soli put on her oversized sunglasses, and viewed what seemed to have been an affluent neighborhood at one time. The houses were run down; people aimlessly walked the streets as if they had nowhere else to go. Out in the open were free games of dominos and the gated alleyways hosted games of dice played for profit. Solimar smiled at the irony that ivory domino tiles played upon a table, practically made the same chinking sound as ivory dice hitting the pavement. Broken beer bottles of all colors littered both sidewalks and streets. Women in white, flowers in their hair were a dime a dozen. Women who pandered their wares near the alleyways charged much more, but it seemed to Solimar that a crisp twenty dollar bill could take a man a long way. Solimar shook her head realizing that poor was poor all over the world, but here, in this place, poor did not compare to poor back home. It seemed harder, darker and

Solimar forgetting her immediate problem, focused on the fact that she had to get her friend the hell out of there at any cost. They pulled up to Mari's address. Soli and Saúl had not spoken to one another during the entire car ride, but he did take her hand in his and she did not resist. He gently squeezed it from time to time, trying to elicit a response from her, feeling regretful over their harsh verbal exchange in the parking lot, but Solimar had remained silent, opting to absorb the poverty, afraid to get into any discussion that would divert her thoughts from her mission.

The driver opened Solimar's door and helped her out of the vehicle. Saúl quickly followed, whispered something into his ear and the driver nodded his consent and returned to his post to wait. They walked up the one flight to find Mari wheeling out her mid-sized suitcase of recently purchased goods, a tall, nice looking Black man at her side. They truly stood frozen in time as the women glared at one another as if they had not seen each other in ages and the men backed off, correctly sensing that this would be an emotionally charged reunion. "Where are you going?" Soli boldly asked. "What business is it of yours?!"

"Bitch, I'm here. You are my business." They stood there, two stubborn and confused women, wounded by their own circumstances, not even knowing anything anymore. Saúl thought to himself that this was certainly not what he had expected and decided to break the tension that hung like frigid air. "Allow me to introduce myself, my name is…" Mari held up her hand and said "I know who you are. You are the Bello Adonis and you know that I'm Marisol, so let's cut the crap." Soli was taken aback by her friend's defensiveness and quite hurt that she would speak to Saúl in that tone. Saúl squared himself behind Soli as did Roberto with Mari, the men now making eye contact one with the other. "Saúl. Would you be kind enough to give Marisol your contact information in the event that she decides she wants a friend again? My cell doesn't have international connection and I'm in no hurry to go running to buy yet another calling card and make phone calls that go unanswered." Mari shamefully hung her head for a minute and when she looked up to see Saúl furiously writing his private cell number on the back of his business card and Soli fighting back tears, she dropped her luggage and quickly grabbed her friend and hugged her tightly. "I'm sorry Soli; I just didn't think you were ever going to come."

"It's okay, it's alright! Don't cry, it's fine now, I'm here." Roberto chimed right in "Thank you Lord Jesus Christ in Heaven and all you other folks up there! This was gonna be worse than the gang fight tonight!" Saúl exhaled realizing that these two goddesses who were at an impasse, diplomatically managed to get past it without international incident or spiritual intervention. "I need a drink!" Saul declared. Roberto said "Shit, I need a whole damn bottle, but before that, allow me to introduce myself. I'm Roberto Robles, a former, well, you know, classmate of Marisol. We studied together for a short time at Columbus University right here in Panama City." The four exchanged cordial handshakes, nervously laughing, some discreetly wiping tears from their faces and they all worked themselves into the limo; Roberto, Marisol and Saúl deciding that a *"cuchitril"* would do them just fine. They weren't quite ready to be seen in "public." Roberto knew just where to go. Solimar, out of the loop, asked "Okay, before I agree to this, what exactly is a *"cuchitril?* Is it a place they sell *cuchifritos*?" Roberto confounded asked "What in the hell are *cuchifritos*?" Saúl started laughing at the confusion Solimar had inadvertently created and Marisol was forced to break it down to the both of them. "Roberto, *cuchifritos* are a variety of fried foods, like croquettes, stuffed potatoes, plantains, blood sausages, you know, *morcilla* and a variety of other foods that come under this category; very big in Puerto Rico, not to mention the South Bronx and Manhattan." Before Roberto could ask Marisol to explain to him where, Marisol turned and addressed her friend. "Solimar, a *cuchitril* is what you would say, ummmm, *una ratonera*, a dump, a dive, a hole in the wall, *me explico*?" Solimar stared at Roberto and Roberto stared right back at her. Solimar broke silence. "You know, I'm not sure I like you taking us to some cuchi joint that don't sell no *cuchifritos*."

Roberto shot back "Well, I'm not sure I like you either, you cuchi cuchi eating *cuchifrita* about to go to a *cuchitril* for the very first time!" Marisol turned to Saúl and said "Are you going to just sit there or are you going to help me mind the children?"

"Nope, I haven't been inside a *cuchitril* in ages and I'm going to get my cuchi on, so you're all on your own!" Solimar playfully tickled Saúl, extended her hand for Roberto to kiss and Marisol breathed a "good grief" as they climbed out of the limo and stepped into the most beautiful hole in the wall Solimar had ever seen; a quaint, discreet out of the way spot, with no advertisement, no fanfare, not even a blackboard outside announcing their specials for the day. Solimar whispered to Mari "I thought this was a rat trap." Marisol said "What would I know Soli; I've never been here before!"

The restaurant seated no more than twenty people, with a pool table in the back room and an unobstructed view that overlooked the Panama Canal. It appeared to Soli like a private supper club or something chic like that although the granite top tables bore no tablecloths. Solimar was breathless and instantly broke into tears, as did Marisol, when they received their throwaway one page menu. There imprinted in big gold letters was the name of the restaurant: El Sol y El Mar. Roberto, knowing that this had struck a chord in both of them said "What is it? You're crying because there are no *cuchifritos* here? I told you that already!" Marisol leaned into him and said "Knock it off. You know why we're feeling sentimental." Saúl winked at Roberto and said "You guys cry, eat, do whatever you want; as for me I'm definitely going to treat myself to a *tremenda borrachera*!" Roberto said "Macho, I'm right behind you, what are you drinking?"

"Duque de Alba por favor." Roberto was impressed. It was obvious that Saúl had money, but now he showed that he had class to go with it. "That shit is what's up; I haven't had that since I graduated college. *"Oye mira"* he signaled the bartender *"Pon una botella del Duque!"* Solimar said "Are you serious? You're getting a whole damn bottle of that brandy from Spain,

El Duque? You really gonna get drunk." Marisol didn't give Roberto a chance to answer, but responded herself to Solimar. "Did you not just hear the man order a whole bottle for the table? I ain't drinking so it's on the three of you fools." The waiter came over with four brandy glasses and poured a generous portion for each patron. Marisol went for a glass first. "I thought you weren't drinking?" said Roberto. Marisol said "I wasn't until he poured it. Why waste it?" They raised their glasses and cried out a healthy *"Salud"* each knocking back their drinks in one gulp, chasing it down with freshly squeezed lemon water although there was no need. The Duke is one of the smoothest brandies you'll ever drink. Halfway through their bottle, Saúl feeling as if he arrived somewhere special in his life, enjoying the affects of the alcohol and the scent of his pretty woman by his side, started talking what we call, *mierda* - shit-talking; the favorite pass time of the happily drunk. "You know bro, this girl here, this *sirena*; she is one tough-ass cookie. I can't even break her down in bed!" Roberto said "She look like you gotta hit her over the head with a hammer!" Mar and Sol were in shock, but realizing that there was no offense meant, they sat back and watched these morons measure their cocks. "Hell, I was trying to get with this one tonight, but you two showed up, so basically, you blew up my spot and totally messed up my game plan!" Marisol said "Hold up, hold up and *holope*; there wasn't going to be a gang fight tonight in the alley behind my room?"

"Ahhhhhhh, nope! I just came by to return your little basket and when I realized that you weren't having me, I came up with Plan B." Saúl fell out and Solimar slightly shook her head at Mari who was already getting pissed off. Roberto continued "You see, I realized that you didn't remember me from college, since you were only in your first or second semester when we met; so I figured if you would remember me, and then spend a little time with me, you'd see that I really ain't no *puta cabron* and whatever else you called me. I'm really a good guy, but for real for real, I did hear that there might be a gang fight, I just wasn't too sure if I heard right, but they usually do it in that alley;

I think they pay the landlord not to call *la policia*." Marisol furled her eyebrows and kept quiet. Saúl cut in to keep Roberto from talking too much having read the look of concern on Marisol's face. "Like I was telling you before Roberto, I been with this one and she is a mess!" Soli cut in. "Then why are you with me and dragged me to Panamá if I'm such a mess?" It was Marisol's turn to signal Soli. Solimar eased up and Saúl kept right on rambling "You see, like this man had a plan today, that got all fucked up because of us, I gotta plan too and my plan is that after I finish off this bottle, I'm going to order another one!" Marisol, Roberto and Saúl laughed until their sides hurt. Solimar didn't find the humor in Saúl's drunken statement; having hoped that he was going to say something just a little different, or at the very least, a tad more eloquent.

As the jokes and festivities started to wane and they were waiting for their second round of coffee in hopes of sobering up, Marisol looked straight into Solimar's eyes and asked "Now what?" Having not given it much thought, Solimar shrugged her shoulders and replied "Fuck if I know girl; you were the one that dragged my ass over here" shrugging her shoulders again. Saúl fidgeted in his chair and Roberto just took another swig. Booze was good, especially today, drinking top shelf! "Listen Mar, let's just go crash in a nice room by the beach. I saw a Sheraton or something on Israel Street and we will figure things out as we go. I already called work and extended my vacation for another week, but I have to go back, so let's just make the best of it. These two jokers can come visit us if they want." Indignant, Roberto said "Jokers? Did this woman just call us jokers?" Roberto was quite insulted. "I'll have you know that I hold a law degree!" He adjusted his jacket and said "That's right. I am a lawyer!" and with that statement he hiccupped. The three burst out in their now familiar laughter and Roberto had no choice but to join in. Mari affectionately pinched his cheek and rubbed the top of his head. Saúl extended his hand for a shake and Soli blew him a kiss from across the table. When Roberto caught it in mid air she yelled "Sucker! Now I know why they call it the "Bar" association!" Saúl rewinding back to a previous comment said "Wait up and back up! What do you know about Israel Street Miss Bebe Soli who has never been to Panamá before in her life?" Solimar answered "I was looking out the car window checking things out, you know to see where things are located; I wasn't exactly gonna let you drive me to somewhere that I couldn't get back from." Roberto said "Watch your back son, you got a live wire on your hands in case you don't already know; if I were you, I'd throw that fish right back into the ocean!" Solimar stared at Roberto through squinted eyes and said "How do you know Saúl found me in the ocean?" Roberto shook his head and exclaimed "What?! I'm getting a headache here and it surely isn't from the Duke!" They laughed some more, finished their coffee and deciding to keep going, drank the rest of the evening well into the night, keeping their eyes upon the sun as it set gently behind the exquisite Panama Canal. They closed down the "cuchitril" and Roberto requested the tab. Roberto and Saúl began arguing over the right to pay the bill. The head waiter defused the escalating argument. "Gentlemen, there is no bill. It has already been taken care of."

"That is totally impossible, what do you mean the bill has been 'taken care of'?" demanded Saúl. Roberto, recalling that the two women had taken a rather long time when they went to the ladies room, and further recalling that he had asked Marisol to keep the booze flowing said "I get it man. I know what happened." Turning to Marisol he said "You didn't have to do this. That bill was an easy $300 dollars." Marisol lied and said "Well, Solimar and I split it, we wanted to treat you guys, you know, looking out for looking out?" Roberto, perplexed said "Well that must be some *gringa Americana* stuff because no chick around here has ever treated me that wasn't my mother!" Saúl concurred. "I agree, and thank you lovely ladies. Next time it'll definitely be on me and you two won't be allowed to sneak off into the bathroom, so make sure you two pee before you start drinking like fishies."

Everybody Meets Roberto

As they left the restaurant, Mari again asked "Now what?" They stood right outside of where they sat some six hours or so ago. They were all drunk from alcohol, others from alcohol and love, and one from alcohol and the richness of the moment. The limo had long since been dispatched. Four drunks, three pulling suitcases behind them walked the streets of Panamá, but none of them even remotely resembled a tourist. "Is it safe to sleep on the beach?" Soli asked Roberto. Before Roberto had a chance to answer, Saúl gently interrupted "Remember how we were born Solimar. We have mothers and fathers; we don't have to sleep anywhere but in a home or a safe environment." This statement struck Mari's heart and she began to cry, nasty drunk girl tears. "I guess that means I have to go to my parents." Soli, worried about her friend, asked "Mari, what is wrong with going home where people love you?" Marisol wiped her tears and finally confessed to everyone "I'm adopted!" I don't even know who I am! I'm not Panamanian, I'm not American; I'm a whole bunch of people that I don't know! Don't get me wrong, I appreciate that these people took me in, but I don't belong to them. They tell me that I'm Colombian and Jamaican, but who really knows?"

"Colombian *and* Jamaican? What the fuck is that Mari?" The two laughed momentarily at Solimar's innocent insensitivity and Roberto's heart just broke. Solimar, now very curious, kept it moving "What happened, *que paso*, like what? What else did anyone tell you about your parents?"

"I don't know what the fuck happened. Supposedly my mother died while giving birth to me and my stupid asshole of a father couldn't figure out what to do, so he left me in care of the hospital to put me up for adoption!"

"So your father was Colombian or were you given your adopted parents' last name?" Mari shook her head no although that did not clear up anything. "My mother, may her soul rest in peace, was the Colombian. Apparently, they weren't married so the hospital labeled me "*Niña Espinoza*" until I got adopted, and the family gave me the name Marisol, but never changed my last name believing that one day, I would want to know the truth, or whatever the hell they were thinking." Solimar nodded, fully relating to the heartache caused by not knowing who you are or where you're going and much less how you're going to get there. She glanced over at Saúl and wondered why she didn't check out Ancestry.com in the hotel's internet room before boarding the plane.

Mari broke Soli's train of thought which was already heading in a totally different track when she said "I don't want to go back to them yet. They are nice people, I promise they are, but I feel like a complete failure!" Saúl gently placed his hand on Mari's shoulder and said "No. Don't go if you are not ready. We can all crash at my parents' place or check into a nearby hotel for the night until we figure things out. Don't cry, please don't do that." This only served to make Mari cry even harder and Roberto, dumbfounded, confused and not capable of dealing with the emotions floating in the air just broke out and slapped the living daylights out of Marisol. "Puta! Stop this shit already!" Wide eyed and back on earth, Mari slapped him back. Soli reached to get in between them, but Saúl wrapped his arms around her quickly and whispered "Let them work it out." With the fury of alcohol in her veins, Soli lashed out and attempted to slap Saúl, but her hand never made contact. He blocked her with the precision of a trained martial artist. "No woman has ever nor will ever slap me, got it?!" He held her right wrist in his iron fist, his right hand securing her left arm behind her back. Staring deeply into her eyes, seeing fear, instead of kissing her, he playfully bit her cheek, but bite her he did. "I'm sorry."

"No, you aren't, but I know for sure you won't pull that bullshit again." Mari sat her ass down on the side of the road and the warm, humid night aggravated their passionate outburst; she was sweating and uncomfortable. Roberto paced around her asking her to please just get up and let's go. After a while, Mari got up, sickened to her stomach feeling nauseous and just wanting a hot bath, cool shower and a clean bed. She said "Come on Soli, we're checking into that hotel you saw right now!" Mari begun to move towards her friend and Saúl set Soli free from his vice-like grip. "Like hell you are! All you crazy ass motherfuckers are coming to my house!" They all looked at Roberto, astonished by his remarkably gleeful outburst and glancing at one another nodded in agreement that his suggestion would be the wise thing to do. Saúl walked over to Roberto, who was lit to the maximum level and happier than a pig in slop and said, "Come on man, lead the way."

Putting his arm over Roberto's shoulder they walked together. The "ladies" followed in tow and to everyone's surprise, Roberto's home was just a block away. A beautifully appointed Victorian home awaited them with bedrooms to spare or share. He let everyone in, called for the housekeeper who came running and politely asked her to please set up a nightcap and bring a couple of cigars from the humidor. Soli and Mari felt like a couple of jerks; moreso Mari who had been prepared to go spend the night in another roach infested room, not capturing quite yet that Roberto had only been testing her willingness to be in his company. Saúl, extremely pleased with the accommodations, graciously accepted Roberto's hospitality and quickly went to the bathroom to wash his face. The four of them were disheveled, tear stained and completely inebriated; each were on the verge of losing their dignity had it not been for the alcoholic, who in drunken wisdom, came to their rescue. Soli and Mari were told that their bedrooms were ready replete with adequate night clothes to wear, if needed. The housekeeper was aware of Roberto's plans for the evening, but was surprised to see that he tagged on another couple into the equation. Soli graciously thanked Roberto's housekeeper and before following her to her assigned guest room leaned into Saúl and whispered "This shit ain't over. You and I have to make some time to talk." Saúl begged off the inevitable battle. "Not tonight Solimar, please not tonight. We are both exhausted and nothing will be accomplished." Soli nodded, letting him off the hook for at least the night. "Do you want me to sleep with you?"

"No, Solimar. It isn't appropriate, but even if it were, I haven't the strength to hold you, much less play with you. You are a pain in my ass and I need some time to get you out from under my skin." Soli examined his face deeply "You think you could?"

"No, I'm just talking more shit to hear myself talk it."

"*Gracias Saúl.*"

"*De nada, mi amor.*"

"I will see you in the morning, *si*?"

"That's only a couple of minutes away."

"Love you." Saúl tenderly kissed her cheek and momentarily played with a loose curl that framed her radiant from alcohol, love and confused face. "Love you back." Solimar followed the housekeeper, realizing that she had just confessed to loving Saúl. Marisol in the meantime was deep in conversation with Roberto, each profusely apologizing to one another and Marisol thanking Roberto all at once. She had grossly misjudged him and felt embarrassed by her actions. She quickly made her exit and was also escorted to her room. The two "ladies" retreated to their private baths, the men stayed up to have one last brandy and a cigar.

"What do you think of them two?" Saúl asked. Roberto puffed long and hard on his cigar. "You tell me, them nuts are your friends." Saúl, answered sincerely. "I just met Soli two days ago and she has my heart tangled up and twisted." Roberto laughed, nodding his head. "I reconnected with Mari yesterday after years of not seeing her and only having had a few dates with her that ended up in disaster and, man, I'm still crazy over her; I always was. When I saw her staying at that joint, I knew I had better step in and try to help her, you know? Man, have you noticed how fine she is? Dude, a woman like that can make me stop drinking. She even offered to cut my dick off with a disposable razor and put the Grim Reaper on my ass!" Saúl laughed and they high fived it. "Solimar is a complete mystery to me." Swirling the last of his brandy, Roberto said "No she's not. She looks just like you!" Saúl, swallowing a lump in his throat, blurted out "We found out today we have the same last name." Roberto straightened up; detecting Saúl's concern and said "It could be a major coincidence." Saúl stayed quietly hoping, contemplating that possibility.

"What gives, bro, what are you really thinking?"

"I rather not even dare throw those thoughts out into the universe."

"Then don't, bro, just go with the flow and time will tell. I mean, you just met her so it isn't like you guys …." Saúl said "I guess you forgot our conversation in the restaurant."

Roberto, trying to make light of his faux pas said "Listen, if you need a good lawyer…" handed him an old tattered business card. They both burst out into their drunken laughter, each woman tentatively trying to hear them from behind the doors of their respective rooms. When they heard the footsteps climbing the stairs, they both jumped into their assigned beds and pretended sleep. Both men stopped in to look over their girls.

"Sleep with the Angels Solimar, *mi cielo, mi fucking puta vida.*"

"Marisol, sleep good tonight, I'm going to need you tomorrow pretty girl." With that each man retired to their private hell, but not so much for Roberto, at least not this night. Tonight felt like family, and that was a blessing to be savored. It had been a long time since good people walked his way. Long time since a woman thanked him and even a longer time since a man openly respected him. He slept solidly, no nightmares or cares, a little boy smile upon his thick lips; a smile that Lydia never missed because although she was only the housekeeper, she always tucked her boy in when he wasn't looking, no matter how old or how drunk he was.

The morning found each drunk in surprisingly good spirits. They all handled their hangovers graciously. They were much too excited to focus on themselves. They wanted one another and were anxious to see what the day would bring. Mari quickly slipped into Soli's room to find Soli all dressed, bed made and almost ready to go. Mari smiled to see her friend looking like a lost little girl, her hair still uncombed. "Soli" whispered Mari "You want me to do your hair?" Soli didn't really want her to, but knew this was an extension of her friend's olive branch. "*Si*, sure." Soli went to the vanity and sat, handing Marisol a hair brush. Mari sensed something wrong in the air, but did not dare question Solimar at a time that seemed rather fragile. She took the brush and begun to work on her friend's hair which nearly reached her butt and had the thickness of a well made jump rope. Mari piled it high and wrapped it into a quite presentable bun on the top of Soli's head. They found some pretty clips in Soli's cosmetic bag and adorned the bun. "Thanks Mar."

"No problem Sol."

"You want me to do your hair?" Mari looked in the mirror, laughed and said "It's done."

Solimar looked at her friend strangely and said "Girl you look like you just stepped out from Animal Planet." Mari laughed again. "I want to look like this. It is the new and improved Marisol Espinoza, no more Betancourt."

"Okay Betty ex-Betancourt Boop, curls do work on you, just please spray them down or something, them suckers are all over creation and you're looking like Medusa." They giggled, small talked about the weight of Solimar's hair on her head and the latest hair styles trying to decide if they should both change their look. The conversation turned towards the inevitable and they decided that they better come up with a plan quickly, but first things first, check on the guys, each of them secretly anxious to see them.

The men, though freshly showered and shaven were exactly where the women left them. They were taking their cognac-laced coffee, smoking and laughing up a storm. Upon the ladies' return to the den they had left only hours ago, they straightened up a bit and Roberto tried to clear the air by waving his hand through the dense smoke. Mari said "don't worry about it Rober. We burn sage and incense all of the time."

Roberto's housekeeper was all smiles when she came to announce that breakfast was indeed ready. Everybody famished, headed to the dining room where they were met instead with Lydia's famous hangover remedy - a wickedly brewed concoction of orange juice, homemade hot sauce that would put Red Devil Tabasco sauce out of business, a raw egg yolk and a healthy shot of brandy. Roberto smiled as he watched the others struggle to get the raw egg down, never mind the chaser, only for the sake of not insulting Lydia's kindness. Solimar pinched her nose as she swallowed, much like she did when her mother forced the weekly spoonful of castor oil down her throat, followed by half an orange sprinkled with sugar. Roberto defiantly sat back, having been put through this ritual one too many times. Lydia sarcastically asked "What, aren't you going to drink yours?" Roberto seriously remarked "You kidding me? You're supposed to rub that on your chest and then put on a cotton turtle neck so the fumes don't escape." Marisol immediately threw up the half swallowed raw egg back into her glass as Saúl, who was already sweating profusely, having downed his portion like a champ, broke into a fit of laughter as he watched Solimar pound Marisol's back, trying to help Marisol compose herself, both now sporting flared nostrils and heat-infused tears rapidly streaming from their eyes, ruining their freshly applied mascara and saturating their once angelic faces. Lydia ignored the show, knowing that this would straighten their drunken asses out and said "When y'all get it together, I fixed a buffet. Welcome to Lydia's Casa de Locos. I am here to serve the ill and the mentally infirmed." As she walked away, she muttered "serve your asses right for getting all damn stank drunk and running all over town looking like homeless hoodlums." When the newly labeled ill and mentally infirmed got it together and seated themselves, behaving more like school children that had just been reprimanded, Roberto held out a chair. "Come sit with us. Today, I will serve." Lydia, reverting back to her genuinely delightful self said "No, *hijo*, it is my pleasure to serve your guests."

"Not today. Today you enjoy the company of the ill and mentally infirmed along with your breakfast." Lydia smiled, walked over to Roberto and boxed his ears. "Nana!" Roberto exclaimed a bit embarrassed. The trio stood frozen, not knowing whether to laugh or keep quiet, but opted for the latter. Roberto chuckled and said "She raised me. She is my Godmother, my Nana and my friend and just decided to stay with me when my folks died. We've been together for a little under forty years now."

Turning his attention to Lydia he went further to state "Let me formally introduce my friends. This one here is Marisol, we studied together at the university and these are her friends Solimar and Saúl that came from the States to visit her." Everyone let out a sigh of relief and begun to heap spoonfuls of eggs, bacon, sausages, flatbread and everything under the sun that you can bring to a breakfast table, including a bounty of fresh fruits. Lydia entertained them with stories of Roberto's childhood, his graduations and all around escapades. Roberto beamed with pride. When the conversation dwindled down and the food was all but gone, Sol y Mar jumped up to clear the dishes. Lydia was totally appalled and begun to protest.

Soli said "I think I heard Roberto say yesterday that he was giving you the day off so we're just helping out so you can get ready." Mari said, "Yeah, that's right; he said that when we were at the *cuchitril*!"

"*Que* nice. Roberto took his new friends to a dump. Can't you show these people that you've got a little bit of class?!" Saúl started chuckling and said "Actually, the place was nice, but last night none of us had much class; I'm afraid to say we definitely forgot our education and our upbringing." Lydia, ignoring Saúl and returning to the subject stated "I don't have days off." Mari quickly interjected. "Well that is what Roberto said so you better talk to him, he's the boss, I think." Roberto was not only blindsided, but thankful to see these women in his house, piling dishes, running the sink, pulling on gloves to get the job done. Lydia looked at her Robertito through her not-so-old yet owlish eyes. "Yes, it is true, Nana. I want you to go shopping for yourself." Lydia frowned. "What are you guys up to?" Saúl put his two cents in to back up the girls and said, "Oh yeah, yeah, I remember now, he did say that yesterday and actually I can have my driver pick you up in about half an hour."

"Driver?"

"Yes Señora Lydia, he can take you anywhere you need to go and if you need to pick up a friend for the day, it will be okay too. He will escort you for as long as you need him and have you home when you are good and ready." Lydia crossed her arms and said "I am not going to give you a hard time because you already have your hands full here Roberto, but don't make me spank you, bad boy!" Lydia looked over at the girls busy cleaning up the kitchen. These two were not like the other women Roberto would bring home late at night. The other girls acted like they were too good to do any housework, even when they stayed for more than a night. They all seemed to have a sense of entitlement, although most were nothing more than common prostitutes, lucky to have decent food and shelter until Roberto tired of them, which was usually rather quickly. Lydia, seemingly understanding of what might be going on, smiled. These two had respect for Roberto and his home. They acted like women that you wanted to bring home to meet your parents and were quickly seeping into Lydia's generous heart. Sol y Mar kept busy, elbow deep in dishwashing liquid and suds, scrubbing pots and pans in the double sink and pretending not to eavesdrop. Lydia turned to Roberto once again and said "The least you could have told these *chiquitas* is that we aren't living in the stone ages, we do have a dishwasher." Having dropped that bit of information, Lydia went to her bedroom, which was more like a mini apartment, to change clothing and put on some lipstick.

Saúl was on the phone while Roberto got playfully jumped by the girls, teasing him, harassing him and saying that he now had to pay for two sets of manicures, not realizing that he had begun his early morning tremors and wasn't ready for their playful banter. He was feeling sick and needed another hit of the proverbial hair of the dog. They sensed that this was getting awkward and stopped as Lydia appeared at the top of the stairs. He reached into his pocket and took a wad of money, without counting it, for Lydia to spend. As Lydia descended the steps, her ebony skin shone and her fire engine red lipstick accentuated her full lips, the only make-up she had ever learned how to apply. Roberto met her at the bottom of the stairs and said "Ma, this is for you."

"Puta! Gracias, I love you" was her grateful response. "Me too! Now don't go picking up anybody to try and make me all jealous!" Lydia smiled "What you think, that only you can pick up? Ha, I don't think so!" The men smiled, the women giggled. They all watched Lydia step into the limo, with the excitement and grace of an elderly Cinderella, taking the extended hand of Saúl's driver, consenting to be treated as she was, forever *la dama*. Before the limousine could clear the curb, Roberto grabbed the cognac bottle and chugged it straight from its glass container. His shakes had made him forget that he had company.

Soli signaled to Marisol and they walked back into the kitchen. Soli simply said "We've got to get out of here Mari, *este tipo* is bad news." Marisol quietly said "I know this dude is bad news Soli, but look how good he has been to us. We can't just dump him like that." Solimar had no choice but to agree. "Let me talk to Saúl. Maybe we can get this guy some help." Mari replied, "I know where to take him if he wants to go, it is a place called Hogar Crea. It is a Christian based rehab center for addicts of all kinds." Soli had issues with it being a Christian rehab, but thought that any help he could get was better than none. She was supportive of her friend's idea and brightened up, cheering her girlfriend on. "Mari. That is an excellent idea, but you are going to have to work on him. Go, go, go to him, and see what you can do for this guy and I'll finish up here, who knows, he might agree." Mari leaned over and kissed her friend square on the lips, at the very moment that Saúl entered. "Hola Bellas, what are you two divas up to?"

"*Buenos dias* Saúl" stated Marisol, embarrassed that he may misinterpret their affection, quickly left the kitchen. "What was that all about?" Soli did not answer him. "Solimar Santana, I asked you a question, may I have the courtesy of an answer?" Solimar turned to face him square on, her eyes spewing anger and desire. Saúl stood his ground as well and they were just about ready to go at it when a loud distraction came from the other room. "Who in the hell do you think you are?"

"I'm Marisol Espinoza." Marisol stated defiantly. "And? You're not my wife; you're nothing, just a puta I went to school with and helped out because I see you're just as stupid as you used to be back then!" Mari came running into the kitchen, "Soli, let's go, we are out of here!" Saúl was not remotely ready to let Solimar out of his sight. "Go handle your business Marisol. I have something to discuss with Solimar right now and she is not going anywhere."

"My business? That drunk is so very not my business." Marisol shot back. "Oh yes he is." Mari stood dumbfounded at Saúl's boldness and accurate assumption. That drunk was her business. He came to help her out of a potentially bad situation and he did. Marisol recognized the validity of Saúl's statement and briefly remembered the class that she had been pulled from when she got deported. That class was the last one on substance abuse. "Will you help me Saúl? I'm trying to get him to consider going over to Hogar Crea. You know that I have to stay in Panamá and I would like to be friends with the guy, but not like this, *me entiendes*?"

"I do understand, but I cannot help you Marisol. I am sorry, but I can't. He needs the tender hand of a woman right about now and I don't want to step on that man's toes. He's good people, *buena gente*, you know? It is just not my place." Mari nodded and with a newfound determination, left to do what she was trained to do. Soli had finished the cleanup and used that interruption to sneak away and try to unobtrusively make her way to her bedroom when Saúl caught up with her and was heavily breathing down the back of her neck. He wrapped his powerful arms around her. She closed her eyes as she heard him whispering into her ear and tenderly nibbling on her earlobe. She couldn't take it. The warmth, his presence, his persistence, his appearance, all of him was driving her insane. She turned around and hissed "You better stop fucking with me." Saúl stepped back, bowed and gestured her to go and said "Run then. See where that'll get you." Soli took the stairs two by two, something she hadn't done since she was fifteen years old or so. Saúl took them three at a time and made it to her door just before she tried to slam it in his face.

Roberto tried to decipher whether he was upset or not, but in actuality, he found the situation quite funny. "What the hell is going on with those two crazy asses? They're gonna break my damn house!" Mari, relieved that Roberto had broken the tension, started laughing and said "Fuck if I know Rober." Roberto was laughing hard and shaking his head, forgetting his momentary outburst only minutes prior. "Fuck, if you don't know, what the hell? We just gonna have to wait them out right here and find out. I ain't missing this one for nothing, nada, zilch, *ni cojones*! This jam is better than Lydia's *novela*, which I check out from time to time!" Marisol saw that as an opportunity to further establish their friendship. "You really check out the soaps?" Roberto patted the cushioned seat next to him, signaling her to join, which she did. He reached for the remote control, turned on the television and said "Here sweetie, come watch last night's episode. I record them for Lydia because rather than seeing them everyday, she likes to pull a marathon on Saturday nights or Sunday afternoons. Let's check this out. The last that I remember, the main dude caught his woman in bed with his father!"

Inside the bedroom, Soli went at Saúl as if she wanted to kill him. She pounded her fists on his chest, pulled his hair and was hissing and crying all at once. Saúl allowed her to have her fit of rage and then allowed her some more. Soli begun throwing things, anything she could find out of her opened suitcase, panties and all. "You knew! You had to have known and you lied to me. My brain can't, don't you see, it just can't process or believe or understand or even think because of you! *No puedo!*" Saúl, realizing that she was close to spent from her own frustration, grabbed her in one massive sweep, and started to undo her tight hairdo, allowing her hair to cascade while rubbing the top of her head, releasing her hair, massaging her pain. Soli stood there, a ragged rag doll, with no strength and less will. He gently cupped her chin and turned her face towards him. "Solimar *mirame*. Please look at me. I know nothing. I swear Soli, on my very soul, I don't know anything."

She looked into the reflection of her own eyes and allowed him to undress her. He carefully laid her down and undressed himself. Spooning her once again, they begun the lullaby and Saúl rocked his not so little, but very limp doll. Again the Guardians appeared, sprinkled a bit more of the left-over heavenly balm on their weary souls and naked they slept, while the demons that tormented them angrily paced the corridors unable to storm into the rooms, which had by now been sealed in blood thanks to one matron saint named Lydia that prayed over the bedrooms before she left for the only official day off she had ever gotten. She sprinkled holy water from the gallon she religiously collected on a monthly basis from *La Iglesia de Piedra*, the Stone Church, upon each doorway, leaving it all in God's Hands.

Sol Y Mar

After their mini breather from reality, Mari carefully and non-judgmentally spoke to Roberto, even offering her friendship as an incentive, although she knew that wasn't the way to go, but she was really in a roundabout way, telling him that she needed their friendship just as much. After a little research and lots of open communication, they came to agree that Hogar Crea would indeed be a good place. It would take thirty days, maybe more, but it would be a good start on the road to recovery for Roberto. He was a little ashamed, but positively responded to Mari's care, trusting that she knew what would be right for him and he agreed, with minimal resistance. They worked the phones, got his insurance information together and when it was all set and done, Roberto broke down into tears. "Marisol. First, I gotta tell you that I like it a lot when you call me Rober; it sort of reminds me of what it could have been if our relationship had turned serious and second, I never had a friend in my life that would do something like this for me, except for Lydia, but she would never dare suggest it being the housekeeper and all. She probably would think that I would fire her and she would probably be right, I might have done that." Marisol gently placed her hand on his shoulder, identifying with his source of pain. "And I, Roberto, never had a friend in my life, except for Solimar, that would take me out of harm's way, not even my ex-husband who got me deported. You don't know how I thank God for my status in the United States at that time; I could have been sitting in some prison over there with only Soli to come see me!"

"Mari, you aren't mad?"

"No. I am many things that I have to work through, but what is mad going to do for me? I have accepted that I have to rebuild my life and God was truly looking out for me because I could have gone to prison here too, but they let me go on my own recognizance and all I have to do is pay some fines, make a court appearance and a couple of other minor things. Seems like my former landlord cooperated and told them that I had nothing to do with it. He saw how hard I worked, waking up so early in the morning, coming home late at night. I think his conscience kicked in after he found out that I got deported and that Ricardo had taken off. That plus, well, I did leave a clean record here and never been in trouble in my life, except for the time that Soli and I went to a Halloween party."

"Let me guess. You two dressed up like *brujas*?" Marisol laughed although she was slightly offended at his joke. "Well, no. I wish it had been that. Sol got dressed up like a street walker and I got dressed up like a sexy gypsy and we almost got arrested for indecent exposure or soliciting; I can't remember which!" Roberto, detecting Marisol's misery asked "Do you want to talk to me about him?" Marisol, still embarrassed by her poor choice said "We can leave that for another day, I mean it is clear that my husband never loved me and used me for his own selfish purposes." Roberto gently pressed on. "How did you meet him Marisol?" Marisol took a deep breath before she answered. Even though she had just told Roberto that she didn't want to talk about it, she felt that she needed to unburden herself. She looked intently at Roberto and saw that he was genuinely concerned for her. She would not deny his desire to want to share. After all, he had shared his inner demons with her; why not put all the cards on the table. "Roberto, I met him the day my Visa got issued, at the embassy; he had been denied several times and asked me how did I manage my Visa. I suppose now that when he realized that I got it, he started to date me .... Look, I don't know, the only thing I do know is that I was used."

"Do you still love him?"

"Yes. I love him because that is what I promised to do when we got married." Roberto saw Marisol in a different light. She really was an honorable person and lovely lady in a heart-wrenchingly painful situation. He kissed Marisol on the top of her head and said "Listen here *muñeca.*" Roberto quickly realizing that she may not be readily receptive to being referred to as doll shyly asked her permission. "Is it alright if I call you *muñeca?*" Marisol, having dearly missed Latin terms of endearment, having been subjected to being called "gorgeous" by one who didn't even believe that she was, nodded her reserved consent. Roberto continued. "I'll pay for you to complete your studies Marisol. I have money. Maybe I have too much, and in time you can forget this *payaso* – this fucking clown and maybe you and I can eventually hook up and do something together."

Marisol was touched by Roberto's desire to repay her concern and decided to stick around for a while and see where things might go. Afraid of the welling of emotions that felt something like love, she hurriedly changed the subject. "I'm gonna make us some snacks" and without a further word, she went into the kitchen and fixed a trayful of sandwiches. Marisol called out to the couple upstairs to come eat, but they were knocked out and never quite made it down to enjoy their mid-day meal. Marisol was growing worried for her friend and was about to go upstairs to check on them. Roberto, with a full stomach and well on his way to La La Land, stopped her from disturbing them. "What do you think is going on with them two?" He looked at her, eyes a bit askew. "Muñeca. Has it been that long that you don't remember?" he asked playfully. Mari hit him softly on the arm with her open palm. "You know what I mean…" Roberto swerved, as only drunks do, did a two step and said "I think they are kissing cousins or something like that." Mari's face went pale. "What the hell?" Roberto whispered "Yeah Chica, Macho told me yesterday that they got the same last name and you gotta admit that they really do look a lot the fuck alike." Marisol's jaw dropped. "No fucking way puta!"

"Yes way! Shit happens in *la vida* and that is why we cannot judge nothing or nobody. You never know." Roberto shrugged his shoulders. "But Soli hasn't mentioned that part to me. I don't get it." Roberto took his friend by the hand, sat her down and said gently "Hey maybe she don't get it. I think that is why they are upstairs right now. Think about it. Macho told me she found out when they arrived in Panamá when the driver was waiting at the airport and had the name sign held up in big ass letters, but he had already peeked your girl's passport before they boarded, and he let her board with no questions."

"Please don't tell me that actually happened."

"Yeah, *Ñeca*, Saúl checked your girl's passport when they were in Florida getting ready to board, but his shit was public knowledge when they got over here. Up until then, they were still only on a first name basis!" Marisol put down her sandwich, went to the bar, fixed herself a double, no ice and lit a small cigar, not wanting to take the time to go upstairs for her much preferred ultra-slim cigarettes and needing a smoke to go with her stiff drink. Roberto, impressed, didn't say a word. After her intake, she turned to Roberto. "Rober, you don't know Solimar like I do. She may be *un poquito loca*, but she has really high moral standards. If she finds out that they are cousins for real, she'll be on the next thing smoking outta here." Roberto shrugged his shoulders, poured himself a short brandy while Marisol kept nervously, but freely talking. "I want; no I need her to stay with me."

Roberto a little whacked, but very intrigued by the intensity of Marisol's feelings decided to test the waters. "So, like what's up with you two? You two are like into each other or something?" Marisol not so patiently answered "Roberto, if we weren't all caught up in this fucked up predicament, I would try to explain the depth of my friendship and loyalty to that one up there, but for now, your question doesn't dignify an answer." Mari continued nibbling at her sandwich, Roberto quietly sipping his cognac. Although not so unusual in this part of the world, the turn of events was more than most people could handle. They opted not to speak of it anymore for now.

Solimar woke up to find Saúl looking at her through shut eyelids. She turned towards him and gave herself over body and soul. They made love and loved again. They cried. No food, no water, just pure, raw passionate loving. The caresses on both their parts were sublime at best. Tenderness followed by emotional pain, followed by gratitude and tears that gave way to smiles. They experienced every emotion humanly imaginable, and some so very unfamiliar. No regret, yet plenty of confusion. Their soulful encounter was a whirlpool of agony and ecstasy, sometimes even causing the agony to be ecstatic in and of itself. Soli kissed Saúl so very tenderly on his lips. "Thank you, *mi amor*, for finding my rosary. I haven't prayed in eons, but you made my day with that." Saúl stroked Soli's hair and said "Thank you Solimar for giving me a reason to want to pray again."

"Do you think we should go downstairs now and join the others?" Saúl kissed her forehead and speaking into her hair said "Like hell, Sol. I'm going to keep you near me, right here tucked under my chin, next to my skin as long as I can."

"*Te Amo.*" Soli whispered as she nuzzled into his strong and reassuring shoulder. "I love you too." Saúl replied as he held her closer, closed his eyes and went back to sleep, drained from everything that had transpired in the last couple of days, drained by the all consuming loving of Solimar Santana.

When Lydia returned later that afternoon, she encountered darkness and a shrilling silence. A cold chill made her body shiver and gave her goose bumps. She entered the house to find Roberto drunk, slumped over in a corner of their parlor and Marisol keeping herself occupied preparing dinner. "Where is everybody?"

"Roberto is sleeping it off and Soli and Saúl are taking a nap upstairs." Lydia laughed. "Siesta time is way over girl, now tell me what's going on?" Mari responded quietly by saying "I really don't know. *No se lo que esta pasando.*" Marisol continued to gather the ingredients for the evening meal. As Marisol began to place everything into their respective pots on the stove, Lydia looked at her approvingly, a slight smile crossing her face. She took her few purchases to her room and when she returned, Lydia sat on the kitchen stool that Roberto always utilized to sit on in order to chat with her as she cooked and thoughtfully said "I think that maybe you should knock on the bedroom door and make sure they are alright. Those two have so much passion; they are liable to kill each other. I'm a little scared."

"Why are you scared?" Marisol asked knowing that Lydia was not privy to the previous conversation she had with Roberto and Roberto definitely was in no position to 'update' her. Lydia instinctively knew that there was a consuming passion between those two and that type of flaming desire can sometimes lead to tragedy. Lydia did not bother answering. Instead she reached for the glass of wine on the counter and drained it. She licked her lips and saw the perplexed look on Mari's face. "Sorry. I thought you poured that glass for me" she said plainly. She went over to the wine rack and pulled out another bottle. "I'll pour you a fresh one. Now are you going to go upstairs, or what?"

"Oh no; I could never do that!" Lydia placed the unopened bottle on the counter and went to the drawer that housed the corkscrew. "Well, if you can't, I will" she said slamming the corkscrew down without opening the bottle. Lydia marched right up the stairs and practically banged the door down. Saúl and Soli leaped out of their skins and pulled the covers over them. Lydia, without waiting for a response opened the door and said "*Hola*. I just wanted to know if you would be joining us for dinner." Lydia had noticed the plate of uneaten sandwiches that Mari had left outside the room on the hallway table. "Marisol made lunch that went uneaten and now she is making a pile of food down there. Roberto is passed out drunk and you two are our only guests and I rather not see good food go to waste." Saúl immediately said "Of course Señora Lydia, we will have dinner together. Thank you for inviting us."

"I expect that you will be dressed for dinner in no more than an hour!" Lydia turned on her newly pedicured feet and closed the door behind her. She took the plate of food downstairs with her, fully intending on wrapping it up and giving it to a family that lived down the block who graciously accepted all of Lydia's generous offerings.

Soli bowed her head in shame and whispered to herself, "I feel like the only whore." Saúl tenderly turned to her and said "Woman, you're not a whore. Solimar, you're the woman that I'm with and plan to be with for a very long time, so come on, hit it and let's go."

"Saúl?"

"*Que pasa, mi vida*?" The quiet that settled into the room was thicker than a London fog on a misty day. Solimar shivered and her bottom lip begun to tremble. "Spit it out, Soli, what is it that is tormenting you?"

"Do you think … do you think it is possible that … do you think we are related in some way, that we might be *familia*?" Saúl's worse nightmare came through in real time. "Soli, what does the "S" in the middle of your name stand for?" Alarmed, Solimar jumped out of bed and said "Forget I asked, alright? It's not that important, but if you really need to know it stands for 'shit.'" Witnessing her conflict, Saúl reached for her hand and pulled her gently towards him and said "No, Solimar, I don't think your middle initial stands for shit and I really do not think that we are family, but if by chance we are, it is probably like really distant relatives. God and His Mother wouldn't treat us that way, you know?" He leaned over and kissed her tear-stained cheeks.

As she dressed for a dinner she did not care to eat and face people she did not care to interact with, her Angel descended, once again pouring answered prayers over her head to calm her tormented soul and help her reason out the situation; it would only be a matter of time before the manifestation of these prayers, but still she had to endure the anguish and the battles yet to come. She reached for her beads and placed them in the pocket of her shorts and said "Come Bello. We must eat and stay strong. I gotta chill and a strange sensation and when I get a feeling like that, something is gonna go down and I want us to be prepared and ready." Acknowledging Solimar's brave resolve, her Guardian Angel immediately stepped back and hid in the shadows, confident that Solimar had received her blessing, but frightened that with this quasi epiphany, Solimar's eyes may open allowing her to see directly into the spiritual realm; a realm that was cluttered and infested with the heaviness of demonic activity; demons whose sole purpose was to cause the downfall of Soli and Saúl, not to mention Marisol and Roberto, and any innocent bystander that would get in their way. The Guardian, whose name was still unknown to Solimar and probably forever would be, knew that her charge had been blessed with the gift of discernment.

Roberto was the first to catch a glimpse of them as they descended the stairs. "Well, look what the cat dragged in! Did you guys have fun or did you fuck each other up?" Soli simply answered, "We fucked each other up in more ways than one." Roberto said "Yummmmmmmmmy. I wish this puta here would fuck me up!" Saúl was in no mood and said gently, but sternly, "Please refrain from calling the women names. I know that sometimes we do that jokingly and they are fresh enough to do it back, but not now Roberto." Roberto stumbled into the kitchen where Lydia had taken back control over her domain. Mari sat dejected on the bar stool, twirling the corkscrew between her fingers that had not quite made its grand opening of the bottle of wine Lydia had pulled out, having decided to better have it with dinner although longing for the glass that Lydia had rather rudely assumed was hers. Solimar and Saúl paced up and down. The tension in the room was exhausting. Lydia quietly served the food that was prepared so lovingly by Marisol. No stories were told. No jokes. No tales of yesteryear. The moment Mari was served her plate, she expertly took the corkscrew to the wine bottle, poured herself a full glass and sipped it. She then showed the bottle to everyone at the table, silently asking if she should pour. Saúl and Soli declined, opting for water instead. Much to her surprise, even Roberto waved the bottle away. He sensed that this gathering was not a cause for celebration. Solimar pushed her food around her plate, Marisol consumed more wine than food, Saúl ate all that he could so as not to insult Marisol's and Lydia's efforts and Roberto was too drunk to lift fork to mouth.

Lydia finally broke the awkward silence and pointedly said "I don't know what is going on here, *pero tengo una idea* and my feeling tells me that you four better figure things out in a hurry because things ain't looking good for none of you." Saúl excused himself from the table. "Señora Lydia, with your permission, I must attend to some pressing business and make an urgent phone call." Soli, who had been biting her tongue, jumped up and said "Yeah, you gotta call your woman, don't you? You were supposed to be home three days ago!" Roberto reached for the near empty bottle of wine and poured what was left into his glass. "*Y ahi estamos*; Mari, here comes the jump-off we were waiting for!" and downed the glass of wine. Saúl, thoroughly confused at Solimar's accusation said "What now woman? What are you talking about?"

"I heard you *estupido* when you were talking on the cell phone back in the hotel in Florida, remember? …. "Ciao Mami, I'll see you tomorrow, I love you." Solimar mimicked and continued her attack "or I guess you already forgot that when we met, my naked ass needed to use your cell phone?" Marisol, Roberto and Lydia's ears all perked up at the revelation of their infamous encounter. "That was my mother!" Saúl said without any expression or emotion, feeling betrayed that Solimar would think so little of him, having spent himself on her, trying to show her how very much he appreciated, admired, respected and yes, loved her. Mari was still trying to wrap her head around the fact that Soli was naked in the hallway of the hotel and all Lydia could do was try to suppress the giggle threatening to escape from her mouth. Roberto, however, broke out in his customary drunken glee. "You see Mari, you see! Soli wasn't worried about him calling his "Mami" when she was getting it on!"

Soli was totally embarrassed now, having shown her naked ass yet again! "I'm going home. You call your driver and get me the hell out of here and send me back to New York!" Saúl, starting to get fed up with Solimar's insecurities suddenly grabbed her face in his powerful hand. Soli tried to free herself, but he squeezed her face to control her just as one would pull on the reins to control a wayward horse. "Bitch! You haven't seen hell yet because you still ain't been inside all of me puta!" With that horrible statement, he let go of her face. Everyone in the room was stunned except for Roberto who was doubled over roaring with drunken laughter stuttering "I thought we weren't gonna be calling them names tonight!" Saúl stormed out the front door and went straight into the night and whatever it held for him. He didn't even bother contacting his driver. Mari decided to stay with Soli in her bedroom for the night. There was not much conversation or speculation to be had, just the furious clanking of Lydia's dishes that she opted to wash by hand and Roberto's snores.

"Sol?" Mari asked as she was getting ready for bed. "What Mar, what?" She replied harshly hoping that Mari wouldn't interrogate her about what had just transpired. Mari did not take the hint. "What's going on with you and Bello?" Solimar, who was in the process of reorganizing her suitcase, gave up and let out a mournful sigh. "Mari, I think we are cousins, we have the same last name."

"Roberto mentioned that to me today. Saúl told him everything that went down between you guys last night, but you know something - that's not so bad Solimar. It's not like you guys are gonna have kids or anything really serious unless you want it to be. Lighten up; we both pretty much missed the boat on the baby thing." Soli's eyes welled up with tears. "Mari, I know this guy for what? Four days now? Come on, this is insane. I just need to get back home and put this all behind me. I'm sorry you are stuck out here indefinitely, but let's look at the bright side. Maybe something could be worked out for you, now that we made connection with a diplomat." Mari sat her girlfriend down on the edge of the bed and combed through Soli's hair with her fingers and watched sadly as her friend crumbled into tears, feeling completely helpless as well. In a moment of vulnerability, Solimar laid her head on Marisol's lap, losing her steel resolve and cried her heart out. All you could make out was Solimar's fear and Solimar's pain. "He left Mari; he left and walked out the door!" It was now Solimar's turn to ask "And now what?" This she managed to say between sobs and tears that were quickly turning her eyes red, soaking Marisol's nightgown. Marisol's battle-weary heart just couldn't take it and she joined her friend in her cry, having no answers to give to her, when she came up with the only idea she could. "We gotta pray again like we used to." Soli simply said "I guess you forgot that I told you that Heaven is not taking any prayer requests right about now. I guess God is still busy somewhere East of Eden fixing shit for the next round of idiots He creates." Marisol, taking advantage that Solimar was literally in the fetal position, her head still on her lap, slapped Solimar's rear end really hard and said "Solimar! You better stop saying that. You know we believe. We are believers. Come on, let's go to the battlefield and take these motherfuckers on!" Solimar was shocked back to reality by the sharp sting she felt on her ass. She sat up and didn't know whether to slap Marisol or hug her. She did neither.

Mari went to her room and returned with the cheap, miniature, plastic statute of the Blessed Mother that she recently purchased and an old, laminated prayer card of the infamous Guardian Angel, watching over a little boy and little girl crossing a rickety bridge about to collapse. Mari found a candle in one of the cupboards, lit it and pulled out her rosary beads. Solimar reached for the ones Saúl found for her. They begun with the Apostle's Creed and Lydia joined them by the second Hail Mary. These three women prayed and cried earnestly from the hearts that they thought they had lost and were no longer entitled to have. By then Saúl had returned and peeked into the room to find this trio of women wailing and praying for him, the other and taking turns praying for each other. His eyes filled and he silently walked away so as not to break their mantra. By then, they were in a trance, a trance that would eventually help them dance. The little demons became a bit smaller and a whole lot weaker, until one by one they dissipated. The Guardians cried "Gloria" and the Warriors maintained position, never leaving their post. The ladies hugged and kissed and Marisol told Lydia that she thought it best for her to stay with Solimar for the night, promising to figure things out in the morning. Lydia nodded and went on to her apartment. Saúl had patiently waited for the session to be over, leaning against the banister when he noticed Lydia coming out of the room. Ashamed, he quietly whispered "Señora Lydia?" Saúl had caught her on her way to her bedroom, ready to retire for the night. Lydia had too much excitement for one day. She looked drained, somewhat tired and very worried. The look on her plump, unlined face made Saúl feel guilty for bringing his newfound drama into this humble woman's life. "*Que, what, que es*?" asked Lydia. "I came to apologize for my disrespect at your table." Lydia slowly made her way to where Saúl was standing. He fully expected to be slapped and he would not have stopped her if she had. Lydia looked up at him for what seemed like an eternal moment, feeling his shame, yet fully knowing that he was a victim of all of the mixed emotions and confusion that the household was presently sharing. He did not expect what happened next.

"Look, I don't know what is going on around here, but I haven't had this much fun since Roberto came in here with a Chinese girl who didn't speak a lick of Spanish and her English was even worse. You better get back in that bedroom, get her girlfriend out of there because girls aren't supposed to sleep together and make a claim on your woman if you don't want to lose her. Whatever the consequences, God knows your heart and hers." Saúl hugged Lydia, kissed the top of her head and simply said "*Gracias* Mami. I will do exactly what you just said." He went straight to Soli's room and found the two of them sleeping, back to back. "Mari." No response. Mari was dead to the world. Saúl whispered again "Marisol." Marisol did not budge. She was in a deep slumber; something to do with the combination of wine and long overdue prayer. He picked her up and walked down the corridor to Roberto's room. He carefully placed her on Roberto's bed, covered her and tenderly kissed her forehead. He went downstairs, collared Roberto's drunken ass and said "Sober up man. There is a gift on your bed. Don't let me hear that you fucked this up in the morning because if I do, I'm taking the both of them with me and we are out." Roberto, a bit dazed said "Yeah man, relax. I haven't had a damn drink in two hours." Saúl leaned over and kissed him hard on both cheeks. "I'm proud of you man. You can do this one hour at a time if need be." Roberto straightened up and said "Shit. I got this. I may be drunk, but I ain't no fool."

    The men hugged each other and went upstairs, each of them retiring to their personal baths to groom themselves for their women. Roberto quietly crawled into bed, after shaving his 5:00 o'clock shadow and applying a dab of cologne. Mari turned in her sleep and said "Soli?" Roberto's pulse quickened. "No, Mari, it is me, Rober." Marisol didn't flinch, but only turned around and embraced him. Roberto was petrified. He hadn't been with a woman he hadn't paid for in years. Marisol continued to sleep. Roberto turned on the little lamp on his nightstand. There she was before his eyes. Shoulder length, brownish/blondish hair tousled all over her face. The color of her skin was rather odd to him. It was like the color of slightly soiled sand, an interesting contrast to his darkness. Her rounded hips stood atop soft thighs, slender calves and ankles. Her belly also was round and bit pudgy and he softly took a pinch. Roberto, in his moment of clarity, studied her every detail down to the pores of her skin and the pimple that was just about to break surface. He did not dare arouse her, but he did not have to. She slowly gravitated towards him, naturally gyrating and Roberto was scared straight. When she finally opened her eyes, she smiled and said "Well I guess I slept my way into your room." Roberto begun to cry and Mari laughed at his sentiment. "Will you get busy already Roberto? It isn't everyday a miracle happens." He began to softly kiss her, butterfly kisses wherever he could land his lashes. Mari was eager. Somewhere along the line, they found a happy medium and begun the horizontal dance that would be lovers do. Before he entered his soon-to-be personal paradise, Mari gently asked "Tomorrow we go?"

"Oh God in Heaven Marisol, tomorrow I will go, but tonight you stay."

Two doors down a similar mating ritual was taking place. However, Solimar and Saúl Santana did not make love. Weary from their all day Olympic marathon, they stayed up talking and trying to figure things out. Soli used everything she had learned from her on-line investigations to find if there was a family link between them. Saúl did not know his grandparents' names and his father being an only child had no real family to speak of. His mother's family had remained in Cuba. Saúl had intended, but neglected to piece together a complete family tree, which, in fact, he had attempted, but from his mother's side only. They came up with no answers and opted for an in-the-buff pillow fight instead. They gloried in their nakedness and their childishness.

In the meantime, Lydia was in her bed quietly laughing her head off. She had the middle room and the walls were thin. Between Roberto and Mari's moans and groans and Saúl and Solimar's incessant laughter, Lydia knew that somehow these four would be alright. Eventually, she pulled a pillow over her head and said to herself "*Gracias Dios Mio*...thank you God that these kids found each other and you blessed me with them."

Morning arrived much too soon for everyone, as the sun poured golden rays through sheer curtains and open windows. The lovebirds and lovers managed to beat Lydia down to the kitchen; her gentle snores replacing the sounds of the previous night that had kept her awake. Marisol was the first to enter the kitchen "Good morning Sol, or should I call you sunshine?" Solimar noting her friend's upbeat step said "Hey Mar, you're looking rather radiant. Is that afterglow?" Mari blushed and held back a grin. Saúl added his two cents "Hmmmm, seems to me that the lady is a tramp after all."

"Hey bro, watch that! No disrespecting the ladies." Roberto went straight to Saúl and hugged him with all of his might while whispering in his ear "thanks man." Saúl was profoundly moved by this gesture of sincere gratitude. He had grown fond of the drunk, the deported one and the loving mother figure he found in Lydia, but he knew that today he would have to take Solimar with him and try to convince her to stay in Panamá and be his wife. The men came into agreement that they should treat the women right and agreed to get busy in the kitchen and make breakfast, but not before Marisol said "Look guys let me get the coffee started before Lydia comes down acting all grouchy and whatnot." They quickly agreed because neither one of them had the slightest clue as to how to use Lydia's sophisticated coffee machine that also grounded coffee beans and had another contraption that made the froth for the cappuccino. Saúl started to get the pans ready to cook breakfast. Soli sarcastically said "Watch him Rober, he can't cook for scratch. The man tried to kill me once with a Cuban sandwich!" Holding up her right hand, as if being sworn in before a judge, she affirmed "True story." Saúl stood there with his hand on his hip, shaking his head. "As mean as you wenches are, I see why!" Roberto replied defending his buddy. Solimar turned to Roberto and stuck her rear up for Roberto to kiss and got another good slap on the ass, this time from Saúl. Mari lifted her eyebrows and throwing up her hands said "Oh well, so much for no disrespect today!" That's when Roberto in a lucid, playful moment wet his hand under the running faucet and sprinkled Mari. Wrong move; big mistake! Within minutes they had started a mini food fight and were laughing their unified laughter, a laughter that came out of love and appreciation. Their friendship was settling in quite easily, despite their confusion with each other's situation, yet they independently accepted their dependency and true respect each for the other. By the time Lydia walked into the kitchen, her immaculate domain was a bloody mess! Pots and pans, plates and cups littered the countertops, pancake mix dripping off of just about everything, not to mention flour all over the floor and even the walls. "What the hell?" Roberto sheepishly looked at his Nana and said "We wanted to surprise you!"

The ladies backed up, cleaning themselves with moistened paper towels. Soli jumped right out of her chair, threw her hands up and said; "*No me metas en esto.* There is no "we" in this one. This is a Roberto-Saúl exclusive venture. *Yo no se* nothing." Marisol as always, quickly followed Solimar's lead and threw them under the bus. "No Miss Lydia, I wanted to make everyone breakfast and then they came in and said they would do it and even though we insisted, they started acting up on us like they do, so you know we just said nothing because they took right on over. They were the ones that started the flour fight." Lydia placed the palm of her hand on her forehead, pulled up a chair, sat down, lit a cigarette and said "Mari, fix me a drink, a real one, *por favor.*" Soli went straight for the coffee and Mari straight for the bottle of Anisette, having noted Lydia's preference to pour Anisette instead of sugar into her coffee. They both served her simultaneously, wide-eyed and scared that Lydia would go ballistic. There are two things that you don't mess with, a woman's purse and a woman's kitchen and the only ones that didn't seem to know that was Roberto and Saúl.

Lydia flicked her ashes into a moist paper towel and seriously looked at the men. "*Pues?* You wanted to surprise me. Well, one of you can surprise me by getting me an ashtray for starters, but wait – were you going to surprise me with this mess you made or were you going to make me breakfast because I don't smell nothing but the Anisette in my coffee cup." The men glanced at each other and scrambled to start cooking. Sol y Mari tried to help when Lydia stopped them, laughed deeply and said "Come on girls, sit your pretty little asses down, relax and watch el show. The clowns are in town and we got front row seats to this circus for free! Step right up ladies, *el show es gratis!*" The ladies served themselves their espresso and with Lydia's permission sweetened it with her private stock of Anisette. They toasted their spiked coffee cups and the three of them watched as Roberto and Saúl fumbled, dropped things and poured sugar into the pancake batter instead of a pinch of salt, not knowing which container contained which. They even had tied Lydia's aprons on and the women were hysterically laughing at them. Saúl finally exhausted from his effort suggested "Can we just eat out?" The ladies simultaneously yelled "Noooooooooooo!" In the end of their failed escapade, they all winded up eating a bowl of cold cereal, buttered toast and of course, Café con Anis.

As Solimar begun to get ready to clear the dishes, having found the dishwasher, Mari said "Solimar sit. Roberto and I have an announcement to make." Everyone went stone cold silent, having no idea what to expect. Lydia, seated at the head of the table, nodded her consent, cigarette in hand. Roberto got up, cleared his throat and declared the sentence that would define him for some time. *"Hola, me llamo Roberto Robles y soy alcoholico."* The room fell silent, nobody budged. Marisol walked over to him and took his hand. Firmly she announced "We made the arrangements yesterday to go to Hogar Crea for treatment. They will be picking Roberto up today at 1:00." Everyone simultaneously looked at their wrist watches; it was already 10:45, leaving them little time to digest the news and talk to Roberto. Lydia stood up, went for a bottle of the good champagne that had been sitting there for years, and unceremoniously popped it. She took out the fine crystal pitcher and prepared a Bellini, champagne infused with peach nectar. She poured five drinks into flutes designed to serve a king. Roberto looked at his glass and asked "Nana, should I be doing this?" Lydia simply said *"Hijo,* nobody goes into rehab dry. I want you to go in there drunk as a skunk, that way they will give you the best attention possible. Now shut up and drink up and if you break the glass when we toast, fuck it. *Salud!"* They all raised their glasses and Lydia was the first to cuddle her boy, running her fingers through his black curly, wavy and somewhat nappy hair. "Baby, this has been a long time coming. I thank God that these old eyes are getting to see the beginning of your triumph." Saúl by then was misty-eyed as he raised his glass again, remembering a time during his teenaged years when his father had to submit to the very same thing. Solimar did not dare interfere in this moment and Marisol was all aglow at her accomplishment. They moved the bittersweet goodbye party to the porch, where they drank as if it would be the last day they would ever drink again, and took turns crying and laughing and telling silly jokes. Saúl excitedly shared. "Hey, I've got a great idea. Mari could come with us to my parents' place until she straightens out her mess." Roberto shot him a look and Mari simply stated "I'm staying here with Lydia. It will be easier for us to commute to and from the rehab. Besides, I'm not ready to straighten out my mess, *entiendes?*" Soli added, "I hear that. I'm not ready either. I probably won't have a job when I get back to New York. I'm AWOL!"

"But I thought you said you called in an extra week." Solimar averted her eyes. "Well, I had meant to Mari, but I got caught up in the excitement of coming here, seeing you and hanging out with that blue-eyed devil over there that I forgot to call."

"I got your back Solimar, *tranquila.*" Saúl firmly stated, kissing her lightly on her bare shoulder. Roberto laughing his drunken giggle said "I bet you do. I bet you got her front and her top and her bottom too!"

Saúl chose to ignore Roberto and turned to Lydia. "Señora Lydia, you have been gracious to us and I wanted to thank you properly. He pulled out a long, skinny jewelry box from his jacket pocket that contained a special gift. He got on one knee and said "Permit me." She nodded and he wrapped her right ankle with a white gold "S" chain anklet speckled with tiny gems, having noted her preference for silver. When she lifted her leg, she instantly knew that he did not want her to forget them. "Saúl, how can I ever forget you and Solimar? That's impossible." She took his face in her hands and kissed him square on his lips. "Hold it right there Madam with your sexy, red hot, juicy lips, that's my man." Solimar joked. Lydia, flattered laughed "And you are my girl. Besides, at my age, *me muero!* But if I was twenty years younger, I would have been giving you a run for your money, *para que lo sepas!*"

The van pulled up and a young, clean cut, nice looking guy got out, leaving the driver behind. He walked over to the porch and inquired "Is this la residencia Robles?" Lydia screamed "Yes, it is! Now come on up and don't trip on those steps!" The counselor was completely undisturbed by the "good luck party" scene he had encountered, recalling that when he had walked into Hogar Crea ten years prior, he had sent the counselor away and partied with family and friends well into the night causing the counselor to return every two hours until it was 1:00 a.m., not 1:00 p.m. "Which one of you fine men is Roberto Robles?" Roberto started to shake. Mari took him by the hand and matter of factly said "Let's go get your things honey." Roberto followed Marisol up the steps, lost and uncertain whether or not he had made the right decision. Lydia politely asked, "Would you like a drink?" Saúl burst out laughing and so did the guy. "You know Saúl; you really are a piece of shit. He can drink Kool Aid, *agua*, soda or gin and juice!" They all laughed the harder.

Upstairs, Mari pulled out a bottle that she had sneaked up. She said "Here Papi, do your thing. In a week or so, I'll be by there." Roberto chugged. Mari cried. Roberto chugged some more and asked "*Ñeca*, did you pack my cigars?"

"Oh shit, *Nene* let me get that!" She ran downstairs to the family room where the humidor was and emptied it out. Frantically, she ran to the kitchen to locate a plastic bag to wrap them in. When she couldn't find the bag, she started to moisten paper towels and wrap each one individually. Marisol was frantic until Roberto came downstairs and said to her "Mari, fuck the cigars; are you sure you aren't going to leave with them?"

"I give you my word that I will be right here with Lydia until we get through this storm."

"I love you Mar."

"I know; and I'm really starting to feel a special feeling here in my heart. Now come on *Licenciado* Robles. This is just some bullshit we got to get through. *Nada paso.*" With that clear affirmation, Marisol ran back upstairs, picked up her man's overpacked suitcase, which she herself had organized, and dragged it down the stairs causing a loud thumping sound with each step. As Marisol handed the suitcase over, she asked the counselor if there were cigarettes and cigars available there for purchase, having made a total mess out of the ones she took out of the humidor. The counselor replied "Sure, there is that and more, but purchases have to be debited from an account set up for him in the main office. For the first thirty days, we don't allow the patients to have money on them, simply for their own protection."

"Gimme *un minutito*" Marisol went running back up the stairs to get her purse. Solimar reached into her Kate Spade, opened the still sealed envelope Saúl had given to her back in Florida and handed the counselor two crisp one hundred dollar bills. "Can you make the deposit for him?" Saúl knew better than to interfere although he wanted to. "Of course, but I didn't bring a receipt book. We usually take deposits at the clinic when we check in. We also do an inventory of the patient's belongings." Saúl stepped in, patting the counselor on the back and said "Man, don't worry about it, we know where you live and trust me, you don't want me showing up with my little gang here." Roberto took his wallet out from his back pocket and took out the money to repay Solimar. Saúl, not wanting to cause Solimar the discomfort of having her "help" rejected, again stepped in before she took offense. "Roberto, put that away *hermano,* you took us into your home and treated us like *familia!*" Saúl meant that as a term of endearment but to Soli, the word 'family' now had a negative connotation. She had spent so much time trying to reunite with her family and now she could only think of the old adage 'Be careful what you wish for because you just might get it' or was it 'Be careful what you *pray* for?'

Roberto once again stepped into Saúl's massive embrace and they hugged openly displaying their brotherly love. Solimar, moved, wrapped herself around them and Lydia joined in. By the time Marisol was back with the money, she found herself pulled into a group hug. The young man stood there patiently waiting. He had witnessed many tearful goodbyes, but none with the love and respect that this group openly shared. The goodbyes were short, but plenty tearful, and the four of them stood rooted watching as the van gently rolled away, Roberto, seated in the back seat, waving as if a child on a school bus, the rest waving with both hands and blowing kisses.

"Sheesh."

"Soli, just say 'shit, damn, fuck' like you always do."

"That's too many words right now. I'm beat!"

As soon as the van pulled away, an unexpected, dark ominous cloud rolled in as if to replace it. Solimar didn't like it. Saúl said "Mamita, we gotta get going. I have business to take care of and we got to get home before it starts pouring."

"I don't even know where you're taking me to Saúl; I'm not so sure that I even want to go." Saúl, alarmed, but with much patience and understanding of her position said "Solimar, if you need to know where we are going, it is called Cerro Azul and I will give all the information to Marisol if it makes you feel safer. Of course, you already know, we are going to my parents' house." Solimar asked "But what am I going to do there? Don't tell me that you expect me to sit around looking pretty and doing nothing; at least here I'm with Mar and could help Lydia around the house, you know?"

"*Mira* Solimar, I have to go see my parents before returning back home to Puerto Rico. In addition to meeting my family, we will take a day to see the sites. You are going to be blown away by the sheer richness of the beauty of this place; *es un paraiso.*" Marisol and Lydia nodded their heads in unison. Both being natives, they were acutely aware of Cerro Azul's majesty. Marisol intervened and said "You know, Soli, the beauty of that place, like Saúl just said, you cannot miss it before returning to the States. It will do you a lot of good. To call it a paradise is an understatement. It is like way above sea level, the weather is absolutely divine, not hot and humid and sticky like here. At night, you don't even need to turn on an air conditioner; it is balmy and breezy. It makes you wanna snuggle up with a nice lightweight blanket. There are forests surrounding it and exotic birds and supposedly wildlife unique to Panamá. There are many trails that will take you through a cloud forest where it is possible to see rare palm trees that can only be found in Haiti or in the Ivory Coast, if the clouds are not hanging so low that they are right over your head. No one seems to know how those palms were able to spread from there to way over here and if I'm not mistaking, also to the bottom of Central America – this is a natural mystery, an enigma that is still being studied the last that I heard. The flowers are vibrant. Soli, they are so beautiful that you feel like they are talking to you, beckoning you to pick them and take them home. Everything is so alive, and the foliage is different from what you are accustomed to, so very abundant and dense in Cerro Azul and nothing ever dries up, and don't be surprised if you come across a jaguar or see an eagle flying over your head. If I recall correctly, before I left for the States, some developer had proposed to build a mini modern day style mall, but the place is still so hidden that you will probably not encounter many tourists. The locals are very hospitable and welcoming. I'm sure you will buy the little town out with all the pottery and custom made jewelry and they sell it all for a song and a dance. Solimar go. You have to go because you will definitely fall in love, and if you do, you may just go home, pack up and come back to all of us."

Solimar, mesmerized, hung on Marisol's every descriptive word, which made a perfect argument for Saúl's case. She rose from her chair, thanked her friend, and turning to Saúl said "Look, I want to go, but where do we go from there?" Saúl said "If I have my way, you will fall in love with the tropics and with me and then we will take off to Puerto Rico in a day or two. Puerto Rico is where I actually live and where we are both from. After that, you decide if you want to resume your life in New York, or as Marisol said, come back to us, be it Puerto Rico or Panamá." Solimar silently nodded and went upstairs to change. As she was changing into her modest attire, Solimar contemplated long and hard realizing that her life was on the cusp of change, knowing that she had to make a decision, right then and there. She returned to her friends, opting not to verbalize her uncertainty. Instead, dressed in a tie-dyed tunic and responding to the music Lydia played filled with Afro-Cuban intonations, Soli playfully made her entrance dancing and shaking her shoulders, her loose hair flying in the wind which was picking up momentum. She extended both hands; one to Lydia and the other to Marisol and in no time at all three women were throwing caution to the wind, momentarily abandoning all of their cares, Marisol sporting denim shorts and tube top, Lydia in her housecoat, barefooted. Even the cloudburst that showered them did not deter their dance, their praise to God for a well-fought victory. Saúl thought that they ought to go back inside but thought better of it and sat back and allowed the women to dance their pain away.

The Angels were still crying "Gloria"; the demons relentlessly and now furiously approaching causing casualties even among themselves. Soli was now fully receptive to the battle that was raging in another dimension, an epic battle that would take no prisoners. She threw her head back and shouted *"Guerra*! It's war for you motherfuckers that don't understand my language!" declared Soli, pumping her fists in the air. Saúl, perplexed and confused, grabbed up his woman and kissed her all over her face, as he always did. He did not know what to do to calm her down and she brushed him off. He turned to Mari and Lydia and they too were deep in the rapture; Marisol further enhancing the moment by burning incense and Lydia dancing what seemed something of a rain dance. Saúl had not seen them like this before and he knew that this would end when it would end and it was not his place to interfere. He could not feel the hand of his Guardian Angel pulling him away, but he could not resist the pull either. Saúl went back inside and sat at the piano. He tried to play a note or two, but felt ever so alone, even to the point of missing his drunken buddy who would have helped him figure this all out. There was something happening and he didn't know what to do about it. His Guardian Angel stood firmly behind him, signaling the *Guerreros*, the Warriors, to take up their post in front of the house, while the Angel protectively wrapped his wings tightly around Saúl shielding him from the others. The demons perceived, or rather knew, Saúl's weakness and though it was a perfect moment to attack, they could not reach him.

After an hour's worth of watching last night's praying women dancing in pain, drinking in the refreshing rain, they slowly winded down as the sun came out, and Saúl called for his driver. Telephone numbers were exchanged, as were hugs, kisses and promises for a better tomorrow. Mari assured Soli that she was certain that she had made a good decision and vice versa, but they were unable to say good-bye. They stared at each other, trying to capture the defining moment that would once again change their lives. Señora Lydia realizing the pain of separation, proudly announced that they would be doing "church" tonight. This lie somehow appeased the girls and Saúl gently helped Solimar into the car and gave the driver an address. He dared not look out the window, knowing that the women left behind were crying those long, streaming, precious momentous tears and not knowing what he'd be encountering at home. His woman leaned into him and fell asleep for a portion of the ride ahead of them, her little girl snores keeping him company along the way.

Saúl did what he could to pray, but was speechless and his thoughts were contrary to prayer for the fear that held him captive. The spiritual realm was marked with both anticipation and dread. Saúl and Solimar Santana were moving right into the combat zone barely armed, or so they thought, not knowing that they were traveling with an invisible entourage. Solimar jumped out of his arms suddenly, startling Saúl, who was already worried over the upcoming couple of days. "*Mujer,* what's wrong! You scared me!" Still Saúl grinned. She was acting like a child who hated to fall asleep in the event that they might miss something. Solimar said "I want to see everything Mari was describing to me." Saúl closed his eyes, inhaled deeply and said "Baby girl, I will take you to that and more, but for now all you can see is the highway that we are on that will eventually take us there, but *mira,* you can get a glimpse of the wonders she was talking about." Solimar looked out of the tinted windows of the limousine and saw a mountainous region with what seemed like foggy clouds covering the area. Saúl said "Come back here and rest yourself; I promise you that first thing in the morning, we are going in and I'm going to make you fall in love with paradise and I'm going to obligate you to fall in love with me." As an afterthought he whispered "you blue-eyed witch!" repaying her off-the-cuff compliment of "blue-eyed devil." Solimar gave him a weak smile, used to their tit-for-tat volley and kissing him on his lips said "you're halfway there Bello."

When they arrived to Saúl's parent's home, Solimar did what she could to seem presentable. She hurriedly put on some lip gloss, wiped her cheeks and quickly ran a brush through her unruly hair. She was pura-Latina, cursed with hair that would frizz, curl and wave when wet. She quickly opened her travel bag and scooped out a glob of conditioner to run through her hair. "Come *Negrita*. Victor will take care of the luggage." He used that wonderful term of endearment, the best one ever used amongst Latinos, whether your skin color was black or white or anywhere in between. Solimar felt shy, exposed and fearful, but she trustingly held on to his hand. "Bello?"

"Que, Mami?"

"Is this really okay?"

"Solimar Santana, I would not take you anywhere where God didn't have you covered, you got that Angel?" Solimar Santana, uncertain, reluctantly nodded.

Home Meets Hell's Angel

"Solimar Santana .... Welcome to my home. *Mi casa es tu casa.* Don't forget that alright?" Saúl's mother came rushing to the door, eager to greet her firstborn and openly favorite child, due to his many accomplishments that made her boastful and proud. "Saúl, mi amor, I'm so happy to see you." She opened up the gate and hugged her son. *"Bendicion,* Mami."

"Que Dios te Bendiga, hijo." Esmeralda shifted her attention to Solimar allowing her gaze to slowly roam all over Solimar's physique, noting that Solimar was "humbly" dressed, thinking to herself 'this must be one of Saúl's little playmates. Why, oh, why does this boy of mine always affiliate himself with beautiful trash? Tie-dye went out in the 70s. What a horror!' Esmeralda was still in touch with one of her son's former girlfriends, the one that was crowned Miss Puerto Rico and Esmeralda did not tire in her hopes that he would return to her, knowing that they could further advance one another's career and produce beautiful grandchildren. However, that had still not been accomplished and she had to now do what she does best. She hypocritically asked "Who is this lovely lady that you bring with you?" Solimar bowed her head, took off her sunglasses and made direct eye contact with her future mother-in-law. The woman stared at Soli trying to make a connection in her head and Soli stared

directly at her. The woman slightly cringed. Soli did not flinch. "Hola Señora, I am Solimar Santana, a friend of your son." She raked her hair and extended her hand which went untouched. Solimar just thought to herself – 'Alright now, here we go with the bullshit' and with that she withdrew the only sign of peace this household would ever know from her. Omar, Saúl's brother, interrupted the awkward moment as he came barreling down the stairs to greet him. "Hey bro …. Whoooaaaa, whose this?!" Saúl said "This is Solimar." Omar bowed down and said "Damn! It is my pleasure to meet you."

"Thank you. *Gracias. El placer es todo mío.*" Solimar responded, trying to use her best command of the Spanish language. As an afterthought, but mostly to get under Esmeralda's overtly perfumed skin, she added "I see where you two are brothers; your brother Saúl had a similar reaction when he first met me." Omar, instantly enchanted, said "You got that right! We know quality when we see it and if it is what I'm thinking, consider yourself family woman!" Esmeralda Santana quickly interrupted "You must be tired from your trip. I'll show you our guest room. Perhaps you would like to freshen up and change your travel clothes into something more suitable." Soli instinctively retorted, "I am not certain that I will be staying the night, but thank you ever so much for your gracious offer." Solimar S. Santana breathed deeply and straightened her posture to fully reveal her slender, yet strong and mighty 5 foot 7 inch frame. Her legs seemed to cooperate and stretched to help maximize her beauty. She and Esmeralda were approximately the same height and Solimar purposely focused on her penetrating gaze deflecting it right back into Esmeralda's dark brown eyes, a tight smile on her thin lips, until Esmeralda had no choice, but to look away. Solimar then shook her head whipping her hair around her shoulder like a matador working his cape. Omar was mesmerized by this act of defiance. No one had ever stared his mother down; nobody ever dared. Victor had placed their luggage at the mansion's entrance, yet still nobody moved. Soli, stroking the length of her hair, casually strutted to where Victor was standing in wait and followed him into the house. Omar watched intently as Solimar walked down the pathway. There was something commanding about her step, her presence. She walked like she was royalty. Saúl snapped his fingers in front of his brother's face, breaking the spell he was under. "Where is Papi?" Omar answered distractedly, "He is in the study looking over the family budget. You know him, always looking over his *pesos!*" Saúl silently walked to the study, found and greeted his father. "*Hola Pa, Bendicion.* I have someone I want you to meet." His father gave his son a warm hug and said "*Si hijo, vamos a ver.*"

The two men walked to the living room. The aged man whose sight was failing simply exclaimed "*Pero que bella*, what a natural beauty." He was immensely taken aback by Solimar's extraordinary presence. "This is my father Solimar - Raul Santana and my mother is Esmeralda." Solimar did not extend her hand this time, she didn't move a muscle. Raul stepped closer to her and took her hand in both of his; he raised it to his mouth and kissed it. "It is my pleasure and honor to meet such an elegant woman. I insist that you grace my table with your presence and dine with my family." Soli gave Raul the respect he elicited by bowing slightly at his chivalrous gesture and warm invitation. It was at this precise moment that Saúl's mother entered the room and the 'hackles' on the back of her neck stood up, as she jealously witnessed Solimar's effortless powers of enchantment. She was quietly enraged by her husband's flirtations with this... woman! She had to immediately think of a way to break the spell that this enchantress was weaving over the men in her family. The tension escalated and Esmeralda attempted to take over an impossible situation.

"Son, are you hungry? We are having an early dinner today, figuring that you would want to retire early from your travels. After dinner, we can have our chauffer take your friend back to her hotel... or wherever she is staying." Soli said nothing. She was intently staring at Raul and all but jumped into his hazel eyes. Visions of a woman with opaque blue eyes came to her, very long, snow white hair flowing behind her, much like Solimar's except for the color. Memories rapidly flooded her mind. Memories of lots of kisses, homemade candies and hugs all for Solimar, a big Black man accompanied this mystery woman at all times, always smiling proudly, cradling Solimar and carrying her close to his chest, never allowing her feet to touch the ground. It must have been a dream. Demons and Angels spoke to her loudly now. "You are Solitita, remember that! Solitita, Solitita, Solitita!" resonated the taunt in her head. The demons had indeed found their way to Solimar in a house so very spiritually void and unprotected. Soli swayed gently from side to side, carefully listening, flashbacks furiously taking her through a tunnel of time and space, not knowing for sure, and yet knowing in her heart.

"Solimar!" Saúl jolted her. "*Que te pasa, mujer?*"

"What are you talking about? I was just saying hi to your dad!" As he took her by the elbow he said "Soli, *mi amor*, walk with me a minute" and gently led her back outside. They turned without excusing themselves. "Soli, *mi vida*, you just went into a trance. Your fists are all balled up and you are sweating." Soli gently laid her hand on his cheek and imploring his common sense said "Then please get me out of here Saúl. I don't belong here!"

"Baby girl, this is going to be your family! I didn't want to ask you this way, but when I went out last night, I found a jewelry store and got the ankle bracelet for Lydia and this for you." He opened a box revealing a two carat diamond nestled into a platinum band adorned with what seemed like a ring of crushed diamonds, resting upon black velvet waiting to be owned and shown. "Nena, marry me, stay in Panamá, please, I beg you." Soli was hyperventilating. She sat on the porch breathing as if she were in labor. Saúl quickly poured her a glass of ice water. Solimar could not see ten feet in front of her. Out of nowhere, a beautiful young woman appeared. She had not the same coloration, was actually rather pale, but there they were, aquamarine eyes, giggling and greeting her brother, her long chestnut colored hair also flowing in the wind. Before Solimar could speak, Saúl was happily greeting his baby sister. "So ....lé! I'm so happy to see you!"

"Sa....úl! I'm so happy to see you too!" They hugged and kissed. She turned to Solimar who was in a near state of shock and bluntly asked, "Who is she?"

"She is my friend and hopefully wife to be. This is Solimar. Solimar meet my little sister, Soledad." He turned to his kid sister and continued. "Actually, you just walked in on my marriage proposal!" Saúl showed off the ring to his sister and Soledad excitedly reached to hug Solimar, but Solimar put her hand up signaling her to stop. This was too much too soon. Solimar was in a state of emotional overload, on the verge of crisis and could not handle any more.

Omar stepped outside, wondering where everyone had disappeared to and cried out to his little sister, interrupting what would have otherwise been an awkward moment.

"Soledad, mi amor, I haven't seen you in eons!"

"I've just been very busy with school stupid; we still live under the same roof, remember?" And as if directing her conversation to Solimar, she continued. "There is no escaping the Santana household or rather the Santana compound. It's been drilled into me that either I leave here married, pledged to a convent or in a sealed coffin!" The siblings affectionately laughed, having heard their father repeat that mantra to Soledad on what seemed like a daily basis and the obvious bond between them did not escape Solimar's understanding or longing. Solimar's eyes opened wider and her pupils dilated. She had heard Soledad's prophetic statement before, except perhaps not as eloquently stated. She got up and prepared to meet her maker. Barely excusing herself, she went back into the study leaving the three to enjoy their family reunion. It was a moment of clarity that Solimar had to take full advantage of or forever lose it. "Excuse me." All stood rooted where she had left them. The rest was the beginning of the inevitable confrontation.

Solimar entered the study to find Saúl's father sitting in a chair having an apéritif before dinner. She stepped up to him and he put his glass down. "Raul or is it actually Raulin?" He stood up with a disconcerted look on his face. Nobody called him Raulin, not even his wife, and his children never heard him being called that. How did she know?

"Si mija?" To hear him refer to her as 'my daughter' only served to enrage Solimar. With that response, Solimar slapped her father across the face and sent the old man reeling. His cries brought the whole family running into the study, to find him sitting in his chair holding his face from the vicious attack on his person. "Yo, Puta, you just slapped my father, what the fuck?!" Omar exclaimed. Omar tried to lunge at Solimar, but Saúl held his brother back. Esmeralda and Soledad cowered in the corner closest to the door. "You miserable son of a bitch, *hijo de la gran puta*! I ought to sweep your porch with you."

Saúl bit down hard, still wrestling with his brother to keep him from attacking Solimar. "Get up you coward. *Levantate!"* Raul obeyed and Solimar went straight for his throat. Mrs. Santana cried, as Soledad held her mother close to her heart, which was palpitating uncontrollably. Soledad, confused, turned towards Saúl who was still holding back Omar. Solimar let out a guttural cry and shouting at her father said "I hate you! I can kill you right now with my bare hands, but you aren't worth it." She hissed and spat directly into his face, and although it was too much to take, nobody dared intervene. "You are a worm! *Puta! Mierda! Desgraciado!"* Soli moved in for the kill. She raised her fist, ready to pummel the old man. Saúl let go of Omar in time to catch her fist mid air and declared *"Basta!* It is enough." Although Saúl had a good hold on Solimar, her raw fury gave her tunnel vision and she only saw the old man cowering before her, the rest of the room a blank before her eyes. "You fucking piece of shit, *chucha madre*, you pig. I'm going to make sure you get what's coming to you, if it's the last thing I do before I leave this miserable earth and go with my mother. Her vengeance is mine, all mine, do you understand me? I can't believe she gave you a second look, much less anything else! Saúl, get the fuck off of me!" Saúl released her. The others gathered around Raul making sure that he was alright. She walked to the entranceway, picked up her suitcase, walked out the door without looking back and headed north. Saúl cried inconsolably, having made the obvious connection and feeling exactly what Solimar was feeling: the bite of betrayal. Nobody dared say a word. He did run after her, but by the time he caught up to her, Solimar was back in trance waving down a cab.

"Stay away from me. Stay the fuck away from me, *comprendes*?!"

"Soli, where are you going?"

"That is none of your fucking business!"

"Let me...."

"Puta, I got me!" she said as she pounded her chest in self-bravado. "I always have and always will take care of my damn self! Get away from me and stay away from me, you and your god-forsaken family from the bowels of hell!"

Saúl profoundly wailed his heart out in the middle of the street taking in the now pouring rain that only a few hours before blessed his woman as she happily danced. He prayed that Solimar would return to Roberto's house. As he watched her load her luggage onto the back seat of the taxi, all the while shooting deadly glances at him warning him to not take a further step towards her, he screamed out hoping that she would hear his heartfelt cry "Solimar, may your life be as beautiful as our eyes and your hopes as ample as the horizon! I love you woman and I don't care who you are Solimar Santana! I will see you again!" Soli frightened by his painful plea, instructed the taxi driver to head towards the airport. Lucky for her, Mari had slipped her the reimbursement money for the flight they had missed and she still had $800 left over from the grand Saúl had given her to put into her knock-off Kate Spade bag. Solimar was prepared to sleep at the airport, but when she arrived, she learned that there was a flight getting ready to depart in 45 minutes, in which she was the last to board, thanks to weather-related delays, giving Solimar enough time to clear customs. She even managed to get a partial credit on Marisol's Florida vacation ticket, having the agent call Solimar's contact at LaGuardia Airport, pulling in an old favor. The flight winded up costing her next to nothing and she was even upgraded to first class. Solimar took this as a divine sign that she had made the right decision to leave this hell on Earth and go back home. As Soli settled herself into the third row, window seat, she felt her soul ripping through her skin as the airplane started to back up from the gate and rolled slowly onto the runway, gaining gradual speed. Solimar started sobbing, but never kept her eyes off the hellish land that had given her so much joy and an enormous amount of pain. The stewardess noticing Solimar's distress came to her aid, gently informing Solimar that she could have whatever she wanted to drink, anything at all, compassion in the flight attendant's eyes. Solimar, quite seriously said "Please just tell the pilot to step on it and get me home as soon as humanly possible." The flight attendant, inwardly amused, nodded and came back with a single serving bottle of Moet & Chandon, a champagne flute and a small plate of fruit and water crackers, adorned with an array of chocolates and exotic candies. "Please try to eat something. When I'm feeling down and out, this usually helps." Solimar moved by her kindness simply nodded her head and whispered an incoherent thank you.

 Soli was on her way home, leaving both Sol y Mar behind her and her pummeled heart in Saúl's hands in a faraway land called La Republica de Panamá, an isthmus, a fucked up wanna be island. A place in the middle of nowhere that ripped the heart from her cowardly chest and kept it for itself. She snickered to herself at her newfound knowledge: an isthmus is an island that is being pulled in two different directions. A place somewhere between Rio Abajo, Cerra Azul and the occupants that she was running away from, remained the essence of Solimar Santana. She chuckled at the irony in her name. The irony that stayed between Solimar and Santana which was her secret 'S' for shit or maybe this time, it had changed to solitude.

No sooner than they reached cruising altitude, Solimar vomited into the "in case of an emergency bag" in front of her and handed the champagne back to the stewardess. This was no time for celebration. The flight attendant hurriedly handed Solimar a few hot towels and helped clean Solimar up, reclined her chair, as well as the empty chair next to her and placed her head on a pillow, covering her in not one, but two blankets, something like the blanket that Solimar had so hoped to have been under with tonight's promise of tomorrow in Saúl's arms.

Existence Begins Where Life Ends

Saúl never even bothered to confront his father, as the truth was now apparent to everyone. He returned from his attempt to stop Solimar only to find the room intact with all of its dismayed inhabitants. He disgustedly left their presence and went up to his bedroom to try and think things over. Eventually, he noticed that there was a lot of foot traffic back and forth past his bedroom door, but no one dared to knock to inquire about his feelings. No one wanted to confront Saúl as to why he brought that woman to their home, knowing the scandalous *bochinche* that might erupt, even to the point of making the tabloids, not to mention the shame that her presence caused to reveal, placing every one, including himself in a compromising position. Saúl honestly did not care what his family thought of his actions or what they felt towards Solimar. His only concern was to call Marisol to give her the heads up that Solimar might very well be on her way back to her. Marisol engaged Saúl in conversation, and he finally gave her the details of what had actually transpired. Solimar and Saúl were indeed half siblings; Solimar's violent reaction and Raul's cowardly response to her allegations confirmed that. Marisol carefully weighed how she would explain this to Saúl, but as a friend and moreover keeping to her profession, she knew that it was her responsibility not to create false hope within him. "Saúl, listen to what I'm about to say with your head, not your heart. Solimar hasn't called me to tell me she was headed back here, so it is logical for me to think that she headed to the airport."

"Marisol, please no, not that, *por Dios*, I beg you, not that."

"*Escuchame bien*. I told you to listen with your head, now I'm going to make you listen through your ears." Marisol channeled her training in psychology and spoke clearly and concisely. "Solimar told me that she had been anticipating some type of filial connection between you two, perhaps cousins, and she wasn't too keen on that either, but she was trying hard to work past it. Don't you think that to confront her biological father, who all but abandoned her, while also realizing that she was having sex with her biological brother, sent her into a rage fueled by the conflict and shock of the situation? Her mind needs time to process the enormity of all this. Solimar is a runner. Runners run. Drinkers drink, got it?"

"I don't want to get it Mari."

"Well, you better because you don't have a choice in the matter. Give it a couple of days, she will definitely call me because she knows that we all promised to be in contact for Rober's sake and that I'm going to find out soon enough what happened anyway. Solimar doesn't break her promises. As long as I've known her she has always done whatever she promised to do, even if she changed her mind about it. That's when I'm going to find out what is going on in her head and I assure you, when she calls me, I will call you."

"But why don't you just call her? I don't even have her cell phone number! Give it to me Marisol! I'll call her myself right now!" Marisol shook her head; Saúl just wasn't processing the gravity of what she was saying to him. Soli needed time to decompress. Calling her now would only send her into a tailspin that she would never recover from. "Saúl, please do not think I am being hard here, but the answer to that is no on both counts. She needs the space to clear her head, figure out how to even formulate the words to begin to convey this trauma when she decides to speak about it, and if you and I start inundating her with phone calls, trust me on this one, she will move to the furthermost part of Egypt if she has to. Best thing to do right now is leave her alone. Trust my friendship, she will be back, but I just don't know when."

Saúl acquiesced and Marisol gently said good-bye to Saúl, assuring him once again that everything would work out in time. Saúl reluctantly hung up and didn't bother undressing or unpacking. Saúl returned to Isla Verde the next day without saying goodbye to his parents. He attempted to leave before the household woke up only to be met by the twins sitting on the porch, waiting for him, coffee cups in hand. Saúl, touched by their concern, hugged them both and the three started crying. Soledad tearfully convinced her brother to stay just a minute longer, and he sat down beside her on the porch swing, putting a protective arm around her shoulder. Omar was obviously hung-over but alert. He opened the lines of communication.

"Brother, I'm sorry man, it's like wow, we never knew anything, we still don't know much, but Papi did acknowledge something like that he might have had another child, but he wasn't really sure." Soledad angrily challenged her brother. "What do you mean, he's not sure? You don't need a DNA test here or some second rate talk show host to open an envelope and say 'Raul, you are the father!' For Christ's sake, Solimar looks like a freaking carbon copy of Saúl!"

Saúl took a sip of his heavily charged coffee and watched his siblings, whom he loved so very dearly, try to work through facts they didn't have, pain that they all shared and confusion that kept them focused on this central issue, and would so for a very long time. Saúl, not having anything positive to contribute kept his outward peace, until Omar asked "Man, you love her, so what now?" Soledad smacked the back of her brother's head and said to him "*Estupido*, what kind of question is that?! He was proposing to her less than twelve hours ago right here!"

Saúl smiled for the first time in the last 24 hours and said to them both "You guys have so much of her in you. She is very inquisitive, Omar, just like you" and turning to Soledad he said "And boy does she have a fiery, quick temper *hermanita*, just like you. I see my woman, our sister in you both and I honestly don't know which way this is going to go." He set his tears free and said "Listen, I don't know how, but I'm going to find her and get her back to us where she belongs. I don't care if she doesn't marry me, but at least just to have her around as family would be sufficient for me." Omar couldn't help himself "C'mon bro, you had to have some clue; an idea, what?!" Saúl softly responded "I had a nagging feeling of some kind, but to tell you the truth, I didn't want to know and by the time we suspected that we were family in someway, I was gone; I was in too deep and for me, it was far too late to turn back. I fell in love with Solimar the very first moment I tried to come on to her and she all but sent me to hell." Omar, hurting for his brother said "Look man, let me pack a few things and go back to the mainland with you. I really don't think you need to be alone right now." Saúl said "That time will come soon enough, but for now why don't you come out for the next long weekend. You just can't leave work because I'm not in a good way." Recalling Mari's advice and applying it to himself he added "Besides, I won't be good company, I have to clear my head." Victor honked the horn, signaling Saúl to hurry or he would miss his flight. He said his good-byes and headed to the very airport that took his love away not a day prior.

Upon his arrival, he found his house immaculately clean, but his pots were cold. He had forgotten to call ahead and let his housekeeper, Rosario, know that he was coming, so she probably just took the day for herself. 'Fair enough' he thought to himself. He hadn't eaten and still had no appetite. All he wanted was a stiff drink, a good cigar and his hot tub, which afforded him a view of the ocean.

He reported to work the following day and the days turned into weeks with no communication from Solimar. He remained in constant contact with Marisol and Lydia, calling them two and three times a day. Marisol did, in fact, receive a phone call from Solimar letting her know that she was back home and was alright and giving her strict orders not to give her contact information to Saúl. Saúl was thrilled to hear that at the very least Mari had gotten word, but became upset when she would not give him Soli's telephone number and to further learn that Solimar did not want his. Marisol wanted very much to give it to him, but she was bound to honor her friend's wishes. Marisol gently tried to break it to Saúl that Solimar was attempting to put this harrowing experience behind her. Saúl broke into a fit of rage and yelled at Marisol "What the fuck, Mari? I don't count here? How about me; doesn't anybody fucking care that I was affected for having fucked and fallen in love with my own sister?" Marisol was very patient and took no offense to his outburst or his liberal use of profanity. "Saúl, you are a very smart and sensitive man. Right now you and Solimar are exactly in the same place and you wouldn't be good for each other at this juncture." Saúl stubbornly said "You know what Mari? We aren't in the same place at all because I can't see, touch or smell her. I can't fight with her or hug her. Fuck! We can't even yell at each other because she is somewhere in New York and I am here and please drop the psychological mindfuck because I rather fight this out with her than find peace without her, so no, we are not in the same damn place!" Marisol bit down and said "I understand and I am horrified for both of you and you know Saúl, that if I could, I'd be on the next flight out myself to try and convince her to let you back into her life and return to Panamá with me until things iron themselves out, but my situation does not allow for that so all I can do for now is what I have been doing, and that is to wait Solimar out." Saúl didn't allow Marisol to finish, but instead rudely hung up the phone. Utterly disgusted and frustrated, he raked his hair and placed a phone call that he hadn't placed in years. He contacted a fellow diplomat who maintained a private stash of cocaine and hashish and asked him to meet him for dinner on the pretense of some made up international business, knowing full well that his *compadre* would bring along something for a nightcap.

Nearly two thousand miles away, Solimar, too, was furiously raking her hair when she found the proverbial pink slip in the mail along with some documents to sign if she wanted to collect a six-month severance pay package. Her little unplanned, extended vacation was frowned upon by her employer. On a positive note, Roberto worked the twelve steps diligently, missing ever so much his Marisol, who faithfully came to visit him with and without Lydia. Marisol and Lydia had improvised and created a make-shift life for themselves in Roberto's house, losing their sorrows and concerns by watching *novelas* and engrossing themselves in the fictitious lives of others, giving them reason not to focus on their own, while riding out the storm that tore through both their lives, having already fragmented their core.

Autumn leaves falling, changing the landscape of New York City from steel to hues of gold and burnt orange only served to irritate Solimar, or was it just that Solimar had become accustomed to the tropical sun and palm trees? Solimar had become a recluse, opting to live her life behind closed doors, in a sanctuary that was all but that. When she did go out, she hid her face behind large framed sunglasses. She didn't want to have to face anyone, thinking that they could see right through her and correctly judge her to be an incestuous whore. Although she felt she was being shunned by society, she forged ahead and found a bit of peace as she had reconciled with the Roman Catholic Church and prayed her rosary daily. She opted for a parish outside of her neighborhood although there was a church three short blocks away from her new residence; she felt more at ease and safe from the 'neighborhood watch.' Instead of picking up the pieces to her shattered life, Soli spent her days daydreaming of what could have been had she stayed with him against the odds, while Saúl cried bitter tears everyday and felt no shame about it.

Back in San Juan, Saúl's hefty package of crystal snow, stashed in his safe, kept him up longer than he needed to stay up, but he wanted nothing more than to stay awake day and night thinking of Solimar, all day, every day, until exhaustion conquered his mind and weakening body and forced sleep upon him, if only for a couple of hours at a time. More than making love to her, he missed her day-to-day qualities ... the raking of her hair, the rolling of her eyes, her thunderous laughter and butchered Spanglish. He missed the way she often galloped into a room with her confidence, tossing her absurdly long hair, which by now Saúl had come to compare her to a thoroughbred horse. Making love to Solimar was a bonus, not the prize. The prize, for him, was in her eyes and because it was this way, he could barely look himself in the mirror. The hashish helped him to balance his high with his daily fantasies. Women called him constantly, but he begged off their attention and tantalizing invitations with the excuse that he would be leaving town shortly. Their relentless demands to occupy his personal time flowed onto his business life to the point that he instructed Jessica, his assistant, to carefully screen each call, but to immediately put through anyone with the Santana last name even though he had a dedicated telephone line for his family members. Security was also alerted to allow in any woman who claimed to be Solimar Santana and not to ask her any questions or for any identification.

    Saúl had just minutes before arrived at his office and was reviewing the international faxes and emails, when Jessica stormed into his office and said *"Perdon Señor* Santana, I know that I have strict orders not to put a woman through unless it is business related or, of course, a family member, but this woman keeps calling and she won't take no for an answer and she is now here having made no appointment and she won't give me her name. I don't know what to do. Should I have security remove her?" Saúl feeling hopeful that it might be Solimar said "It's fine Jessica, if she is that persistent, she must have an urgent need, show her in please." Jessica breathed a guarded sigh of relief and said "Thank you, I will see her in and will await your call in the event she is not the woman you are expecting." Saúl contemplated then discarded the idea of asking for a description of his guest, remembering that if "this" got out, it could bring on a scandal of monumental proportions.

Saúl straightened himself up, crossed his fingers and thanked God that his crazy love had come to her senses, remembering when she said something about not wanting to know his name, but asking where did he reside. Solimar now knowing that he was a diplomat would facilitate her finding him. He sat and tried to maintain his composure for the sake of the delicate situation he was about to encounter.

He was slightly shaken and quite dismayed when the woman escorted in by Jessica made her entrance into his office. It was Gina; Gina Gomez, more commonly known as Gigi. "Hola, mi amor, it has been much too long and you haven't answered not one of my calls in months." Saúl, gravely disappointed, but ever the gentleman kissed Gina on her cheek and said "Forgive me; I've been up to my neck in work." Saúl nodded to Jessica signifying that calling security would not be necessary, but the look on his face told her that this was not the woman he was expecting. "Would you care for a beverage? *Un café?*" Gina did not vocalize her answer. She shook her head no. Jessica looked to Saúl. "Thank you Jessica that will be all for now" and Jessica, relieved, closed the door securely behind her.

Gina did not sit in the chairs across from Saúl's desk, but sat on the loveseat, crossing her legs, revealing her beautifully shaped legs and said "*Querido*, the last I knew of your existence, you were in the States, in *La Florida* to be exact. You were calling me daily, but then you dropped off the face of the earth. Naturally, I would become concerned. You vanished and well, you know how much I must have missed you." Her words were measured, calculating and cold although the lilt of her voice, dripping with honey, could readily invite a man with less discerning taste. She concluded her rhetorical inquiry with the sweeping of her hair away from her ample cleavage which was proudly displayed in her low cut blouse that barely covered her nipples. Saúl was not impressed or interested. Gina wasn't a lover, but a sexual conquest and a poor one at that. In all reality, she was a predator, hunting for a rich, trophy husband and all in San Juan and neighboring towns knew Saúl was an eligible bachelor. Saúl barely escaped her clutches the last time he saw her. Now she was back on the prowl, but did not realize that her time was running out. Trying to hide his annoyance, he asked "Gina, what can I do for you? You see that I am here and although I was meaning to call you ..."

"What's up with the Gina? So formal when you always call me Gigi?"

"Gigi, I am not really available right now to get into a long, drawn-out conversation about what has been going on in my life or yours for that matter."

"Then why don't you just come here and give me a real kiss. No need for excuses. I forgive you without you having to ask or talk about what has transpired to keep you so distant from me. Don't forget, we had agreed that when you returned we would discuss our potential engagement, so now we can start to do just that. I found a princess cut emerald ring that I'd like to show you. I'm not so sure I want to go with the traditional diamond." She very subtly, but unmistakably seductively, shifted her weight slightly to allow her mini skirt to ride up just a little bit higher, revealing the uppermost part of her thigh and a hint of the curvaceous round of her ass. Saúl closed his eyes and when he opened them, he did not see Gina, but his memory of Solimar whom he loved and missed with all of his heart. Saúl, who was leaning on the side of his large desk, motioned for her to come to him. Gina stood up and walked over to Saúl to retrieve the prize she had come to claim. She draped her arms loosely around his neck, knowing that her breasts would be high and tight and in his direct view if he allowed his gaze to fall. Gina was quite adept at what she did. As he took Gina into his arms and readied himself to kiss her, he paused and looked deeply into her eyes. Gina shivered slightly with anticipation and was prepared to have sex with him on his desk, as they had done so many nights before when the offices were closed. She guided his hand up her skirt, signaling him that she was ready to receive him. Natural to Gina, she wore no undergarments, her large breasts, recently lifted, requiring no retainer. She didn't like to fumble with clothing, not when she knew that an office quickie required her to quickly jump back into her clothes before anyone would notice; one of the many details of her inducement. Her moist heat slightly dampened the tips of his fingers and he looked deeper into her hypnotic eyes, trying to lose himself, unable to deny his erection, nor his need to be loved. He had denied himself carnal pleasure in the hopes that he would see his Solimar again. Gigi's gorgeous, cat shaped green eyes implored him to take her, but they were not Soli's, a reflection of his own. With his free hand, he ran his fingers through her 'corn silk' blond hair, but it was not Soli's wild and tangled mane where his fingers and rings would often get caught and trapped in. Her porcelain skin was not Soli's creamy milk chocolate that he had come to think of as whipped mousse, and would often steal a nibble or lick from. The smell of Gina's skin was beyond exquisite. She had found and was finally able to afford the classic, Chanel No. 5, Mari's favorite, but it was not Soli's unique mixture of cigarettes, Sangria and some cheap Victoria Secret body spray that completely took over his senses, especially when Solimar's sexual heat came to surface, rendering him senseless. Saúl softly pulled away, cursing himself. He hadn't had sex since Soli and was in need of warmth and passion, but he knew that not only would this further complicate matters with Gigi, he'd regret it the minute he climaxed. Nothing about her even came close to Solimar Santana. Nothing ever would. He broke the impending spell. "Gina, you are one beautiful woman." Gina confidently whispered "Well that is obvious."

"But, I can't be with you." Gina immediately disengaged from his embrace and in disbelief said "Excuse me?"

"Gina, I cannot be with you." Gina indignantly shot back and said "Saúl, I didn't patiently wait for your non-return calls to hear this nonsense. Of course, we can be together. I truly understand that the distance these last couple of months has created an impact on each other, something of a divide, but you are back now. All we need to do is get out of here, pick up where we left off and get something to eat, drink and spend the afternoon at my place. We will work this out. It is no big deal. We are together now and that is all that really matters." Saúl bowed his head and said "Gina, it is a big deal and we can't eat, nor drink, make love or talk our way out of it. I have changed and I can't change back."

"Okay, Saúl, *esta bien*. I get it. You had a little fling with an insignificant gringa that turned your head and so you'll go back and forth, back and forth until you grow tired. I understand how men work perfectly, and you are no exception. I will wait until you tire of her although I am highly disappointed. It is obvious that we belong together to live in our paradise of an island, but alright, I accept your terms and can deal with an occasional indiscretion, *que mas quieres, mi amor*, what more can you possibly want that I cannot give you?" Gina was a bit nervous, but knew that it was in her best interest to keep calm, cool and extremely collected; this was no time to show how she really felt and potentially lose the opportunity of her lifetime. Although not particularly happy with Saúl and his roving eye, Gina was well aware that she would live comfortably with him, having been to his home and having escorted him to various events and business-related functions. Gina had noticed him having dinner with other women on more than one occasion, but kept this knowledge to herself. Since he favored outdoor dining, bumping into him on a date en Plaza Las Americas or in Old San Juan, as she shopped, was common. She dealt with his affairs without making any noise except for the time that she decided to stop by his home unannounced and found him frolicking in the hot tub with the most gorgeous, amazingly striking African American woman, who was also a fellow diplomat. At this Gina exploded, creating a distasteful scene that caused his colleague a faint, yet amused smile. She wordlessly stepped out of the hot tub exposing a body that ought to be exhibited naked on a runway with nothing but jewelry and shoes on, took her time getting dressed, as Gina continued to lose her composure and sense with every passing gesture of this woman who had Saúl's undivided attention. She turned and thanked Saúl for his exquisite hospitality and planted a kiss full on his lips. Ignoring Gina, she said "I will see you at our next convention. I think it is in Belize, but I must double check my itinerary. At any rate, my husband will be attending that one, so why don't you invite your friend here and maybe we can have a little 'extra' fun?! She winked at Gigi and said "Take care little one" and let herself out with the grace of a sprinting gazelle. Saúl laughed at his companion's lack of sophistication and jealous outburst, but controlled his desire to rid himself of her right then and there, as he thought it best to keep her around for aesthetic purposes, his mind already contemplating his trip to Belize. After granting him forgiveness, Gina firmly decided that she was going to make him hers. After all, he owed her for all of her forgiveness!

Gina continued to listen to Saúl "No, Gina, no; this is ever so much more complicated. This involves family. I can't explain and honestly, I don't want to nor do I have to explain anything to you. You and I had a good time, but our good times were limited to the bedroom. We talk about nothing other than the latest fashions that you want to wear and what high profile events you would like to attend. You don't even know what my favorite food is and you could care even less. For crying out loud, you can't even order me a drink without getting it wrong! We are not right for each other." Gina quietly listened, affording Saúl every reason to keep speaking. As he begun to pace his office, she crossed her arms over her massive bosom and waited, giving him time to let it all out of his system, while she made mental notes of everything he was saying to her. "Gina, hear me out. I know we had discussed that perhaps we would consider marriage someday, but that was then and this is now and I apologize for entertaining that thought with you. I was wrong to do that." Gina closely examined her freshly manicured fingers and asked "Are you finished?" Saúl, anxious to end this conversation said "Yes, Gina, I have nothing more to say other than that I appreciate your understanding and I am deeply sorry if I misled you in any way."

"Is that all Saúlie?"

"Please don't call me that." It reminded him too much of the name he repeated in his head a thousand times a day: Soli. Saúl took a long stride towards his former lover and begged "Please don't be angry at me. I do have feelings for you, just not the right feelings." With that declaration, Gina snapped and slapped Saúl's face, a thing he never would have expected or would accept from a woman, man or child. Solimar tried to slap him once and failed, but he could tell that she really didn't want to slap him, but Gina meant to strike Saúl's face just as hard as she did. His own mother never slapped him; even when he deserved to be. "If you attempt to do that again Gina Gomez, I won't be accountable for the repercussions that you will suffer," he said with an eerie calm. Gina was not scared nor did she waver, but stood her ground, locking her stare into his, digging her heels in and shooting fiery daggers of anger and hatred. "If I find out that you have another woman, I won't be accountable for the repercussions that she will suffer! What do you think? That I don't know? That I haven't seen you parading all over town with a variety of whores, not to mention that fucking *morena* I caught you with in your house?!" Saúl, realizing that being tactical would not work on Gina said "From your response, I can tell that you have been keeping tabs on me. So let me confirm what you already know. Yes, there is another woman. No, let me take that back - not another woman, but the woman that I love because for me there is no other woman, but her!"

"Well then, let's see who beats who at his own game?" Gina took a broad stance and waited for a response, having thrown down the gauntlet. "Gina, mind your words and your actions. Let us not forget that I took you out of a bordello, gave you a life worth living for and did this all while jeopardizing my position." Saúl walked over to his credenza, located behind his desk. He wanted to put as much distance between them as possible. If she tried to slap him again, he would have to restrain her and have security escort her out, an embarrassment he did not wish to bring to his place of business. "Gina, I never loved you, never told you that I did and the engagement idea was all yours, but I didn't have the heart at the time to say no. But who are we kidding here? You don't love me. I'm just a means to keep your pocketbook filled while you live an opulent lifestyle which you have already abused because you never earned it. I should have listened to my mother when she said 'You can't turn a whore into a housewife!'" Gina, stunned and taken aback asked "Is that why you always insisted on wearing condoms with me, because you think I'm a common whore?" Saúl's heart sank, but he had to come clean. "Of course, but it is not what I think, I definitely know that you are a lady of the night and that you tried to pass yourself off as a patron of that club we met at although you were working there that evening. I can show you your file containing your arrests, your aliases, one of which is Gemma Garcia - or is that your birth name? Frankly, you look more Spaniard than Puerto Rican to me and I also have your employment history all of which are fictitious – I checked. The owner is a friend of the guy I went there with the night I met you, and told my friend that he'd comp us both the favors for the night, hoping that I would become a recurring, paying customer. Lucky for you, my friend had his eye on the younger one with the short auburn hair and you got stuck with me alone, if not sweetie, you might have found yourself working overtime on the house!"

 Gigi closed her eyes and took a deep breath. When she opened them, she had not one tear to shed; only the realization that the game was coming to a quick close and she had no cards of value to play. Saúl, realizing that he had pretty much shut Gina down, having used her past against her, compassionately continued "But, I didn't save you from your lifestyle Gina; you saved yourself by not charging me that night; you could have double-dipped and kept the money all for yourself, but you didn't. I saw you wanted out of the game and I allowed myself to become a means to that end, and it worked. I saw you for you and it is killing me to tell you that I don't love you, but please give me at least some credit for having helped you out of a life you don't belong in, that no woman fucking belongs in!"

Gina "Gigi" Gomez walked to the loveseat, picked up her authentic Carolina Herrera handbag, smiled, dry eyed and said "Then, well, I wish you love and happiness Saúl. I really do hope that this woman is worthy of you; I thought I could be, but you've made it eminently clear to me that this is just not the case." As she started towards the door, Saúl stopped her. "Gigi, stop, wait. I will have my attorney get in touch with you in a day or two. He will bring you some money to keep you for a while. You won't have to sign anything; I do trust you." Gina smiled at him with irony and said "I appreciate that Saúl, but I'm no longer a hooker, or as you would say, a lady of the night; I was just trying to get to the next level and it didn't work between us, but I do think I can make it work for myself, just using another avenue. As you already know, I have other possibilities, but more than that, I specifically came to tell you that I enrolled myself in a business academy and thanks to your generosity; I was able to pay most of the tuition up front. In a year or so from now, I will be opening up a spa, and with the clientele I've picked up throughout the years, I won't have to work on my back. I was going to name it Saúl's Serenade, but I think I better stick with making a name for myself. You have taught me much and that is all the help I ever needed, so I give you *mil gracias.*"

"Will I see you again someday?"

"Sure, why not?" Saúl walked her to his office door leaned in and kissed her forehead, caressed her hair and inhaled her lovely scent. Gina brightened up and extended her well manicured hand. "Amigos?" Saúl took her hand and kissed it; for the first time not wanting to let it go. Although she had a long way to travel, he felt proud of her and despite the fact that he knew she did not love him anymore than he loved her; he felt a newfound respect for her, and knew that she wouldn't do anything to hurt him or his well-respected name. "Amigos." Gigi walked away with her clearly defined purpose, a freedom of no longer having to depend on men for her sustenance. She turned back and said "Hell, Saúl, if you need the gringa to get a make-over, you'll know where to send her." Saúl smiled at her tenderly and said "I hope you know that if you ever need a reference to open your spa, you know where to come for it!" Gina nodded seriously, but then as a final, playful good-bye said "Humor me a minute, Saúl." Saúl having relaxed a bit said "Sure Gigi, what's on your mind?" Gina paused and said "What do you think if I open a male strip club instead and name it Gigi's Gigolos?!" Saúl balked; Gina laughed and walked away saying "Think about it." They separated amicably, hopeful of their respective futures, albeit apart, but they were both at peace with their treaty.

Saúl returned to his desk, leaned back and rested his legs upon it. He called Jessica to bring him a cup of coffee and make sure that Gina had cleared the building, instructing her to hold all of his calls. Saúl went to his private bathroom to masturbate, cursing and recalling Solimar all at once, Gina's scent still on his shirt. When he calmed down his primal need, Saúl enjoyed his coffee knowing that it was time to act. He called a friend of his, a private investigator and set up a meeting. He knew that his friend was good at his work and was totally discreet; after all he had been the one to deliver the goods to Saúl on Gigi. A few days later, Solimar Santana's data was hand delivered to him. With the very limited information Saúl had about Solimar, he was able to obtain a complete history of disconnected cell phone numbers registered in New York City, her date and place of birth and an expired P.O. Box. They just couldn't get a current address. They also found her last known employer, but she was no longer there. He laughed at the irony that his little one was a paralegal and managed to obtain a copy of her transcript from Baruch College, only having finished paying off her schooling fifteen years after her graduation. Upon collecting her severance pay, Soli immediately moved from her tiny, but rent-controlled studio in the Lower East Side of New York City and crossed over the George Washington Bridge to the area where she had met Marisol. She was in Jersey now, and did not want to be found. She left no forwarding address, manually transferring all of her correspondence to yet another P.O. Box address and disconnected her cell phone number, opting to purchase the pre-paid plans. Soli had gone underground and she made absolutely certain that nobody would find her without using resources that were out of her control. She didn't fight for her lucrative job as a paralegal for a renowned law firm, although she had planned to go on to law school on their dime. She accepted that she had blown that opportunity. The firm had agreed to pay 80% of her tuition and let her pay back the 20% balance in small increments which would be deducted directly from her paycheck, but her little jaunt had cost her dearly, and the future appeared bleak at best. Solimar now earned her living tending bar at a local spot drinking herself into oblivion along with her fellow drunkards, following Roberto's forgotten footsteps. Solimar was so paranoid that she even purchased brown contact lenses, which made her eyes look a weird hazel, and dedicated time each morning to pinning up her hair, hiding it under scarves and hats. Saúl and Mari were insane with worry over the disappearance of Solimar. Soli even stopped confiding in Mari. She couldn't afford taking the gamble that Mari would crack under pressure and send Saúl after her. With everything that she had on her mind, she didn't realize that her period was now two months late. Besides, it could just have been a sign of stress, which of that she had more than enough to stay her period for at least a year.

Life Takes On Life

Solimar longed for the tropics and its transparent ocean, but humbly found solace in the carefully gated shores of the Hudson River which was walking distance from her new apartment. While contemplating her lot in life, watching life pass her by, she made a decision to visit her mother's grave which was long overdue. She rented a compact car, went to Metro Plant Factory and purchased a trunk full of perennials, as well as a few gardening tools. She somehow remembered the way to her mother's grave located somewhere in Brooklyn and walked the cemetery, pulling her red wagon behind her, until she found her mother's plot. Solimar, in overalls and a blue bandana, started pulling weeds and digging deep into the soil. Silently, she planted the last gift she would give to her mother verbally saying "Mita, I'm not coming back. I know that you aren't here, but it breaks my heart to see these weeds around your resting place, but I know you're not here. I know that you are *en mi corazon*. I just want to put in these plants and flowers so that they can bloom forever and please, just come with me wherever I go. I'm not afraid of ghosts. Mom, please, *por favor*, stay next to me in this life until I go join you." Solimar worked with unrestrained energy, her hands bleeding as she dug into the cold, hardened earth, having forgotten to purchase gardening gloves. Halfway finished, she laid directly on top of her mother's grave to take a breather. She looked up to the sky and started making shapes out of the clouds, a game her Mom had taught her, as they laid next to each other in the great lawn of Central Park.

Solimar looked hard until, in her delirium, saw the image of her beautiful mother, robed in white, smiling, blessing her daughter and whispering to her in the mild wind that everything was going to be just fine and promising that she would never, ever leave her side. Contented by her illusion, Solimar Santana finished gardening with the help of a grave digger that was on break, but had been observing her the entire while. Having experience and compassion, not to mention better tools, he finished off her planting, washed her blistering hands with an antiseptic and sent her on her way promising to personally look after her mother's grave. Solimar jotted down his number, slipped him a hundred dollar bill and said she would call him from time to time. He was grateful and took off his hat, bowing down as she walked away.

    Solimar continued her routine of visiting the river, a couple of times a week. She'd walk there on her one day off, which was Wednesdays and on Saturday mornings as she didn't have to report in until 5:00 p.m. She would sit on the weathered wooden benches and watch the ripples in the water made by the kids skipping pebbles. She entertained herself watching the older guys fishing, casting their lines from the few designated piers, hoping that they did not take the fish anywhere to be sold and laughing with them when one reeled in something that looked like a boot. Devoid of all thought, prayer and sense of self, she'd watch the lovers walking hand in hand, the old man and young boy who religiously fed the ducks on Saturday mornings and the occasional cruise ship sailing by. Solimar, incapable of feeling envy, was happy at the thought that these passengers would land on some beautiful sunny beach, where they would be served fancy drinks with chunks of fruit and tiny umbrellas and happy people would dance the night away, and maybe even fall in love. She was so wrapped up in emptying her mind she didn't even notice that she occasionally would rub her belly in soft, slow circles. She drank, ate, worked and slept when she wasn't fighting off the demons in her head, or perhaps they were real visitations of the disembodied, yet again. She bathed twice a day and covered her beautiful hair with a white scarf when she wasn't wearing one of her many hats, and wore clothing that would not make her attractive, except when she had to go down to bar and hustle her tips. It was then that she wore mini skirts and halter tops; eye candy for the fellows and money for her pocket.

    Honestly, she had slowly come to despise anything that would resemble or remotely remind her of God and while meditating on this one Wednesday afternoon after having cleaned her home and paying her bills, she impulsively tossed her rosary, the one that Saúl found, into the Hudson River. It was precisely at the moment when the beads hit the water that a woman showed up, whom sort of reminded her of Lydia and approached and asked "Was that an offering?" Solimar confused by the question asked "An offering of what?" The woman simply said "Oh nothing, I just came by here today because I am offering my basket of goodies to Ochun. You know she is the Goddess of the River and if you are nice to her, she will help you get the desires of your heart if God agrees that they are right for you." Solimar cut her eyes at this woman. "I haven't the slightest idea who Ochun is nor do I care." The lady smiled and simply said "I understand. You have been deprived of your roots, but that happens to all of us. You would not throw a rosary into the water if you did not intuitively know that you were making an offering. My name is Olaya, and if you don't mind, I would like you to help me make my offering." Soli had a momentary flashback to the time when another religious 'zealot' tried to 'educate' her, but this one seemed different. Solimar asked "Why are you making an offering?"

    "Well, I've been praying for a new friend to come into my life and I think I found her, but am not sure just yet, but at any rate, I like to give my gratitude in advance." Solimar, bored, tired but slightly intrigued asked "What do you want from me?" Olaya simply said "Don't ask me. Ask Ochun. She is the Goddess of Love, Prosperity and Beautiful Things that you cannot begin to imagine. I want nothing other than to be your friend because you look like you really need one and actually,

I probably need one more. My husband of 39 years recently went on and we were always too busy to make time to have children of our own, but I am honored to say that we have many, many godchildren."

Solimar, moved by this no-nonsense approach said "Okay, how do you want me to help, like what do I have to do here?" Olaya shyly handing Soli the basket said "Here is my basket; take each piece of fruit, each flower and throw it into the river individually and just believe that you are a Child of God and that the Angels and the Saints will provide for your needs as long as you try to reach out to them, anyway you can." Solimar, before obeying, asked "Can't we get arrested for this?" Olaya laughed and said "I guess we could, but who is going to arrest an old bag like me teaching a young girl like you how to feed the ducks? Besides, there are shrimp in there too. Do you think they can arrest us for throwing shrimp into the water?" Solimar really liked Olaya's explanation and wholeheartedly applied herself to the offering she was about to present. With all of her fury, confusion and anger, she begun to hurl fruits like a baseball pitcher, yet delicately tossed flowers into the river. After a few throws, she begun praying, begging, asking anyone up there that would listen to please assist her, deliver her from her shame, pain and guilt as Olaya watched in reverence and nodded the approval of a sage that understood the need to thread together and thereby patch a tattered soul. When the basket was empty, Soli, now out of trance asked the lady "How much do I owe you?" fully expecting to be charged for the privilege of throwing the woman's groceries into the river. Olaya smiled and said "Child, you've blessed me with your blind faith. If we could be friends, I would be more than happy." Soli smiled, undisturbed that this woman was calling her 'child' perceiving that she was genuine about her reference and said "I'll tell you what. I'll take your number, but right now mine is disconnected and when I get my service back, I'll give you a call some time, if that's alright with you." Olaya wrote her number on the back of Solimar's book of matches and said "Go with God, the Angels and the Saints and don't lose those matches." Solimar did just that, feeling oddly liberated.

The following morning Soli woke up vomiting. She knew she was pregnant, but had just been ignoring that godforsaken possibility. She knew she had better take care of this before it interfered with work. She got herself together and went to the local drug store. The pregnancy test did confirm her suspicions. Soli, oddly, felt no fear and wasn't affected by the results. She surmised that a quickie abortion would resolve it all and then she could close this chapter of her life forever and ever, Amen. Solimar went back to her bed and placed her right hand on her belly. Another sacrifice or offering. She did not cry, but instead poured herself a glass of fresh milk and drank it down. The phone rang.

"Hello."

"Solimar, it's me Karen from work."

"Hey Karen, how did you get this number?"

"You put it down on the release papers."

"Shit! Sorry Karen, I didn't mean anything against you." Karen was not offended.

"Solimar, a man called here looking for you." Solimar went cold and hot at once, a knot in her stomach and her head reeling, feeling two seconds away from faint.

"Please tell me that you didn't give out my number."

"Of course not girl, but I got his and told him that I would give it to you." Solimar blew out a deep sigh of relief. "The guy's name is Ricardo Betancourt and he said he needed to speak to you right away because he is in trouble of some sort, but didn't want to give me details. I guess he thought you could get him a lawyer or something." Solimar quickly jotted down the number on the back of an opened envelope, using the pencil she had stuck earlier in her bun and thanked Karen. She immediately dialed Panamá, taking caution to block her new phone number. Lydia answered on the second ring. "Lydia, its me, Sol."

"Solimar, where in God's green earth are you?" Lydia squealed into the phone. Solimar tried to make light of it "I'm here on God's green earth." Lydia annoyed, but contained replied "You don't fool me, but okay, I'll put on Mari for you because she's about to snatch the phone from my ear." Marisol cut right to the chase. "Solimar Santana, what the hell? Have you gone nuts? Where in the hell are you? We've been worried sick over here!" Solimar was not prepared to disclose the full details of her whereabouts and kept to the subject at hand. "Marisol, ummmm Señora Betancourt, I have news for you." Marisol pulled up a chair at hearing her married name. "Ricardito tracked down my office information and he called there. He is looking for me to help him. Apparently he is in trouble with the law." Marisol inflamed at hearing her husband's name said "You are kidding me, right? Fuck him, Solimar, after what he did to me, you would consider helping him?"

"*Tu estas loca, o que?* I just wanted to run it past you first, in the event that you wanted me to do something about it like in me meet up with him and drop his ass off in Panamá with no return ticket. Follow? If I recall correctly, he's still on your Visa and he left out of the country illegally. I wonder how the bastard made it back in."

"Although I love the idea of pulling that kind of evil shit on him, there will come a time to deal with him, but now is not the right time. I need my divorce papers finalized, but keep that thought in mind for the future. By now the asshole already knows I've been deported and probably ran out of money, the way he runs through it, living all high and mighty. It won't be hard to set him up and get him over here, but that is a talk for another day. My divorce papers come first and if he comes to Panamá now, he can contest them and then I'll really be stuck with that son of a bitch. Things are moving along here, slowly, but we are doing alright and the thought of Ricardo makes me sick! Frankly, I don't want to be on the same continent as him, never mind Panamá!"

"But isn't he free to travel to Panamá on his own?"

"Of course he could; he will just have to get clearance from the embassy to return to the States and since he is on my Visa, guess who they will need to contact? Me, and I won't be hard to find; everything that happened is documented in the embassy and I have to report to them from time to time and keep them informed of my whereabouts. We're still married and that is part of the conditions until we become legal residents, but even that now is impossible." Solimar quickly agreed.

"Soli, I'm extremely worried."

"Marisol don't worry, I can handle Ricardo's stupid ass." Marisol blurted it out "Solimar, I'm not referring to that. Saúl is on his way to the States *hoy*."

"What do you mean Saúl is on his way to the States today?"

"He thinks he may have found you."

"Mari, are you sure he is not coming on business? The guy is constantly in and out of here on business; that doesn't mean it's all about me."

"Well I don't know for sure because he said something about the United Nations when he was talking to Roberto, but it sounded to me like he had also hired a private investigator and let's face it, what would he being doing that for?" Solimar slapped her forehead with the palm of her hand. 'Fuck! If that asshole Ricardo could find me, how hard could it be for Saúl to track me down?' Solimar quietly weighed her options, but instantly knew that running was no longer one of them. "Well, Mari, you and I both know that I don't want to see Saúl ever again, so if he comes here, I'm not going to respond, and I really doubt he will find me because he never knew my cell phone number, never got my address or where I worked, or even for that matter what I do for a living. He doesn't even have a picture of me."

"Oh you are sadly mistaken Chiquita. Yes, he does have a picture of you."

"Mari, you didn't! We didn't take pictures, remember and unless you gave him one ..." Solimar was starting to get testy.

"Please girl. That man describes you down to the tiny beauty mark you have on your left *teta,* you know, the one that pops out right over the bikini top and talks about the nine freckles you have sprinkled across your nose in vivid detail. I don't even think you knew you had nine freaking *pecas*."

"Marisol, stop! It was a week-long love affair that ended in the worse possible way. He is my half-brother. If you, of all people, cannot understand my position here, I really don't know what to say. Incest is not exactly my cup of tea and if I should see Saúl again, the only thing he can do for me is treat me as his older sister. I have nothing more to give him and nothing more to take. Unless, of course, everyone is now thinking that a freggin' nut house would be good for me too!"

"But Soli, you are not being fair here. Nobody knew. You didn't set out to fall in love with your brother and neither did he set out to fall in love with you! You're blaming him as if he knew. It wasn't his fault and the guy is broken-hearted!"

"Oh, and I'm not? *Yo estoy aqui* having a super-sized all you can eat fiesta everyday, right? I just came back home, rearranged my life because I had nothing better to do with it. And let us not forget that this little tryst of mine caused me a job and the opportunity to finish up my law degree. You know I can't afford to pay for that shit, and besides I was dismissed anyway. Please don't take it like I'm blaming anyone, but I am blaming myself for being the asshole of the century and following him to Panamá; I should have followed my instincts and just came back home to my normal, boring ass corporate life."

"Solimar, for the love of God, you were a victim of unforeseen circumstances and so was he. The damage has already been done so why not just try to fix it?"

"Fix it? You've got to be kidding me or have your brain cells turned into canned peaches? *El hombre is mi hermano!* Let me spell it out. He is my B R O T H E R! I can't dilute his blood from my veins; I can't wipe out his DNA out of my cells anymore than he can! This conversation has absolutely no purpose and is bordering on the absurd. There is nothing that can reverse the fact that I fucked my brother and my brother fucked the shit out of me and we loved it! I am ashamed! *Yo tengo vergüenza!*"

Marisol, trying to find a solution to a problem with no tangible solution said "*Nena*, it is not like you two are going to have children. Let's face it, what are the chances of you having or even wanting a child at this stage?" Her words cut through Solimar like a blazing hot knife through cold butter. The tears welled in her eyes as she held her belly, but she tried to remain calm. She had to keep it together. She knew that if she told Mari about the baby, all bets would be off and she would immediately get on the phone and tell Saúl. Her words slowly seared Solimar, and although Marisol sensed her friend's fear and sadness, she continued pressing the issue, not knowing Solimar's predicament and simultaneously trying to make a viable argument for Saúl. "You and Saúl can come to terms, agree to disagree, whatever. You guys can even get married, adopt, whatever the hell, but please at least hear him out when he shows up!" Although her tears were a steady stream, Solimar kept herself quiet and did not breathe a word about the child that she had already condemned to walk amongst the unborn. "Calm down Mari. Let's see if he does show up first and I'll just handle it from there. I thank you for the heads up, but I can't think about this now and eventually, Saúl will move on. He is a wonderful guy, good looking, well put together, financially secured and I'm more than certain that a woman is not a problem for him to get; trust and believe he probably has a little black book the size of the New York City yellow pages."

"Solimar Santana, you are a very stubborn person. You should have just stayed with us here in Panamá and taken your family head on. What the fuck are you doing over there anyway with nobody to do it with? I'm sorry to have to tell you this, but the way you left was so wrong. Saúl did not deserve to be treated that way. He is not Raul, and by the way, I'm glad you went for the old geezer's throat although I was appalled when Saúl told us the story!" For a minute, they giggled their Solimar/Marisol giggle. "Mari, for real think about it. It was five, six days, not years or even months for that matter. With a little more time, this episode can be erased and we can all move on with our lives."

"Okay Solimar, have it your way, like always, but here is the deal breaker. If Saúl comes back here empty-handed, meaning without having found your Puerto Rican ass, I'm not going to keep covering your butt. It is not fair to Roberto and I and its not even fair to Lydia to be caught up in your melodrama, as horrible as it is, and as supportive as we may want to be. We have spent even more time with Saúl now than with you and we have come to love and respect him. He has helped us get Rober back on track; we are in the process of re-establishing Rober's former law practice and Saúl has already sent us clients. He even flew in to visit Roberto at the rehab and stayed with us a weekend. You fucking know that Rober would give you a job in a heartbeat, without even looking at your resume. Since you left, we have been there for him and he has been there for us. I feel like a good piece of shit friend not telling him how to contact you and letting him hire a private investigator instead."

"But…"

"But nothing Solimar, the man has lost weight, only shaves and goes for hair cuts when he has to go on business. Although he looked good, when he came by here, his hair was long enough to pull into a ponytail! He disappeared for a week and come for us to find out that he went to that little island off of Puerto Rico, Vieques, just to be alone and he even considered committing suicide!" Solimar's heart skipped a beat. "What did you just say?"

"You heard me. Saúl almost drowned himself in the ocean, drunk as a skunk on Sangria, your favorite drink, not to mention a near overdose of cocaine and hashish!"

"What are you saying Marisol, I don't understand. Saúl doesn't do drugs."

"Well, he does now, or who knows, maybe he used to in the past; it's no big deal, we all did anyway. I don't know, but he put a concoction of all of that garbage in him and went right into the ocean like a fucking zombie *loco* trying to die in el Sol y la Mar. You rather leave that legacy?" Solimar not wanting to acknowledge this or the acute confrontation of Marisol's last question said "Marisol, I thought that one day you told me that the correct way to address the Sun and Sea in Spanish was el Sol y el Mar." Marisol went ballistic and started screaming at her friend. "Are you serious right now? Are you? You know what Solimar, you're a real fucking asshole, I was just fucking trying to tell you that this poor bastard tried to drown himself and you want to question proper syntax?" Solimar, who was already choking back tears, said "Look Mari, this is all too much for me to handle, but please, keep on telling me what really happened, who rescued him?" Marisol calmed down, but her tone still carried an edge. "He rescued himself and his crazy love for you helped save him. To hear him tell it, he said that when he walked into the water and the ocean floor bottomed out, he was feeling himself letting go, going towards the light, but then he remembered some 'inspiring' moment you guys had on the beach together or some shit like that. Obviously he had to have been hallucinating because he said that you swam towards him and pulled his drowning ass out of the water!"

"Marisol, he said all of that?"

"Girl, it gets better. He said you were a fucking mermaid! Obviously, he made it out by himself, but he did say he was way in over his head and the waves were beating the crap out of him. I guess he remembered how to ride the waves and managed to get himself to shore." Soli placed her hand on her bosom and thanked God that Saúl survived. As much pain and heartache as she was in, she didn't want anything to ever happen to him. At that moment, she was too spiritually broke to make the connection with Olaya and the 'offering' she had wholeheartedly presented to the Goddess of the Sea, at Olaya's instance; the very offering that would be traveling downstream until it reached the ocean. "Mari, please don't be so hard on me. I'm going through my own; I just can't; *sinceramente no puedo.*" Marisol was growing tired of trying to talk sense into her friend. "Okay, okay and o fucking kay already! Just try to get yourself around the fact that the man sleeps, breathes, eats and lives you; if I hear your name one more time, I swear I'm changing mine! When he came to see Rober, he even dragged me to the mall under the pretense that he needed to pick up a few things and took me right into Victoria's Secret to buy that body spray that you use. He uses the shit as air freshener! Solimar, he bought out the store and put in an order to be shipped to his house in Puerto Rico, right then and there! He even smells like it and doesn't care!"

"Marisol, *basta ya carajo*, you're giving me an Excedrin headache here, and I don't have any."

"Fine Solimar, I'll let you go because you are giving me chest pains here from hell and I can't take shit for the heartburn either. Besides there is someone here that wants to speak to you. I'll talk to you whenever you get over yourself." Marisol was so incensed that she didn't even bother to say good-bye or God bless you. She handed the phone over to Roberto. "Hey Bella."

"Roberto?"

"Si, *cariño* how are you doing?"

"So, you finished the program? Congratulations."

"Yup. I'm a graduate from the how not to be drunk school. Clean as a whistle for 69 days."

"Wow. Rober, I am happy for you and highly impressed."

"Listen, I'm glad you called and that Mari gave you the heads up, but, changing the subject a bit, I want to tell you that Mari is pregnant. We tried to get a hold of you sooner, but lady, you are not so easy to get a hold of, changing numbers every other week. We are getting married next month and we want you to be our *Madrina,* our Maid of Honor." Solimar instinctively rubbed her belly. "But then of course, Saúl would be the *Padrino,* you know that he is definitely my Best Man. We also want you both to baptize our child, so, well, you figure that out. Eventually you are going to run into Saúl again, so you might as well stop running."

"Wow. I will see what I can do about getting some time off, but that might be hard. I have a new job."

"Listen Sol, if money is tight, I got your ticket and you know that you have no expenses to worry about here. I know Macho is going crazy looking for you and I'm being open and honest with you here. He definitely is on his way to New York, but has no idea as to where to find you or so he says because last we spoke, he had a private investigator trying to track your skinny behind down. We haven't told him anything, nor will we until you clear it and say that it is alright, but when it comes to the baby, well that is on you and him...If you want, I'll give you all of his contact information right now and you can save yourselves all of this unnecessary agony by calling him yourself."

"Thank you, Rober, but I have to decline your offer. I'm not ready to talk to Saúl, but I do want to be there for you and Marisol and definitely for the baby's baptism. I just need a bit more time so that I can confront him on my terms. As for the wedding, I really don't know; I've got a little business to settle, but I'll do what I can to get over there to witness you guys get married, but if not, for sure, I'll be there for the baby. I'll do anything, even if it means seeing Saúl again. Are you guys definitely getting married next month, so quick?"

"Actually, we aren't sure on that one totally. I've never been married before and would like a church wedding, but we still got to get Marisol's divorce finalized, so probably not, we might wait until after the baby is born and do it up right, reception, honeymoon and all."

"That works even better. Tell Mari that I will call her very soon and we can work through some details."

"No problem Bella."

"Oh, by the way, how's Lydia; how is she handling this, she's alright with it?"

"Are you kidding me? She is up to her neck in yarn crocheting and knitting baby socks and things, happier than a kid in a candy store. I almost had one of my balls deflated when I sat down on the couch the other day by one of those big ass knitting needles!" Solimar smiled with all of heart since she last left her smile, along with everything else about her in Panamá. "That is so incredible. Wow. *Un bebe*! I'm going to be an auntie! I'm glad you two are doing so well."

"Well, I have to say that I'm not happy that you aren't doing so swell, Soli, but okay, for now, we will leave it at that, but you know I've got to say that you should definitely give Saúl a chance even though the situation is totally messed up." Solimar didn't want to hear anymore about Saúl and went silent so as not to encourage further advice or discussion. Roberto, picking up on the unspoken message that her silence loudly delivered ended the conversation.

"Ciao Bella, and take good care of yourself, huh?"

"Ciao and don't worry, I am doing just that." Soli didn't know what to feel, nor could she feel anything. Her thoughts were flooded with the knowledge of Saúl's suicide attempt and the fact that he was coming to New York. She dwelled momentarily on the poetic notion that Marisol would soon be married and how appropriately life had treated her to eventually change her name from Marisol Espinoza - Marisol full of thorns to Marisol Robles, the Oak Tree. Mari was pregnant and so was she. Soli knew that Saúl would find her. It was only a matter of time.

She accessed her internet and started combing the listings for abortion clinics in the area. As she glanced around looking for paper and pen, she took out a cigarette and lit it. On the back of the matchbook she saw Olaya's phone number and called her. Olaya answered on the first ring and simply said; "Don't worry girl, I know you are going through rough waters, but it will be well for you." Solimar shook and trembled so hard that she couldn't even put the cigarette in her mouth. She never gave Olaya her phone number. How the hell did she know she was calling? Solimar openly started crying and Olaya gave Soli her address and asked her to please come by anytime. "Can I swing by now?"

"Yes, little one, if you want, swing by right now, right now is as good a time as any."

Soli jumped into her oversized sweats, called for a cab and flew into the setting sun that marked the early evening, hurrying the cabdriver. Olaya was anxiously waiting for her at the door and what Soli encountered as she entered Olaya's home instantly comforted the core of her soul. Soli walked into a miniature paradise. Soft, gentle instrumental music played, a glass door cabinet filled with all types of sacred books and poetry beckoned her to educate herself, aromas of burning incense and exotic herbs visually filled the air with delicate scented spirals, an assorted array of plants, some hanging, others sprouting up from exotic pottery placed on the floor awakened her curiosity, along with the multitude of flowers and a beautiful turtle that greeted her at the door, not to mention the tapestry, rocks, African art, food and candlelight and a tiny balcony, that seated two, overlooking the Hudson River, adorned in amber paper lanterns and seven jeweled wind chimes. Olaya, impeccably dressed from head to toe in white had already prepared a bowl of fruit and yogurt for Solimar. She handed Solimar a spoon and a linen napkin and said "Welcome to my humble abode." Solimar blurted it out "I'm scared." Olaya laughed and said "Eat up girl, the battle is not yours to fight, but you gotta be strong for the things that are to come. I see that you are definitely with child." Solimar, not ready to discuss this quite yet, picked up the turtle and placed it on her chest. Olaya patiently waited for her answer, but then said "You know kiddo; you really don't have to answer that question. Native American Indians believe that turtles symbolize fertility, perseverance and long life. It is not strange then that the first thing you did was pick up that turtle off the floor and placed it near your heart or that the turtle greeted you at the door. They normally hide." Astounded, Solimar questioned Olaya. "How could you know this?" Olaya laughed and said "I am a seer. Some people would call me a witch but I have no craft and cast no spells; I only speak what my Spirit tells me and what I see from people, or better yet, what people want me to see. Your face shows deep anguish, yet it is glowing so prettily. The Virgin Mary must have looked liked you right about now when she was carrying the Baby Jesus in her belly. Bet you it's a boy. This child you carry will bring you much joy."

"No, you are very wrong Olaya; this child will never see the light of day. Tomorrow, I will schedule the earliest abortion possible because the child has no father and it would not be fair for me to raise it alone. I, like you, also have nobody."

"As the legend goes, in that book called the Bible, maybe you've read it? Jesus had no father either. Mary was about ready to get dumped by Joseph until something or another happened and Joseph found out that Mary was pure, or some mess like that. He stayed around and took on the role of Jesus' father. Why can't something wonderful like that also happen to you, or have you no faith left in anything?"

"Olaya, I am flattered to no end that you would want to compare me to the Virgin Mary, but I'm sure you see that in every pregnant woman. Besides, this was no immaculate conception. Truth be known, this child was conceived in the darkest corridor of hell." Olaya bit hard down on her lip and took her time before answering. When she answered she took Solimar's hand and with tears forming said "Listen here little girl and listen real good. Hell does not produce babies; hell kills babies and does so gladly."

"But even in the best case scenario, I can't do this alone!"

Olaya smiled and said "You are alone because it was your choice, but if you need a babysitter, you can count on me and all this without me not even knowing your name." Solimar embarrassed said "I'm sorry. My name is Solimar." Olaya repeated it several times, trying to engrave it in her mind forever. She said "That is one beautiful name, can you translate it please?"

"Sun and Sea".

"And you are from?"

"Puerto Rico."

"I see; the rich port of the Caribbean. I visited there once many years ago with my husband. We went to a place called Luisa or something like that for a yearly carnival called Mayombe."

"Loiza Aldea! That is where all the witches are!"

"That is simply an untruth. Yes, it was settled by Africans and it is a truly a financially impoverished place, but the richness in culture is unprecedented. Loiza is one of the gatekeepers of our tradition only next to Cuba, keepers of the sacred drum."

"Where are you from?"

"Nigeria, but I was raised in Britain. I've never been back to Nigeria although I intend to go there to live and finish out my life. I have the same ancestry like that pretty Black girl that is short, has long hair and a big forehead, the one that sings the blues…. What is her name again?

"Sade."

"Yup! That is her."

"Why do you dress in white?" Olaya laughed and asked "Do you prefer me to dress in black and not be seen?" At this they laughed honestly, ate their fruit and yogurts and talked well into the evening, Solimar became mesmerized by her new turtle friend while Olaya kept warning her that turtles do bite and to stop poking the poor thing. "What's her name?" Olaya looked at Solimar as if she had lost her mind and asked "Who, the turtle?"

"Yeah."

"Hell if I know!"

"But why doesn't she have a name?"

"What makes you think she is a she?"

"I don't know; she feels like a she, besides I've never seen a turtle that was brown; I thought they were all green."

"So go on and name her. I won't mind." Olaya took a sip of her sparkling water and waited while Solimar smiled the eager smile of a little girl that had just been given permission to take a piece of candy without her mother's consent and said "Alright. Her name is Hickey." Olaya spat out her water and laughed hysterically, reminding Solimar of that infamous night when she met Saúl. "Hickey! What the hell kind of name is that?"

Solimar, amused, replied "Its short for *jicotea*, which means turtle in Spanish." Olaya said "Thank the Lord, now that makes sense, I thought you were going somewhere south with that one!"

After their laughter simmered down, Solimar said "I feel a bit embarrassed; I was raised to always bring a gift when coming into someone's house for the first time. Like a sign of hospitality." Olaya propped her elbow on the table and rested her chin on her hand, staring deeply into the oceanic depth of Solimar's aquamarine eyes. "Your presence and laughter has offered me friendship, need I say more than that?" Solimar held back the tears that threatened to once again fall and said "Well, this has been the most fun I've had in a couple of months and I thank you Olaya."

"I am glad you feel this way, you have made my heart glad as well, but with your permission, I would like to ask my mom a question before you go." Astonished Solimar said "Your mom? Your mom is here?!"

"My mom is here" pointing to her heart "and here" pointing to her mind "and here" raising her arms. With that she pulled out four little round coconut shells from the refrigerator enclosed in a ceramic container. She pulled back a curtain that revealed an altar and started reciting words that Solimar did not understand. Solimar started to outwardly show that she was getting nervous. "Shhhhh Solimar .... No harm will befall you." Solimar now entranced, watched this simple ritual. When Olaya had concluded the sprinkling of water from what looked like half a carved out coconut shell, she took the oracles in her hand, passed them over key areas of Solimar's body and yelled "Ma Yemaya is Solimar's child destined to be born?" She dropped the coconuts yelling "Obi" and there they stood all face up. Olaya danced with happiness. "A child will be born and when he is, you will remember this day and take him to the closest body of water and offer him up to God in thanksgiving." Solimar cried. "You don't understand! I can't, I cannot."

"Yes you can, and you will! Even Christians don't believe in abortions and they massacred just about everybody in their path in Jesus name! Why do you think that precisely at this moment of your life, you showed up at my doorstep? Not for tea and crumpets that's for sure! You came for answers and you got the most important one in your life. If I didn't know any better, I'd guess you would be a daughter of Ochun herself!"

"Who is Yemaya?"

"Funny that you would ask that, my friend; Yemaya happens to be Ochun's sister …. Yemaya being the Goddess of the Ocean; Ochun, as you already know is the Goddess of the River, but with your crazy temperament you just might be Oya's daughter!"

"Okay, I'll bite. Who in hell is Oya?"

"Watch your mouth girl. The question is: Who in heaven is Oya?"

"Sorry. I didn't mean to be disrespectful."

"Oya is the Goddess of the Wind, the Angel that escorts the dead to safety, the Greatest Female Warrior, but don't go getting no ideas; only a High Priest can determine your Guardian Angel and this through a series of things that I cannot do for you."

"But, wait a minute, I found you at the river and you were making an offering to Ochun. I don't get it."

"Being sisters and that the river spills into the ocean and seeing that I have no access to the ocean directly, I ask Ochun to please take my gifts to her sister, Yemaya, got it?"

"So it could be that I can be Ochun's daughter because we found each other by the river and you are Yemaya's daughter!"

"I like the way you think. You connect the dots pretty quickly and try to make sense of things. It could be, but that would be only speculation on our part."

"I really want to know!"

"All in good time dear, you will know everything you need to know to carry you through this adventure we call life, like it or not, but God is so wonderful that you can walk away from the things you do not want to know, something we all have called free will. Now go on, call the cab people. I have to have a stiff drink and you gotta get some much needed rest, you're starting to get dark circles under your pretty blue eyes."

"I don't want to go yet." Olaya smiled tenderly and hugged her new friend. "Okay then, help me peel some fruits and other things; lucky for you, you're already wearing that white rag on your head because you can't have one of mine, and I will do a rogation over your head." Solimar submitted and while peeling fruits couldn't help, but ask "What in the world is a rogation?"

"It's a supplication, a prayer and by the time you leave here you will have a fruit basket on your head, looking like Chiquita Banana or Carmen Miranda and you will sleep with it on tonight.... Now pass me the cotton."

After their simple ritual, which consisted of more prayers that Solimar did not understand, Olaya carefully placed the fruits and oils atop Solimar's head and sealed it with her white scarf. She gave Solimar careful instructions and explained that this is a sort of refreshment for her little hot-tempered head. Solimar touched by this woman's act of faith and kindness said "I don't know what to say. I'm speechless, grateful and I will be back, if only just to play with Hickey." Olaya simply responded "You are so full of love. Take Hickey with you and be done with it already. I won't sleep tonight if you don't and something is telling me that you will either bring Hickey back someday or I'll see her by you, so go on, please, take your friend Hickey."

Solimar obediently picked up her new friend, kissed Olaya and took her cab back home, Hickey safely nested underneath her sweat shirt, not knowing that Saúl was landing at Newark International Airport, right about the time Solimar was changing into her pajamas. He gave the limo driver an address and they sped off, Saúl begging the driver to take the shortest possible route. There was no bridge to cross. He was already in New Jersey. When he reached his destination, Saúl dispatched the limo, certain that he had the right address. He was determined to pitch a tent and sleep outside if necessary until that magic moment arrived. He didn't have to wait long. Solimar was bringing out her garbage in her raggedy, oversized PJs and ugly fuzzy slippers and the white scarf securely tied around her head looking like a Puerto Rican version of Aunt Jemima before they modernized her look and gave her pearls and a hairdo. She spotted him first, dropped her garbage and ran to the back of the house. Saúl entered through the front and by then was at her door, which she had left unlocked. Solimar came around the back entrance hoping that he had not detected any movement. Not seeing him, she disposed of her garbage and walked into her tiny first floor apartment to find him sitting in her kitchen, feeding Hickey a piece of lettuce that she had chopped up and left on the counter.

"*Hola* Solimar."

"Hello. Long time no see little brother." Saúl lingered a while and she watched him place Hickey into a little tub of water that Solimar had also prepared for her. When he was done, he spoke directly to her pulling no punches. "Solimar, I am not playing this game. If you don't want to have anything to do with me, tell me right now."

"How can I not want anything to do with you? You're my fucking brother, no pun intended." Saúl casually responded "Correction, I am your half fucking brother and that being through no damn fucking fault of my own."

"Correction noted."

"Well then?"

"Well then what, Saúl? You want the story, here it goes. Your piece of shit father left my mother when I was not yet two years old. A lifetime later I learned that the dishonorable bastard made a really nice life for himself while my mother and I struggled just to keep our heads above water. Not even a birthday card from that son of a bitch to acknowledge my existence. But that wasn't punishment enough. I fuck his son by sheer accident, bad luck, fucked up karma or cosmic joke and wind up preggggg." Soli realized she went too far, but trying to eradicate the last sentence said "And that's the Reader's Digest condensed version." Saúl dismissed her last statement. "Marisol is pregnant. It can't possibly be that you are too." Solimar hoisted herself up on the countertop of her little kitchen. "No, I didn't mean to say that, really." Before she finished Saúl said "Don't lie to me Solimar. Are you pregnant?" The fire in his eyes implored everything that she had to give, telling her without saying it, that she better come clean. Solimar knew that she would not be able to win this battle and acquiesced. *"Si."* Saúl furiously raked his hair, this time with both hands, walked right out the door into the night, spread his arms and yelled in the middle of the street for all to hear "My sister is pregnant people!" Solimar begun to cry not knowing if she had just pushed him over the edge. He came back in and she said simply "Don't send out birth announcements; you are celebrating way too soon. I guess you have the right to know that I'm having an abortion next week."

"Like hell you are!"

"Saúl, for the love of Jesus, Mary and Joseph and all the Angels and the Saints, this baby can come out autistic, retarded, all fucked up!"

"I don't give a shit if it comes out with no face and three legs. For love of Jesus, Mary and Joseph, the Angels and the Saints, you are going to have this child Solimar!" Solimar hopped off the counter and reached for the liquor cabinet, which was directly underneath where she had been sitting. "Go ahead Solimar. Have some Sangria and pour me a glass while you're at it so we can toast! According to you the baby is already doomed; add a little more, a fourth leg would be just fine with me!" Solimar turned on him with the ferocity of a lioness. Her breathing became quite raw and her eyes spat out venom. She defiantly pulled down the gallon of store bought Sangria, no longer the freshly prepared kind, poured a drink and gulped it down in front of him. Saúl laughed at her pathetic attempt to anger him. "If I recall correctly, our mothers smoked, drank, worked and fucked while they were pregnant, and we came out alright, at least I did."

"That's it! You leave here right now! You wanna be an uncle and a dad all wrapped up in one, have me be my kid's mother and aunt and to boot, have the kid be its own cousin you sick fuck?"

"I'll be that and more Solimar S. Santana" hissing an emphasis on the secret S. "I'll be my sister's husband and my nephew's father if you would let me."

"Correction, estupido, I'm your half sister."

"We don't do halves in Spanish, and you well know that. We are what we are."

Solimar, her back leaning against the refrigerator, slowly slid down and crumpled to the floor. All that she had built up within herself in the last weeks was swatted in one fell swoop. "I can't do this Saúl; I just don't have it in me."

"So, you wanna kill us Solimar, is that it? You rather kill our child, who incidentally, without a shadow of a doubt, will be a mini version of us and will be crazier than hell on roller blades? You want to do that? You're sitting here telling me that you want to kill my son or my daughter or my retarded kid and I'm supposed to say go ahead Solimar, here's the money?" Solimar kept quiet as the barrage of questions and accusations flowed effortlessly from his lips. "You would deny a human being the right to live because you are uncomfortable with his or her existence, or worse, be uncomfortable being its mother!? Who in the hell died and made you keeper of someone else's life? I should strangle you with your fresh face announcing that you're going to have an abortion next week, like if it was a fucking picnic in the park! Or would you like it better if I started pummeling the living daylights out of you, beating you down and saving you the trouble of aborting?! What is it money? What already speak the fuck up?!" Without allowing her time to defend her principles or her sentiments, Saúl Santana kept the heat on, ranting and raving, finally spilling out the depths of his soul and love for her in a manner that she never expected from this otherwise eloquent and gentle human being. "You, Solimar, are a blue-eyed witch, you know that? No fuck that! You're a blue-eyed fucking *hija de puta* fucking motherfucking ungrateful bitch! You didn't call me knowing full well that your friend had my number; you left me standing in the pouring rain, sick to my fucking stomach, worried, crying like a motherfucking lost five year old and you know what? You ain't the only one that has the corner market on hatred in their heart. You don't think that I despise our father for doing what he did to you and your mom? That I lost respect for him and my worthless mother too?! No, it is all you, you, you, not me; I don't fucking matter here for nothing! I don't see that you tried to kill yourself; No way, not Solimar *Santa Ana*.

Solimar just ran to cover her fucking little *plancha*, flat ass, but you sure are ready to kill an innocent bystander, you little fucker! Where the hell is your fucking *cabeza* or have you lost all of your marbles?! I'm starting to get the real feeling here that you never gave a shit about me, that I was just a passport to get you over to Panamá to see fucking Marisol! What the hell am I doing here anyway trying to win you back? For what?! I've got a fucking Miss Puerto Rico in my back pocket and a gorgeous puta up my fucking ass ready to marry me tomorrow if I say so. Either one of them can make me forget your sorry skinny ass in a New York minute and neither one of them would cost me half the money or twice the fucking headache that you have given me! But you know what, if it wasn't that I believe that you are pregnant, which by the way, you left the pregnancy kit in the bathroom, I'd be fucking out of here, but I'm not leaving my child and neither are you, you fucking, fucking, I don't even know what to call you anymore, puta!"

    All this he yelled at her, after having picked her up off the floor, standing her up on her feet and slamming her back against the refrigerator, both fists pounding each statement, his face inches from hers. Solimar realizing that Saúl was getting out of control, feeling his pain simply uttered "I'm sorry."

    "Oh, you're sorry. Isn't that just absolutely fucking rich? Solimar '*maricona*' Santana is sorry. Let me show you what sorry looks like *putana*!" He grabbed her by the nape of her neck and forced her to look into the mirror she hung in her foyer and made her stare long and hard, her face an inch away from being pressed into her own reflection. When he noted that he was making her confront her hidden demons, he placed his face next to hers, joining her so that they could see not just her reflection, but theirs. He whispered into her ear "This is the epitome of what sorry looks like Soli, but we are in this together whether your fucking evil, perverse witch ass likes it or not. If you're taking us to hell, I'm going down with you and you know I only travel first fucking class; you can go coach or better yet, travel in the god damn luggage compartment for all I care!" Solimar pulled gently away from the mirror and leaned into Saúl's chest, not having the strength to even put her arms around him. He pushed her away from him with his index finger and poking her said, "Look, I'm gonna get me a hotel room around here for the night. I'll call you when I book it so you better give me your fucking number. If I don't hear from you with the only decision I want to hear, I'll be jetting out after my conference at the U.N. on Tuesday; I'm so disgusted with you that I can barely look at you! *Sirena* my ass, you are a bona fide *desgraciada,* you full blown witch from hell! I should rip your eyes out and leave you in the dark where you belong and keep them bitches as souvenirs, but no thank you, I've got a pair of my own and I can see what's right and what's wrong!"

As he started towards the door, Solimar realizing that there would be no tomorrow, no second chance, cried "Saúl, please, *no te vayas, por favor,* don't go!" He stood at the door with his back toward her, his hand on the knob, emotionally exhausted, his head hanging low and without turning around asked "What the fuck is it, *bruja*?" Solimar repeated her plea. "Saúl, please, don't leave. *No te vayas, por favor.* I've made my decision; it is just that I can't do this *solita!*" Saúl, hearing her brokenness, slowly turned around and with no hesitation opened his arms. "Come Negrita Bella, if you can't do this, let me take full responsibility and do it for us." Solimar ran the short distance and leaped into his arms, wrapping her legs tightly around his, clinging to him like she had done in the past, that infamous day on the beach when they sincerely discovered each other. She received his forgiveness and clung to his magnanimous heart. Saúl gently lifted her off of him and said "Here, put on your ring, be a woman about it for Christ's sake, and stop acting like some low life that doesn't deserve the time of day! Tomorrow is Sunday and we've got to go to church, we gotta give thanks for the baby." Solimar woman upped and allowed him, her man, her blood brother and the love of her life to reach into his pocket and place the sparkling gem on her left ring finger without even asking if she'd marry him. "I can't go to church with this on my head."

"What do you mean with this on your head? I thought we just finished resolving all this shit!"

"Okay, *calmate,* you can't see that I have my head wrapped?"

Saúl laughed "I see that you have your head warped." Solimar was in no real mood for jokes. "Solimar Santana?" Soli bowed her head. "We aren't children of an inferior God. Life dealt us a hand and as players, we got to play that bitch out to the bitter end, am I coming across clearly, *me explico claramente*?" The hot tears flowed freely from both of them. "How did you find me? Roberto and Marisol gave me their word ... they betrayed me too?"

"No *mi amor.* They protected your wish to the end. You just forgot to swear La Señora Lydia to secrecy. She broke into their bedroom, got the contact information and in turn swore me to secrecy, but I know she doesn't really give a flying fuck what you think about it; she was only scared about Roberto and Marisol finding out, you know, because of her job and all, but deep down she only cared that I would find you and bring you home. She loves you, and I don't blame her; you have that strange affect on people." Solimar walked to the fridge and poured herself a glass of cold milk. "I think I am turning into a pussycat. I've been downing this stuff on a regular."

"That's my girl." Saúl stared at her intently. Solimar, May I kiss you now? I have missed you like if my soul was absent from my body. I have been miserable, not really as good as I used to be at work, I ... I ... I even tried to kill myself, but then I realized that if I did, I wouldn't have the chance to find you again, and even if I made it up to heaven, it'd be a damn long wait before you would join me because I wish you nothing but life, including the life growing inside of you." Solimar, once again, successfully held back her tears, but her heart was pounding, shattering all at once and vowed to herself that she would never discuss with him that Mari had revealed his failed suicide attempt. After all, how many failures did she not have notched under her belt? "I think a two carat diamond ring entitles you to at least a little *besito.*" In one quick stride, he was upon her, kissing her milky lips.

"Ummmmmmmmmmm, milk really does a body good Bella." He held her with all of his might until he felt her relax into him. Soli pleaded off lovemaking and Saúl agreed quickly ... "Baby, chasing you is tiring and let's face it, I'm only a few years younger than you. I can wait until morning; I can wait until forever, what the hell?"

They settled into Soli's bedroom, played with Hickey for a while, taking turns letting her crawl over them both and welcomed the serenity that fell over the night, the calm after their own personal storm, staring into the blue-white stars in each other's eyes. Crying silently, thanking God, submitting themselves to God's will and enjoying the fact that they didn't have to hurt or make love to each other in order to be madly in love. They finally fell asleep while Hickey somehow managed to crawl to the foot of the bed, leaving the lovers to their own, feeling loved herself. Animals are often separated from their moms, dads and siblings early on in life and Hickey found a comfortable somewhere between Solimar and Saúl's feet wondering if she should bite them in the morning, just to let them know that she was there.

The Guardians joined in shouting a "Hallelujah" chorus. The Warriors, as always, silently manned their post. The demons that had followed them from one part of the world to the other walked out the door with a renewed determination to return, and Olaya broke night watching vigil, peeking from her bedroom window, sending blessings, lighting candles and praying until she saw the first sign of the sun rising over the river.

Begging off church, Saúl and Soli went to the local diner instead, note pad in hand ready to commence their plans for their future together. Both Saúl's and Soli's phones were ringing incessantly, but neither picked up, allowing voicemail to do its well-paid electronic job. They had a complicated life to plan ahead of them, but plan they would. They diligently spent the next week brainstorming, lovemaking, stopping in at church when the sanctuary was empty, all theirs to enjoy and yes, going to the doctor. The *"bebe"* was developing well and was nearly clearing the first trimester. They were advised not to fly, so instead Saúl booked a cruise to Puerto Rico. He wanted his child to be born in the land of their forefathers, their native land, also guaranteeing American citizenship with no hassle. Solimar begun to make arrangements to sell off her furniture and things, but there wasn't enough time. Saúl suggested that she just pack her summer clothes and donate the furniture to charity. Marisol's belongings stayed in storage. Saúl paid a year's worth up front, because Marisol had long since forgotten her life before Roberto and neglected to make the monthly rental payments. When they went down to check on Mari's stuff, the warehouse was about ready to put her belongings up for auction. They decided that the best thing for Hickey would be to set her free and drop her in the river before boarding, that way she, too, could make her own way.

    Back in Solimar's cramped apartment, Saúl settled into her small desk to do some work of his own, when he heard Solimar's footsteps and the name he hadn't heard in some time. "Bello?"

    "Yes, love, I was just catching up on some work I've been neglecting. What is it?"

    "Before we leave, I want to share with you a special friend I met." Saúl put his pen down and said "Oh, oh, another lunatic like Mari?"

    "No and yes." Saúl was intrigued. "Okay, give it to me, who is she or is it a he?" Saúl winked at her, but she ignored his little harmless dig. "Her name is Olaya, she is from Nigeria. I think she practices, you know …"

    "Santeria?"

    "She does not call it that."

    "Well, if you let her do a rogation on your head, she must know something."

    "She knows a lot. Hey! What do you know about rogations?"

    "*Nena*, you keep forgetting that my job takes me all over creation and I meet different people, learn different cultures, different ways of thinking and believing."

    "You don't think I did witchcraft on you, do you?"

"Of course you did. The day I met you and you're doing it right now. It is a natural force in you, you little *Brujita Boricua!*"

"Please. Before we go, let's take her out to dinner; she was so good to me; took my heart and soul in when I was at wit's end and only asked for my friendship in return. Now that we are moving, I may never see her again."

"*Llamala.* Give her a buzz and ask her what she's up to tonight. There is a Cuban restaurant that recently opened up, not too far from here called Las Palmas Del Caribe that I really want to check out anyway."

"How do you know this?"

"Solimar, just get on the phone and make plans."

"Why are you so good to me?"

"If you'd like, I will tie you up and spank that ass with a wooden paddle until it is beet red instead." Soli stuck her tongue out and headed for the phone. Olaya picked up at the second ring, but this time it was Solimar whom surprised her. "What's up Oli?" Olaya choked from the cigar smoke in her mouth. "Girl, my husband used to call me that in private, I guess you're starting to develop your spiritual awareness and divining spirit."

"I called to ask you if I can take you out to dinner tonight that is if you don't have any plans of course."

"I've never once turned down a good meal in great company."

"We have loads to catch up, and I have a surprise for you."

"I don't like surprises girl. Do you? Hmmmmm. Don't answer that. Have you been to the doctor yet?"

"Yes Ma'am and the babe is in good shape."

"You stopped those cancer sticks?"

"Trying."

"Drinking?"

"Trying."

"Drinking milk?"

"So far, three quarts a day; gonna have to start investing in the gallons."

"The babe will be fine."

"Did you cook the turtle?"

Solimar laughed and said "No, Hickey is very well taken care of, she's my shadow!"

"What time you gonna come around for me?"

"8:00?"

"Boy you are really testing the waters here. I ain't been out on a Friday night after 8:00 since I saw the first wrinkle on my face."

"Take a nap. We're going to have fun. You like to dance?"

"Of course not, Yemaya only stays watching over the ocean all day and all night long. No fun for her!"

"You are kidding me right?"

"I am kidding you."

"Alright then, let me go see what I can wear and you do the same, I'll call you when I'm in front of your door."

"Wear white so you can be seen."

"I think I will definitely be wearing white sometime soon, as soon as tonight!" Solimar went for her noon nap, leaving Saúl to his work. Saúl, having overhead the conversation, waited for her to fall asleep, kissed his woman, sweeping back her hair off her face and went out shopping. Unbeknownst to Solimar, he was quite familiar with an area that was settled by Cubans in the early 1960s, where his mother grew up, not very far from where she was living. He loved that it was now settled by practically all of Latin America, and was sure that he would find a shop that would provide precisely what he was looking for. This time of Solimar's much needed rest afforded him a time of reflection, reconciliation and he often stopped by the local church and asked God practically on a daily basis to watch over Solimar and their child. He loved Solimar, yet loved his time away from her, giving him a reason to run right back home to the lunatical woman whom he cherished. When Solimar woke up, she found a nicely wrapped present at the foot of her bed; Hickey nestled on top of her head, having found a perfect nest in her matted hair. Saúl leaned against the doorway to her bedroom and watched as she tore into the gift like a child on Christmas morning, tearing paper and ripping bows with absolutely no decorum. Nestled in the white tissue paper, she found a simple white pollera, a traditional Panamanian outfit for women. He found the one specific to the women that are nursing. It consisted of an off the shoulder ruffled blouse and a simple layered skirt. He even got her white ballerina slippers embroidered in silver thread and beads and a matching tiny purse, big enough to carry her identification and perhaps a lipstick.

"Do you like it?"

"I love it."

"Do you love me?"

"Saúl, if I didn't love you, I could not love myself." He moved Hickey out the way and kissed her tenderly and said "get dressed, we gonna go shake the skeletons off our asses. Here are some white flowers I found in the corner market. I'm gonna make you a bath out of them fit for a queen, although you are truly a *bruja*."

"How do you …"

"Soli, I just know."

After her exquisite milk and flower bath, Soli emerged as she did from the ocean when he first laid eyes on her believing her to be a mermaid, not understanding that what he saw was just the woman ordained for him, the yin to his yang. He watched her dress and asked her permission to brush her long, wavy hair. For a moment he remembered Gina's silky hair and felt compelled to tell Solimar that he had kissed another woman in her absence. "Solimar, I promise you that I have not been with another woman."

"Nor I with another man, Bello, but where is that coming from?"

"An old girlfriend looked me up and stopped by my office. She was before you, way before you, when I didn't know love at all, but please I have to tell you that when I explained to her that she and I could no longer have an amorous relationship, I felt really bad … I don't know, for a minute I saw you and went to kiss her, but she is the polar opposite of you in every way and I could not, so instead I kissed her cheek and I kissed her hand."

Solimar took the hairbrush from him and begun to groom herself. She said nothing. What was revealed really did not require a response. "Soli …. May I suggest something different for your hair today?"

"Que?"

"Do that big bun thing that Mari did for you when we were in Panamá, that way it shows off your earrings." Solimar bent over and had Saúl brush her hair from the nape forward. When he had managed to get it smoothly gathered to the crown of her head, she wrapped both hands around it and secured the massive pony tail with a thick rubber band. She then proceeded to twist, twirl and pin until she achieved the desired look, allowing a few strands to escape. Saúl decorated the bun with fresh flowers, gently placing each one around the bun to form a crown. He sprayed hairspray on the flowers to keep them from wilting before their time. "You look spectacular, and before you ask, I learned this while helping our sister dress for a festival in Panamá …. She was really amazing and graceful. It hurts me that you were not there and you never had a chance to be part of a float in a parade." Solimar smiled and shook her head and said "No, no, no. You are wrong *hermanito*. I once marched in the Puerto Rican Day Parade right there on Fifth Avenue! I was a baton twirler!"

"You should have been on the Loiza Aldea float with all the *vigilantes* and masked people and the voo-doo and hoo-doos my little witch!"

As Soli sprayed her fragrant spray, Saúl timidly said "you haven't responded to my confession." Solimar Santana got up from her vanity and hugged her brother. "Little one, if that is a confession, marrying you will be the easiest thing I will ever have to do in my life." Saúl sat on the bed and said "Although some may think I am cursed, I really am blessed. You know Gigi also gave me a free pass even after not doing right by her." Solimar tapped him lightly on his shoulder and said "Listen, little brother, don't get the shit twisted. We had a brother/sister moment, but recognize that I am your woman and will put my foot knee deep into your ass if you wanna keep talking about Gigi." Saúl brightened up with happy tears streaming down his face. "You look so beautiful. Like a *reina*."

"And you are so Puerto Rican. You think that maybe we can get this party going, *mi amor*?" He took her slender hands and kissed them both. He turned them palm up and did the same.

"Oh my! My knight in shining armor or should I say *Principe Azul*? Is that some new shit that I don't know about?"

"No Soli, it is what I came up with just for you. You are my lover and my sister and so much more, don't you think that you should be treated like beyond royalty? I will be eating from the palm of the hands I just kissed for the rest of my life."

"You already have."

Solimar gave him a kiss on both cheeks before offering him her lips. Saúl gently grazed her well lacquered lips and said "Mama, we gotta go, I'm sure Victor is already waiting for us at the door." Victor, the driver, bodyguard and loyal friend to Saúl gently rapped on the door for the third time and Saúl opened it. Solimar in her enthusiasm cried out "Victor! What a pleasure to see you, oh my God, I cannot believe that you are here with us."

"Si Señora, it is a pleasure to see you once again."

"Ummm, drop the Señora part; I'm not quite there yet." Victor smiled and affectionately hugged Solimar cordially, kissing both of her cheeks. The men patted each other's backs and the three went off into the crisp evening air, looking forward to picking up Olaya. Soli invited Victor to join them for the night of fun ahead of them; however, he respectfully declined the invitation stating that he had other business to attend to.

"Oh, that must mean you have a girl at every port."

"Soli!" Saúl exclaimed.

"Well, is it true?" Solimar demanded from Victor. Victor smiled and said "I am not that fortunate, but I do have benefits with friends." Soli looked at him askew. It was common for people from other countries to get well known American phrases ass backwards. "Friends with benefits you mean?"

"No, I mean benefits with friends. Besides, the love of my life is my Mom and she lives in The Bronx, right across the bridge there. It's been a while since I had a home-cooked meal and I want to have some that only mothers know how to make." Everyone nodded their head in agreement, got inside the limo and kept silent until they arrived at their destination. "Oh, we are here, let me call Olaya!"

Olaya timely appeared at the door, a vision in billowing clouds of white. The hat she wore resembled an Egyptian crown and her long chiffon sleeves flowed right down to her long fingertips. Victor quickly opened the back door for her, where Saúl and Soli stunned by this glorious vision stared in awe. Olaya, having expected a yellow cab at best exclaimed "Oh my goodness!" but moreso to see Solimar accompanied by a man that looked just like her. "Oh my goodness indeed, Oli, you look stunning! Allow me to introduce you to my fiancée and half-brother, Saúl Santana." Saúl kissed her slender, yet deeply wrinkled hand and Olaya said "If I had known it was going to be this much fun, I would have agreed on 10:00 o'clock, just to make the night last longer."

Nocturnal Life

The three visions in white floated in, turning heads, raising questions and speculations. Saúl had called in his reservations and specifically asked for the best table available, preferably one of the booths. They settled into one of the two exquisite corner booths, the size of a small bedroom overlooking the Hudson River. The Full Moon hanging low, practically at their reach, beckoned them to acknowledge her as their silent guest. It seemed to be that beauty had a way of imposing herself, giving them little choice but to acknowledge her splendor while staring deeply into each other's eyes when they weren't admiring her delicate, rainbow colored halo. The curtains surrounding the booth afforded them an element of privacy while granting them a view of the ongoing festivities. Olaya quietly figuring out Saúl; Saúl quietly figuring out Olaya, and Solimar, knowing them both, hoped that she would receive a good report from them. She needed them to like each other, although she wasn't sure why.

When the waiter addressed Saúl to commence the taking of his order, Saúl held up his hand and said "I will not be ordering, nor will the ladies right now, but please bring us your finest champagne and you decide what would be best for these beautiful women to dine on tonight. The only thing you have to concern yourself with is that the beautiful one sitting next to me is pregnant, so make sure that whatever meal you have prepared is fit for a *bebe*, as well." The waiter, a bit astounded said "*Pero* I don't know, are you not sure what you want?" Saúl said "*Esta bien*. If you don't know what we may like, please send the chef, and no worries Papo, your tip is guaranteed." The waiter ran off in a hurry to get the chef who presented himself quite rapidly. "*Buenas noche*. My name is Emilio and I will be personally seeing to you this evening. How may I be of service?" He asked graciously. Saúl introduced himself by name, as well as his companions with an undeniable pride that radiated from him as he let their names roll from his tongue, making sure that they would be addressed properly. "I would like for you to look at these amazing women and prepare for them *un banquete* of your finest culinary delights that would befit royalty. As for me, I'm just *un guajiro natural*, a hick from the sticks or as we say in Puerto Rico, *un jibarito*, so I wish to have a good old churrasquito, a nice skirt steak, rare, with whatever else you want to put on the side. The ladies will have your finest, but please remember that my little one here is pregnant, so go easy on the spices." The chef eagerly replied "*Con mucho gusto, es un placer*. I will begin to prepare your repast right away, but allow me some patience as I cook everything from scratch." Saúl nodded. "Take all the time you need. We intend to close down this place tonight, but send appetizers, in small increments. I don't want my delicate ladies to faint in anticipation of the masterpiece you are about to prepare for them tonight!" The chef bowed slightly and returned to his kitchen, mentally doing an inventory of his pantry and barking orders for his assistants to stop what they were doing and help him plan a menu. He was excited at the thought of serving a meal fit for a king and his royal court, as he had grown weary of the standard fare, which incidentally Saúl ordered for himself.

Olaya asked "What are you two up to, you blue-eyed little ones?" Saúl, letting out a sigh of relief answered "Fun. I want nothing more than fun and surprises. It wasn't easy chasing this other blue-eyed little one around. Tonight, I just want to relax, have fun, and as we say in Spanish …. Throw the windows out the door and forget that the last few months ever happened."

"I like your answer, let's just hope these idiots don't bring us cow brains and liver!"

"Oh damn!" Saúl said realizing that he probably should have asked Olaya something of great importance. "Should I have asked if you have any dietary restrictions that the chef should know about?" Soli concerned looked at Olaya. Olaya shook her head no. "I have been all around the world and I have tried many different cuisines…" She paused and asked "Do you think he might serve us fried scorpion or monkey brains?" Saúl raised his eyebrows so high they almost touched his hairline. "I surely hope not, but if they do, I'll send it back!" Once again, the champagne glasses went up in a cheer … Soli, obediently monitoring her intake, but after feasting on platter upon platter of everything from beer marinated chicken chunks to shrimp cocktails, raw clams and oysters, eggplant slices broiled in a delicate tempura batter, smashed garlic plantains and grilled octopus, Soli cried *"No puedo mas"* when the waiter came over with her special dish. "Señora, the chef made this with specific instructions for a woman who is carrying a child. *Bacalao a la Vizcaina*. It is a filet of cod, triple soaked to remove the excess salt for you, covered with an array of seafood cooked and saturated in a delicate cooking sauce and then baked in parchment to perfection. It is fresh, very clean and he even steamed a trio of fresh vegetables for you, asparagus, squash and broccoli rabe with almonds and herbs and baby red potatoes!" Solimar put up her hand said "Thank you, *pero no gracias*, I will take it home for tomorrow, but if you give it to me now you will know for sure what a pregnant woman is like when she has had too much to eat." Saúl gently waved him away and Solimar watched him enjoy his skirt steak and Miss Olaya enjoy her small cauldron laden with ox tails stewed to perfection in red wine and pearl onions over steamed white rice. They each gave Solimar a piece to sample and openly shared their dishes with each other.

Over coffee, Olaya could no longer bear the obvious and the brandy in the Sangria helped her along. "How in the world did you two not know that you are siblings? A blind man can see that, even Ray Charles and he is blind and dead!" Saúl bowed his head, straightened up and seriously said "How could I pass her up either way? It was better for me not to know." Soli interjected her response. "What were the chances?" I mean I never thought that God could be so cruel."

"Cruel? Did I just hear this girl say God was cruel? Honey child, God just put together two very imperfect creatures, like He does us all. I'm still trying to figure out something here, so help me: Either Cain or Abel must have been with Eve because as far as I read, they were the only ones roaming the earth aside from her husband, Adam. One woman, three men; Bible don't say nothing about Eve having a daughter, which if that was the case, it could have been that one of her sons could be with his sister or with his mother ... see where I am going with all of this? There is a whole lot of missing information and you two innocents just winded up in the right place at the right time for a purpose. Saúl concurred. "I have no problem believing your theory. Frankly, I think this is a divine design. I never felt love like I feel for the blue-eyed one next to me." Solimar said "I am really trying to believe that we are not outside of God's range."

Olaya noting that Solimar was still uncomfortable with the subject said "Okay, let's dance people, I got to shake these old bones, get me some exercise and work this food off before it creeps down to my already heavy-ass behind." The three took to the dance floor, laughing, clapping and shaking it up. When a man came for Solimar, Saúl instantly dismissed him by putting up his hand. When the man turned towards Olaya for a dance, Saúl once again put up his hand. Saúl danced the two women with much patience and loads of love, taking turns twirling them and them turning him. Olaya returned to the table first, claiming fatigue, but mostly to allow the couple to have a dance or two of their own. Saúl took his lady by her hand and walked over to the band requesting that they play a special song. The band begun to play "Preciosa," Puerto Rico's national anthem, a lovely sonnet, perhaps that some would call a bolero. As Solimar nestled into Saúl's arms, the band turned up the heat and broke into the salsa version of the song causing Saúl, an accomplished dancer to test his woman's skills. Solimar passed with flying colors. She did not miss one step, allowed him to dip her, spin her and have his way with her, even publicly rubbing booties together, broad smiles adorning their faces. They returned to their table sweaty, giggling and Olaya beamed with pride, happy for both of them. "You two are quite a show. You look good up there, shaking your bon bons!" She then turned to Saúl and said "Thank you for protecting my honor." Saúl replied "I really didn't. I know you could hold your own, but he was already sloppy, drunk and I didn't care for the tattoo of the cross-bones and skull hailing a woman's name on his forearm. Had he not rolled up his shirt sleeves and exposed himself, I still wouldn't have let you dance with that character; he just gave me a negative vibe. That douche bag wasn't a proper suitor for any woman, never mind me allowing him a dance with one of mine."

Silence fell heavily for a minute and Olaya asked "When will y'all be heading home?" Solimar answered rather melancholically "We are heading out in less than a couple of weeks, nine days from tomorrow to be exact. I can't fly so, ironically, we will be traveling by sea."

"I'm going to miss our short-lived friendship."

"Our friendship will go on forever Oli, it will just be distant, but we will stay in touch. Actually, my dearest friend recently got deported to Panamá and by the grace ..."

"Of God" chimed in Saúl finishing off her sentence "We found each other as a result. We met in Miami, while we were both 'de-stressing', Solimar from the deportation process of her friend and me from work. We met casually on the beach and to make the long story short, due to the fact that my family lives in Panamá, I took her with me and we were able to locate her friend."

"Wow. Girl, you didn't tell me all that!"

"Oli, the shit gets even better. If I had not lived it, I assure you that it would be a soap opera. A lot of factors did work to finally bring us together, starting with the rosary I threw into the river." Saúl turned and said "You did what? When did you throw our rosary into the river?" Olaya said "I got this Saúl. If your ass wasn't pregnant right now, I'd be tossing you into the Hudson myself to make you fish it out!" Solimar became a little jittery, rearranging half empty glasses and piling plates to ease the waiter's load, until Saúl and Olaya laughed at her expression and nervous movements. Solimar didn't exactly join in, but the two had a good one at Soli's expense.

When they were ready to wrap it up, Olaya finally asked Solimar "Do you still have doubt in your heart or is it that brain of yours that never stops thinking making you doubtful?" Solimar trying to avoid the topic of conversation simply said "Oli, if you like we can fly you out to Puerto Rico when the baby is born; maybe you can show us how to present the baby in the water." Saúl nodded in immediate agreement. Olaya, overwhelmed with happiness and honor, started sobbing, aided of course, by all of the drink that she had consumed. "Oh children, I can tell you how to do that over the phone, you shouldn't spend money so foolishly these days."

"Your hands on our child will be the first investment we make for his or her future. Say you will come." Saúl humbly implored this from Olaya.

"It's a boy, you know that right? And he may well be an Ibeyi."

"What's an Ibeyi?"

Saúl's tears silently streamed. He knew what that meant, but it was a concept he had not conceived, although his siblings were fraternal twins. "Twins, Sol, it could be two ... I believe that could be. Then is it a deal Miss Olaya?"

"It is a deal, but only if I can make another deal with you." They both simultaneously asked "What?" Olaya said "If I don't ever make it back home to Nigeria, can I entrust you to spread my ashes on the River Niger, when the time comes, and if you can't get there, the ocean, any ocean will do." Saúl bowed his head in agreement, but then shyly said "Olaya, I really do not mean to pry and please feel free to tell me so if I am, but it is my understanding that Santeras or practitioners of your faith cannot be cremated, am I mistaken?" Olaya said "No, son, you are not mistaken, but those are man's rules and I wish to follow what my Spirit tells me. Will you do it?"

"Yes. It will be my honor." Saúl confirmed. "Although I don't think you will be departing this planet anytime soon, I give you my word and if nothing else, I am a man of my word and accomplish whatever I set out to do. Now, can we stop talking about death and celebrate the life we are expecting?"

"Done deal." Olaya, knowing now for sure that she was going back to Puerto Rico, made a firm decision to re-acquaint herself with the romantic language she somehow had forgotten, having only learned bits and pieces along the way. She asked Saúl "How do you say 'done deal' in Spanish?" Saúl crossed his forearms and instructed the ladies to do the same. He then further instructed them to take each other's hand creating a three-way handshake. When they were all joined together he said *"Trato hecho."* Still holding hands, Olaya squeezed and repeated after him flawlessly. *"Trato hecho.* I will see you two in *siete meses* in Puerto Rico. *Siete* being Yemaya's number. The Goddess of the Seven Seas, or if I recall correctly, *"La Reina del Mar."* What a coincidence, huh Solimar?" She smiled with a twinkle in her eye knowing otherwise. Solimar affirmed, not wanting to let go of either one of their strong hands and said *"Trato hecho."*

The Enchanted Island

Ten days from their first dance together and the unforgettable night they made their treaty with Olaya, the Santanas found themselves boarding a cruise ship from Manhattan Island to Puerto Rico ... immigrants in reverse. Solimar left all of her furniture to Olaya to keep, to sell, to donate or to do whatever pleased her. She didn't have the heart to set Hickey free, therefore, the turtle came along for the excursion in a brand new habitat. They relaxed, slept plenty, took in the sunshine and ate enough to regain some of the weight they had lost during their separation and subsequent depression which caused them both much suffering, not to mention Saúl's little stint of cocaine abuse that prevented him from nourishing himself, having temporarily destroyed his appetite. Solimar had never been on a cruise and was ecstatic to be immersed in both sun and sea. Ever attentive, Saúl made sure that Solimar's every desire and pleasures were fulfilled. He took every picture-taking opportunity offered by the cruise line, including the one offered in the children's playroom, where the girls stood behind a giant cardboard rendition of a faceless mermaid, until they replaced the cut out with their own smiling face. Saul loved this picture the best and promised to have it framed and put on his desk when he got back to work. It was his resolve to capture every moment of his woman's delightful experience, sometimes watching her from a distance as she'd close her eyes, throwing back her head and sensuously inviting the wind to flow through her heavy locks. He watched her sleep, watched her dress, took in every smile, every wink, every bit of food she put into her mouth, as if he were masticating every morsel himself. Saúl had no idea in his heart if he was being a brother or a lover, but it did not matter to him. The love that he felt for this woman could not be defined. He couldn't quite understand the pendulum effect of his emotions, but managed to balance them to the best of his limited ability, never losing his equilibrium. He lived inside of her smile, inside of her body, in her. Saúl Santana ceased living as he knew life before her, but lived to please his found treasure in whatever way he could, which was of minimal or no challenge. Solimar was simple, but far from a simpleton; sweet, but not saccharin; intelligent, yet not worldly; inquisitive, but only in search of knowledge or truth; humorous, but her humor was sensitive, never sly or cunning; spiritual, but not religious, always respecting other people's view of God and not imposing her faith; sensuous but not overtly sexy, and above all, Solimar was humble. He appreciated that she was forever thanking him both verbally and with her kisses. She kissed him every time they did something new, every moment he presented her with the simplest of gifts, including a bauble he had won while playing the arcade games, which she proudly wore that day and promised to keep as a souvenir. So many women that he had dated never took the time to say thank you, but expected more; some of them had the nerve to be appalled if he invited them to a run of the mill restaurant, but not his Solimar. She indulged equally at the finest tables, but often opted to grab stuff from the buffet and eat it on deck or in their suite. He noticed that she often shopped for bargains, Saúl having to remind her more than once that cruises were all inclusive unless you went to the shops. They spent their afternoons playing cards and slots, but it was her childlike exuberance at winning $20.00 or $30.00 that made him feel that he had hit the jackpot. Her excitement and lust for living in the moment was contagious. Oftentimes, Solimar would catch him catching her, watery eyed. She sometimes fell into those watery eyes almost as if falling into the ocean itself. Soli never confronted or questioned these moments, instead she'd either wink at him or slightly bow her head acknowledging his love. They played as children do, often getting into little fights; they loved as lovers do when everything is perfectly right, abandoning themselves completely, walking around their suite nude and making love on their private balcony. They agreed not to further ponder on or discuss their filial connection, opting to enjoy the cruise instead and focus on what awaited them in the Enchanted Island. They turned their attention to their favorite time of the day, which was just when the sun was setting, or if they were awake, sunrise – the sun seemingly losing itself behind or peeking from the expanse of the ocean until it revealed or hid itself. They made sure to eat their dinner before then, followed by a walk on the relatively empty deck while everyone else enjoyed their extravagant meals, just to catch that precise moment when the sun was setting behind the sea. They anxiously, yet patiently anticipated the precise moment when the sun would, in its blinding glory, reveal itself halfway over the horizon; these were the mornings they lived for, promising themselves that they would try and honor the sunrise on a regular basis when they settled into their home. It was the perfect symbol, the mirror image that embodied Solimar. Saúl and Solimar were living their perfect 'SeaSun' – the affectionate composite he made up when he tried to translate her name into English. There was no translation, but they laughed every time Saúl referred to her as such, Solimar chiding that the nickname would probably better fit Marisol. Saúl never failed to express to Solimar that her presence to him was represented and captured in those miraculous moments.

Solimar, feeling supremely loved and gaining confidence, even once dared to ask Saúl to make love to her on deck and he smiled, shook his head and said "No, Bella. Remember how we were born. We have mothers and fathers, sisters and brothers and beds to sleep on and make love upon." Solimar wrinkled up her nose and retorted "Not fun." Saúl said "Wait for me right here my dear, I will bring you fun and then some." Solimar, intrigued and anticipating some fanfare paced the deck in anticipation only to find Saúl calmly walking back towards her empty-handed. No surprise there. When he arrived he said "Bella, close your eyes please." Solimar filled with curiosity, anticipation and trust, closed her eyes and spread her arms ready to receive a hug. Saúl took out the spray bottle that he had stashed in his back pocket, filled with ice cold water and sprayed her face. Solimar did not react, but allowed him to keep spraying her … he drenched her hair, splashed her shoulders, her entire body down to her feet. Finally Saúl cried uncle and gave up trying to rouse Solimar. When she heard him mutter "I give up," she opened her mouth wide inviting him to spray the water into her mouth. After doing so and emptying what was left in the bottle into her inviting orifice did she then open her eyes and said "Bello, now that was fun!" Saúl realized that he had her life in his hands, but if she only knew how much more power she had over him, he'd gladly just hand his life over to her voluntarily.

On the seventh day, Solimar asked her future husband if he would dress up a bit as she had special plans for the night. Saúl asked "What on earth are you up to Solimar?"

"*Nada, mi amor*, I just want to go dancing because we haven't visited the club yet and our honeymoon ends tomorrow!"

"Oh of course we could go dancing! It is good exercise for you and the baby!" Saúl loved the idea that Solimar was getting used to the idea of becoming his wife. "Soli, you can't possibly imagine what a true honeymoon I have already planned for us. I consider this little excursion a prequel to the sequel." Soli giggled and said "I do not doubt that the sequelae I will have to endure after all injuries sustained will heal even the most unbelieving believer." Saúl, a bit taken aback by her statement said "Do you mind explaining yourself Missy?" Solimar amused, yet confused that he didn't understand what she was trying to say, sat at the desk, turned on his laptop and said "Give me *un minuto* here." She navigated her way to Dictionary.com and typed in sequelae. "Come Mr. Diplomatico, here is the definition of sequelae" and she commenced to read out loud "Sequelae is an abnormal condition resulting from a previous disease, plural for sequela." Saúl, not knowing if Solimar was seriously educating him or mocking him, laughed and said "Can you possibly be any crazier?" Solimar spun her chair around to face him. She crossed her eyes and said "You see. The sequela is already kicking in!" Saúl, more in love than ever with this playful, intelligent and beautiful woman, shook his head and said "Come on, let's get out of here *loca,* I guess the next thing you're gonna say is we got some telephone numbers to pick up, after all, this will be our last round!"

They excitedly dressed, behaving like a couple of teenagers going out for the very first time to a night club. Solimar dressed in a silky satin, floor length dress, which hung off of her left shoulder, the color of the creamiest whipped cream. The dress also had a modest train and to Saúl, she resembled a Greek Goddess draped in a toga. She let her hair flow, having blown it straight, pinning back both sides with orchid-adorned combs, creating a flowery crown on the top of her head. She applied just a hint of makeup as the sun had already kissed her various times and there was no need but for a bit of lip gloss to accent the glow of the tan, but more especially the glow of her pregnancy. "Solimar Santana! You look ravishing!" Saúl by then was dressed in the traditional "guayabera," a workman's shirt, pretty much worn throughout all of the Caribbean, except, I guess being a diplomat, his was spun from the finest linen and hung from him as if it had been custom made by hand to his specifications. He wore creased jeans and sandals and Soli could not feel more proud to walk with this self-confident, self-made man that could easily mix the two with ease. It spoke to her heart, her humility and her pride. She made a mental note to remember that, not realizing that she did not have to put any additional effort into doing so. The combination of those traits was already inherent in them, having been deposited into their shared genes. "Let's go baby brother; we are going to get our real party started!" Solimar announced this as she raised her elbows and began to swerve her hips with a Latin rhythm that captivated Saúl's soul. Saúl followed his woman, enjoying every bit of her laughter and precocious ways. He had not noticed that she was walking barefoot as only her little white color toe nails peeked through the sweeping dress and he assumed that she had sandals on. She led him to the stairwell leading to the top floor. "Soli, the *discoteca* is down ... stairs, I think."

"Why go down, *mi amor*, when we can go up?" Saúl, recalling that infamous moment when her raw naked beauty was inadvertently revealed to him, winked at her and tried to kiss her right there in plain view as she stood only but one step above him. Solimar offered her neck to him and said "Just wait a little longer then you can kiss me all you want."

Soli led the perplexed Saúl to a part of the ship that he hadn't seen before. They stood before a grand entrance, and the doors opened automatically, as if on queue and revealed the Captain's Quarters. The enormous room was filled with wall-to-wall floral arrangements and a small banquet, a banquet that would feed six to be precise. Only the sun setting lit the room, creating a golden bluish hue, and of course, the many candles that both scented and enhanced the romantic lighting. It was a room that was reserved only for the use of VIPs on special occasions. Saúl being a diplomat, and accustomed to special invitations, thought nothing of the fact that he and Solimar would be invited to have an intimate dinner with the ship's captain. The captain of the ship strolled in and introduced himself and after some short pleasantries said "I believe that I have a marriage ceremony to perform." Two strangers, one male, one female, impeccably dressed, remained silhouetted in the shadows, so as not to intrude until their presence was required. They were the witnesses handpicked by the captain, employees of the cruise liner. Saúl's eyes widened as he grasped the magnitude of the impending moment. Solimar placed her hands on her hips and exaggerating, pushed her barely visible belly forward. "Well? Are you going to make an honest woman out of me or not?" Saúl smiled and said "Solimar Santana... will you marry me?" Solimar turned her back on him. "That's not a proper proposal!"

Saúl looked at her. "What? Do you want me to get down on my knees?" Solimar maintained silent. Saúl, looking for help, turned around to see that every person in the room had pulled out a crisp, white linen handkerchief for him to kneel on. Saúl put his hand on his hip and shook his head, as Solimar coquettishly peeked over her shoulder. "If the captain wasn't involved I'd say this was mutiny!" The spectators softly giggled as the captain handed him a cream colored decorative pillow to match Solimar's dress and Saúl took it and got down on one knee. "Solimar Santana?"

"Yes?" she said still keeping her back to him. "Would you do me the honor of being my wife?" Solimar ran her fingers through her hair. "I don't know... this is so sudden, I would have to think about it, can I have at least a moment to consider the ramifications of this commitment?" Having let the question seep into Saúl's mind, Solimar quickly spun around to face him and took a step forward as she intuitively knew that Saúl was about to give her a good slap on her now blossoming rear end that was inches from his face. With a mischievous smile that would launch a thousand and one ships, besting Helen of Troy, she said "Of course I'll marry you, you blue-eyed devil!" Saúl stood up and whispered in her ear "I love you, you blue eyed *bruja*, now marry me already!" They deeply kissed the kiss they were supposed to kiss after the marriage vows were exchanged.

The captain had the couple married on international waters within ten minutes if not less. Solimar had purchased the thin platinum circles that would never leave their left ring fingers at the jewelry store down below. She had spent the last of her savings, but still had her modest 401K plan which she intended to give to her husband to help offset the expenses affiliated with the cost of relocating and the subsequent uprooting of her life. Solimar spoke carefully and firmly recited a bit of prose she had in her head. "I, Solimar Santana take you Saúl Santana to be my lawful wedded husband through all the things that life offers us. I vow to respect you, look after your needs, submit myself to your wisdom and be your partner in crime, never minding the time. I give myself to you body, mind and soul, child in my womb and promise to never forsake you or doubt you for as long as we both shall live." Saúl, unprepared, repeated the standard vows, his anonymous witness handing him his soon to be wife's wedding band. Having nobody present to object, the officiating party had nothing more to add or do other than to say "I now pronounce you sister and brother, but above that and before God, I pronounce you husband and wife. You may kiss your wife." Time stood still, they all felt as if they were now standing on the edge of the horizon with the majestic sun and roaring sea at their feet. The newlyweds stared into each other's eyes and instead of deeply kissing his bride; he kissed her on both cheeks and on her forehead and nose leaving her lips for last. He kissed her hands, not forgetting to kiss both of her palms. "Congratulations Mr. and Mrs. Santana." They all laughed at the irony. Solimar wouldn't have to change her name, only her title. Solimar had spoken to the captain beforehand to make sure that their kinship would not hinder their marriage. She had also done some research to verify the validity of a shipboard wedding. As long as they were married on international waters, their kinship could not be used by anyone to challenge the authenticity of their union or use their filial relationship as grounds to nullify their marriage. The captain, touched by her story, responded to her earnest inquiry by gently saying "It would be a pleasure to marry you and there will not be an added charge of any kind. Plan your surprise wedding best as you can, flowers, food, whatever you would like to make your day unforgettable. The only thing I cannot give you is the wedding bands and the dress. The jewelry store and boutiques are separate entities. Beyond that it would be more than an honor for me to marry you." Solimar, moved by the captain's generosity, invited his wife and asked that their witnesses would then be treated as guests instead of servants.

  The six sat at a beautifully appointed table, feasting on surf and turf while listening to the pianist, flautist and violinist that the captain contracted as his personal gift to the newlyweds.

Capitan Carlos Juan Ramirez had fallen deeply in love with Solimar's symphony, who represented a daughter that he would never have as his wife was barren or maybe the barren one was him. In his own mind, the wedding that he performed was a gift to God, to help these children understand that they were not at fault for the path that God himself had carved out to be their destiny.

Saúl, after enjoying their sumptuous meal, asked to be excused as he needed to bring his wife to rest for a while due to her condition. Everyone nodded in agreement and Saúl asked if they would please join them at the midnight buffet because by then Solimar would be craving a glass of milk and another slice of the decadent wedding cake. After a nap, a shower and a kiss or two, the newly married Santanas jumped right back into their beautiful clothing and climbed the stairs to the top deck. Saúl noticed then that she had no shoes and asked his beloved wife why. She looked at him with a mock smile on her face. "I thought that Spanish men liked their women 'barefoot and pregnant'?" Saúl laughed heartily. "My girl, you've got much to learn. Now, seriously, why aren't you wearing shoes or should I even ask?" Soli slightly pouted and said "Bello, I just wanted to be as natural as possible, come to you with nothing, but me. If it had been up to me, I would have married you the way God sent me into this world, with absolutely nothing on." Saúl pinched her cheek and said "I didn't realize that my wife was such a romantic, but put some damn shoes on. I would hate to have to be the one to take a splinter out of one of them little feeties."

"Ah, little? Size nine pal, and don't you ever make me prove it you!" Soli then held up her ring hand. "You married me, and that includes my little feet… and by the way, when I get too big to reach down, you're going to be washing these little feeties and painting my toenails!" Saúl raised his eyebrows, made a face and said "I don't think so, but we will work something out; don't want you walking around with crusty, stinky feeties!" Solimar threw on her ballerina slippers and they firmly joined hands, made their way upstairs, and upon their arrival they encountered a deserted deck albeit decked out with a red carpet. El Capitan was calling them to hurry. "Soli, Saúl, c'mon we are ready to start!" Carlos Juan urged them. Intrigued and vastly confused as to why there was no one on the upper deck where the mid-night buffet was customarily served, Solimar asked, "What's going on? What are we starting?" Lili Anne, Carlos Juan's wife, steered Solimar to a beautifully decorated peacock chair that she had carefully adorned with ribbons and bows and said "Sit *hija,* you've had a long day." There were three other peacock chairs alongside and as each took their place, Saúl to Solimar's right and the captain and his wife to her left, the fireworks begun. Saúl and Solimar, completely blown away, instantly broke into tears, raking their hair, kissing and hugging each other, while the others were clapping, cheering and urging them on. "Don't cry, don't cry, everything is going to be alright" came the soft voice of the captain's wife. She pulled Solimar to the side, wiping her tears and said "My husband and I are first cousins. Our family disowned us for marrying, so we understand ever so much what you are feeling. When my husband told me about you two, we figured out the predicament for ourselves. We never had children because we were fearful, you know, but we regret not having done so, even if the child had come out a little sick. So now, you see why my husband gave special attention to your wedding? Do not be afraid like we were. Celebrate your love and your child who will be born soon enough and leave all in God's hands. The Lord really does love us, if we can only believe, everything is possible, and although all is not beneficial, everything under the sun is permissible." Solimar was unable to form a sentence; the knot in her throat preventing her from verbalizing her sentiments. Saúl straightened up and after wiping his own tears, handed Solimar his damp handkerchief and asked Captain and Mrs. Ramirez if he could at least have their contact information so that he could send them the baby's birth announcement. Captain Ramirez immediately gave Saúl his business card and said, "Listen if there is anything you need, we live right here en Isla Verde." He immediately started jotting down their cell phone numbers on the back of the card. *El capitan* walked with Saúl around the deck for a more private, *mano a mano* conversation. As the fireworks continued to light up the night sky, the captain offered Saúl a Cuban cigar. "Aren't these illegal?" The captain lit his cigar without a care. "Not on international waters they're not! Besides, don't you have diplomatic immunity?" They laughed and talked what men talk about while Solimar cried her heart out and Mrs. Ramirez fetched chocolate covered fruits and cake for her new friend, bonding with her. They ended the night downstairs in the disco, captain and all, dancing to everything the disc jokey played, including, of course, Marc Anthony's rendition of the Puerto Rican National Anthem, "Preciosa," a staple to the last night of partying on this cruise ship. Indeed, they were approaching home. Solimar was ecstatic that this was the song Saúl had requested when they had their very first dance.

Unlike all newlyweds, they chose not to consummate their marriage that night. The depth of love, respect and processing of their confusion, as well as the newfound revelation rendered them content with little need for physical gratification. Instead, Saúl played with Soli's hair, twirling it in his fingers while kissing her face a thousand times, and like the brother and sister that they are, they nestled into each other, humming their now familiar lullaby. The ship would be docking in San Juan early in the morning, still having much left to do. Tired and overwhelmed by the evening's festivities, Solimar promised to give her husband a good mounting in the morning, in lieu of breakfast, but tonight, she just wanted to cuddle and feel his warmth on her back, his breath, a whisper on her neck.

The rising sun was their alarm clock, and they rose to a quickie lovemaking session, gathered their belongings and grabbed something to eat before touching their homeland soil. Before disembarking, Saúl pulled his wife to himself and thanked her for the most perfect wedding a man could hope for. While still in his embrace, Saúl asked "Solimar, would you consider changing your name?" She immediately pulled back and looked at her husband as if he had gone nuts. "To what can I possibly change my name to Saúl?" Saúl matter of factly said "You can change it to Solimar Santana de Santana." Solimar laughed and laughed until she couldn't laugh anymore and found herself choking on her very laughter. "You wanna shove it up my ass twice, don't you?!" Saúl seriously watched Soli laugh, and when she came to her senses, she said "Don't you see that I have the best of both worlds? I get to keep my maiden name and have my married name as well?" "Saúl said, "I gave this much thought and it is an old Spanish custom to keep your maiden name yet show that you are married by placing the "de" in between the two names!"

"Saúl! It is also a Puerto Rican tradition that women are allowed to keep their maiden names without the changeover, but I have all of that and then some. I am Santana through and through. I need not go shout it to the world! Or do you want the baby to be whatever we name him ... Santana y Santana like they do in Spain? Saúl pondered a bit and said, "What if we both hyphenate and be Santana dash Santana?" Soli was getting a little pissed that Saúl was pushing this so hard. "Listen you; I'm not giving in on this one here. I'm your wife and our father's daughter and my name is a living testament to that bullshit so you're just going to have to live with that one!"

"Soli, I just want you to be *mia,* mine!"

"*Estupido,* I am *tuya,* yours, twice over! Saúl, a bit dejected said, "It's all good Bella," but he was unable to conceal his disappointment.

They were the last two to disembark Noah's Ark and as they did, Saúl whispered into Solimar's ear "*Escucha mi pregon que dice...*" Knowing the verses to that song, hearing and envisioning the violins, trumpets and timbales playing in her head, Solimar lifted her right arm over her head, keeping her left protectively over her belly and started dancing to the music rocking out, shaking her ass down the aluminum blank, knowing all along that her husband was telling her 'Listen, to my proclamation, my cry, I am giving you the best that I am.' Excited by her man's endearment, she shot back the ensuing musical scale "*Lo le lola lelo la la, la la le le le la la la*" Saúl grabbed his woman mid-way and they started dancing to the music that sprung from their hearts. When their feet touched down on Puerto Rican soil, Solimar kissed her husband hard on his lips and said "Pa, I got it. Ruben Blades from Panamá gave that song to Hector LaVoe from Puerto Rico. I see the connection, don't work me so hard, if not I'll just have to make love to you right here and now and this time, I don't want to hear how we were born or who the hell we belong to!" Saúl smiled at his wife, as she led him by the hand. He declared "*Caminando*. We're walking towards the sun and sea *sirenita!*"

The captain watched from the upper deck, having made sure that no one from the room cleaning service would look for them and ask them to vacate their suite, giving them a little bit of extra time. He knew they were rocking the boat making love as it were, and as he watched them, he only wondered what Saúl could have possibly said to her that made Solimar dance her way off the ship, shaking her ass, practically naked, wearing the infamous blue sarong with a thousand coins sewn into the delicate fabric. He laughed heartily as he watched Solimar calling the shots, taking her husband by the hand, Hickey's cage swinging carefree in the breeze from her other hand, walking confidently into the will of that whom we collectively call God.

La Isla Not So Bonita

The newlyweds excitedly arrived at Saúl's home. Although far from the mansion his parents owned in Panamá, the house was an ample four-bedroom, split level Adobe or Santa Fe style structured home, filled with an abundance of cactus plants, pottery and an airy bohemian feel that dominated the atmosphere making Solimar's heart leap with happiness and comfort. She admired her slight reflection on the terra cotta tiled floors and instantly knew that she would spend her days traipsing around barefooted for the coolness that it offered. Solimar was enchanted by Saúl's talent for making a bachelor's pad seem like a safe haven where no less than six people resided, three being children. The vibrant colors, hidden nooks and uncluttered space gave Solimar not only a feeling of peace, but a sense of belonging. Saúl had explained to her during their cruise that his home was simple and only contained the necessary furnishings. He further explained to her that the purchase of "pieces" was an art form to him; therefore, he took his time connecting with furniture, artwork, linens, etc. as he intended to possess them forever and did not mind spending the sum necessary, as long as the item pleased his senses and was in concordance with his vision. He regaled her with stories about getting things so dirt cheap that he would be embarrassed to disclose their worth, yet those were the pieces most treasured by him because they usually were handmade, and often times were made by children learning their parents' craft. However, he assured Solimar that she was free to do as she saw fit to turn their home into her own, with the hopes that he would convince her that this simplistic way of living afforded a much needed sense of tranquility. He went on to tell her that he had fallen madly in love with that particular style of architecture and the "feel" of its cool warmth during one of his trips to Oaxaca, Mexico and a subsequent trip to Phoenix, Arizona. Solimar was captured by his utter romanticism and practicality without even having toured the home. The colors were blindingly breathtaking – Mango Orange coupled with Lime Green; Vivid Teal coupled with Majestic Purples and on went the combinations that were aesthetically mixed and combined. She did not need to see more to know that she had arrived at exactly the place where she had longed to be. She hugged her husband and said "Bello, I really doubt that I will be changing a thing." Saúl smiled, slapped himself on the forehead and said "Oh damn, Soli, I didn't carry you over the threshold! Get back outside!" Solimar quickly obeyed and allowed her husband to properly welcome her into her new home.

Having heard the commotion from the kitchen, located in the back of the house, Rosario, Saúl's housekeeper, quickly came forward wiping her hands on her apron. Solimar was greeted by yet another housekeeper, yet one not quite as warm and welcoming as Lydia, as Solimar perhaps erroneously expected that the wiping of the hands on the apron would signify an upcoming handshake. Soli made a mental note to exercise her power and keep this one in deep check. Upon their arrival, Rosario had been attentively preparing Saúl's favorite meal for lunch and set the table that he favored, the wrought iron bistro set out back, which afforded him a distant view of the ocean, but was close enough to allow him to hear the crashing of the waves and what he believed to be *'el grito de las sirenas.'* Although now he had his own siren to contend with, whose soulful cries had lured and seduced him with no effort.

Upon him introducing Solimar to Rosario, the housekeeper became noticeably ill and immediately excused herself stating that her cellular phone was vibrating and she did not want to be rude by answering the call in their presence. Soli and Saúl looked at each other, shrugged their shoulders, agreeing that they would have to learn to endure this negative reaction on a regular basis. It was undeniable that they were related and not necessarily as husband and wife. Solimar made a further mental note, and if her intuition was serving her correctly regarding Rosario's behavior, something smelled a bit fishy and it wasn't lunch. After giving his wife a quick tour around her new home, Saúl became increasingly frustrated that Rosario had not yet come out of her bedroom and called out for her. Rosario appeared, a little more composed and said "*Perdoname Señor*, it was just that..." Saúl curtly interrupted her. "Rosario, my wife is pregnant. She cannot go without eating for indefinite periods of time. After lunch, you will have to sit with her in my study and talk things over because from this day forward she will be preparing our menu, and if she desires to do so, she can prepare the meals as well." Rosario nodded in silent agreement. Saúl went further and stated "I would appreciate it if you now set the table in the dining room. This is, after all, my wife's first meal in her new home, and on this and other formal occasions, her place is to be seated directly across from me, occupying the other end of the dining room table. Should she entertain in my absence, she is to occupy the head of the table. The rest of the time, we will take our meals in the small room off of the kitchen, and she is then to be placed to my left, which is her right, understand? There will be more than enough time for my wife and me to spend our days lounging out back." Rosario stunned at all of these directives, complied without uttering a single word. His constant reference to "my wife" slightly irritated her. She was convinced that Saúl was a sworn bachelor and the women that he brought home always ate in the back, never in the formal dining room, much less his room of preference, the nook off of the kitchen.

After lunch, Rosario asked Saúl if she could have the rest of the day off. Saúl had no problem with her request, fully cognizant of the fact that both Solimar and Rosario needed time to adjust to their new living arrangements. After Rosario bid her good-bye for the day, Solimar and her husband began the process of learning how to function as a married couple, but first they made love for the third time that day on a brand-new mattress that Rosario had "forgotten" to remove the industrial-strength plastic off of; not that it mattered, they made love just the same.

As they maneuvered around, trying to find their comfort zone as married people, Saúl opted to telecommute and work from his home for a while. He worked the phones, fax machine and computer night and day out of his well-equipped home office. Saúl's driver took Solimar from one doctor's appointment to the other. Occasionally, Solimar took a day to tend to her manicure, pedicure and hair appointments. Saúl was adamant that Solimar would not drive until after the baby was born. The days were relatively easy and the nights were blissful, but Solimar was becoming increasingly restless. She hadn't even called her friend to tell her that she was now married and living in Puerto Rico, and had wondered if they, in fact, had gotten married themselves. The emotional drainage that she had endured did not allow for much more, although she was restoring her balance slowly thanks to Carlos Juan and his wife, Lili Anne and their loving attention. The older couple were enamored of their adoptees, and stopped by frequently to check in on them, often inviting them to dine with them as well.

Lili Anne, a striking and immensely confident woman who easily stood 6 feet tall, towering generously over her husband, gladly took it upon herself to show Solimar around, which proved to be a great help for Saúl who had fallen behind in his work-related duties. La Señora Lili Anne Ramirez was tantamount to a local celebrity and this facilitated Solimar's transition quite nicely, as she was now being recognized by name in the local shops, restaurants and even by the street vendors. Lili Anne, protectively introduced Solimar to Puerto Rican society as her niece from *Nueva York* who had just married *un diplomatico* and relocated to *la isla*. Having no family of her own, there was no real way to check if her statement was true or false although Solimar had subtly recognized the fact that Lili Anne and her husband were highly regarded and respected in their community to ever be challenged or questioned in any way. Saúl, concerned about Solimar staying home alone while he went abroad on business, had arranged for Solimar to spend a few days with Lili Anne at a hidden, exclusive spa while he traveled to New York and Carlos Juan off to yet another port. When he launched this idea over an early dinner at the Santana household, Solimar begged off, shaking her head and Lili Anne asked a rhetorical question. "Do I look like I need a damn spa treatment?" Carlos Juan chuckled and said "Brother, I think you just made a big no-no." Saúl confused said "I'm sorry, I just thought…"

"Don't think, Saúlcito, Soli and I talked this morning about you guys taking off tomorrow and we agreed that she would spend the next three days at my house." Saúl, giving himself his place, asked "And you ladies made these plans without consulting me first?" Carlos Juan coughed, excused himself from the table and hurriedly made the chopping of the head sign to Saúl while shaking his head and waving his index finger, signaling no! Solimar, a bit confused as to why Saúl was jumping the gun said "Wait a minute, wait *un minutito* … do you think I was just going to take off and not tell you?" *"Estas loco o que?"* Lili Anne looking rather bored and raising her glass said "The pride of Puerto Rico – I still remember him as the Menudo kid, Ricky Martin, sang something about living *la vida loca*. It is time for me to welcome you guys into living the *married vida loca.*" Solimar disconcerted by the fact that Saúl would be capable of thinking that she would take off without informing him said, "Listen here, Saúl. The conversation between Lili Anne and I took place only a few hours ago. I was going to tell you right here and now that I thought it best for me to spend some time by her, seeing that Carlos Juan is also leaving on business, as well as giving Rosario a few days off. I mean, why keep the sanctuary lit if the only one in it would be me? I rather hang out with Lili Anne, take in the sights and go to the beach with her instead of sitting around watching novelas and game shows waiting for you to get back home. Is that so bad? Besides, you took the liberty of planning a spa treatment for both of us! Don't you think that was a tad presumptuous on your part?" Saúl blushed while acknowledging that Solimar's argument was quite logical and apologized to Lili Anne who waved him off without a word.

Carlos Juan returned to his seat and said "Are we all resolved here?" Lili Anne kissed her husband's cheek and said "Aren't we always?"

"Lili Anne, by now you must know that I hate it when you answer a question with a question."

"Carlito, after 48 years of marriage I know you do hate it. That's why I do it, to grate on your nerves." Saúl shook his head and said "Soli, we need marriage counseling because knowing you, instead of grating my nerves, you'll be grating *mi cojones*." Soli gave Saúl an evil, mischievous grin confirming his suspicions. Mercifully, Rosario entered with a dessert tray filled with flan to which Lili Anne and Solimar reacted to with childlike glee.

The foursome enjoyed their flan, which Solimar had prepared recalling her mother's recipe and proudly took the credit for it. Rosario lurked in the long noon shadows, enviously plotting how she could get this pregnant little witch out of her house and be rid of her for good. Her English lacked fluency, but she knew enough that she could fend for herself and could tell that Solimar's Spanish was much more limited than her English. She figured that without Saúl around, who would be departing bright and early in the morning, Solimar would be at her mercy, subject to her subtle antagonization for the length of his trip. That was her second mistake, underestimating Solimar. Her first having occurred a year ago or so when she took the liberty of coming on to Saúl on a night that Saúl erroneously made the fatal error of inviting her to share a night cap with him. From that day forward, Rosario had eyes only for Saúl, and although she did witness a parade of women going in and out of his bedroom, she never saw a woman twice in his house, except for the one that went by the name of Gigi. However, she never really saw Gigi as a threat, instinctively knowing that she was not the one for Saúl, even though Gigi tried her hardest to land him as her husband. This one now was different from all the others. She came already married to Saúl, obviously pregnant, and toting a turtle in a cage. 'Who brings a pet turtle with them on a cruise?' Rosario pondered and the answer came rather quickly, "Only a *bruja*." Solimar came into Saúl's life with no fanfare and no advance notice. She appeared as if an apparition, except her presence was natural, not ghostly and had a sense of permanence. The only warning she had gotten was one phone call Saúl made from the cruise ship instructing her to immediately purchase a top of the line mattress for his bed and replace all the sheets and blankets with new ones from the linen specialty store that he frequented, and have the old ones disposed along with the mattresses. He instructed her to purchase white sheets only, as he would take care of the rest upon his return. He did not want his new wife to sleep in a bed or upon sheets previously soiled.

Rosario made her entrance and shyly asked "May I remove your dishes? Is there something else I can serve you?" She addressed Saúl but it was Solimar who said "Well, as a matter of fact, you can take a two hour break, if you like. The dishes will be right here when you get back." Lili Anne glanced at Carlos out of the corner of her eye and made it a point to remember that she would have to train Solimar on how to effectively deal with her housekeeper. Lili Anne intervened "Actually, Solimar needs help packing. We are going away for a few days. Please prepare a small luggage for about four days? We will be spending it at the beach, so she will not be requiring too much." Rosario immediately said "Oh *si Señora, no problema,* right away." She never once acknowledged Solimar's stare or orders. Lili Anne placed her hand on Solimar's thigh and squeezed it, signaling her not to move or say anything just yet. Rosario went to tend to her newly assigned duty, abandoning her idea of antagonizing Solimar and thrilled that Solimar was leaving for the night tonight, leaving Saúl alone to prepare for his business trip, also reveling in the idea of her having the house to herself. She hurriedly ran up the stairs, putting together a new plan of action in her head, when she heard Solimar yell out "And don't lock the suitcase! I'll be upstairs in a little while to check on you!" Saúl became incensed. "Solimar Santana!" he sternly said, but not loud enough for the maid to hear. Carlos Juan quickly defused the situation. "*Tranquilo*, nothing happened. Let's get packed and going. Tomorrow you and I must be up early to travel. Let the women handle this. It will be fine." The subject was immediately dropped, and Solimar got up from the table and started piling the dinner dishes into the sink. "Solimar, you are now officially driving me crazy. There is no need for you to ..."

"*No empiezes conmigo* Saúl. I can see that you want to start in on me again, but I know, I know, you say it a hundred times a day 'Don't forget how we were born Soli, we have mothers and fathers and blah, blah, blah.'" Solimar retorted with a petulant toss of her head causing her hair to practically slap her face. Saúl realizing that Solimar was upset got up from the table and said "Come Bella, I'm missing *mi sirena malcriada* already." Soli gave him a light punch to his stomach and said "I know that you are just trying to calm me down, but lucky for you, it's working." Saúl nodded his head as Lili Anne decided it best to escort Soli out of the room.

Lili Anne and Solimar went upstairs to find everything in perfect order. Rosario had packed everything Soli would need and then some. Lili Anne, after carefully inspecting the contents of the luggage, closed the suitcase and without as much as saying thank you to the housekeeper, said "Come *hija*, we are going to have the time of our lives without the men for a few days." As an after thought, she turned to Rosario and said "Watch the house."

"It is always my pleasure, *Señora*." Rosario bowed slightly to Lili Anne still ignoring Solimar as she had just about enough of her insolence. Solimar couldn't contain herself; she needed to get the message across to Rosario that she was totally pissed off. "Rosario?"

"Yes." Soli looked up, took a deep breath before continuing to speak to her. She had expected to be addressed as *'señora'* as she had addressed Lili Anne. "Why didn't you pack up Hickey? Is it not obvious to you that we are always together, or did you actually believe that I would leave her in your care?" Rosario had had it up to there with Solimar, and not checking herself blurted out the unthinkable. "I don't know where that disgusting *jicotea* is! It roams all over this house like if it owns it." Lili Anne stepped in between Solimar and Rosario and pointing her index finger said "You find the turtle, even if it means that you have to crawl under every bed and sofa in this house. When you find it, you put it in its little house; she's travelling with us. Have I made myself clear?" Rosario, dumbfounded, but responsive to an authoritative voice automatically complied saying "*Si Señora.*"

Saúl took the ten minute ride with them to see them home, kissed his wife good-bye and drove back missing his woman, but already his head immersed in the projects that awaited him. His mind was filled with his agenda for the next few days. He was tired, happy and just wanted to go to sleep, but instead, he was met by Rosario, who had been waiting for him at the door. Concerned that she had not gone up to her quarters, he questioned her. "*Y que Rosario*, is everything okay, did something occur that I should know about?" Saúl asked her this simple question, quietly noting that she had already slipped into her pajamas, although bedtime was still a couple of hours away. Saúl had a lenient dress code for his housekeepers and the occasional extra help he would hire on an as needed basis. They were allowed to work out of uniform, as long as their shorts were Bermuda style or Capri length. He expected their tops to have a modest neckline and their shoulders covered, preferring button down shirts He required them to wear the standard uniform when tending to formal dinners or cocktail parties. However, it was of utmost importance to Saúl that no woman be allowed to walk around his home in a housecoat or nightgown. He absolutely insisted that they wear full length pajamas to bed and put on a robe in the event that they needed to use the common areas after hours. Rosario, up until now, had always abided by this logical rule, but on this occasion, although she did wear "pajamas and a robe," the ensemble appeared to be very sophisticated and subtly enticing two-piece loungewear worn underneath a sheer robe that she had forgotten to close properly. She let her pretty, wavy brown hair loose, cascading around her face, instead of the tight bun she usually wore when she worked. Saúl took inventory of her and realized that she really was a very attractive young woman. Rosario had an especially sensuous glow to her that night. Although she was a short, stocky type of a girl, her weight was inviting, not unpleasant at all. She had the thick curvy Latina type body that Latin men would fight over, as no one could dispute her hour glass shape. Her dark eyes, set in alabaster skin, danced, shifting back and forth. Her dimples deepened with her smile. Oddly enough, after five years of service, he had never noticed that she would rake her hair back, like Solimar does when she is angry, or as he does just to get the hair off of his face, unless he hadn't noticed the nervous habit because she always wore her hair in a ponytail or pinned up in a bun. Could it be that she was mimicking one of Solimar's adorable attributes? He gave her the benefit of the doubt. "*No, nada*, Saúl, I just, I just wanted to talk with you for a minute, if you have a moment to spare." Saúl purposely overlooked the familiarity and said "sure, what is it?"

"Would it be acceptable if I take a drink with you in the living room so we can discuss a few things that have me concerned?" Saúl, accepting the fact that Solimar and Rosario were not yet on the best of terms, took it upon himself to fill the gap and deal with the administrative duties of his household until Solimar could fully take control. "Sure Rosita, I'll get it myself. Sit and relax, you've had a long day. *Vino tinto, si?*" Rosario immediately took the "Rosita" reference as a go ahead without realizing that it was nothing more than Saúl's tender sarcasm for having crossed the line first and referring to him by his first name without ever having been invited to do so. She nodded her head at the suggestion of a glass of red wine and thanked him. Feeling sexy, self-assured and on the verge of triumph, she gently tugged at the delicate bow that held her top together, exposing a glimpse of her cleavage. Saúl came back with a glass of wine for her and a cognac for himself. "*Que te pasa* Rosario, are you quitting on me?" Rosario, empowered by his doubt carefully said "No, absolutely not, but, well you know that when your mother sent me to you, it was going to be on a temporary basis while I found work in my chosen field of study, but now I have worked for you for five years, and..." Saúl cupped his brandy glass by the stem, swirling it to slightly warm the amber liquid. He took a small sip and said "Rosario, if this is about a raise, you got it. I realize you have more work to do now that I have a wife and a baby on the way."

"Oh no, no, no. It is not that at all. It is just that I was thinking that instead of living here five days a week, I should stay the entire week with you, with a weekend off each month."

"Why would you want to do that Rosario?" Saúl asked sensing that Rosario was up to something other than a raise in salary. Rosario noted the change in his tone and the seriousness of his look and decided to change her plan, originally planning to state that she wanted to be more available to Solimar to help out with the baby. "Well, to be totally honest with you, the family that I rent the room from for the weekends have decided that it would be better for them economically to rent the room out permanently. They have asked me to pay the full month's rent, whether I occupy it or not or leave so they can find a full-time tenant that will pay approximately triple what I am paying now for the weekends." Saúl said "I completely understand. Our economy is in very bad condition and people are doing whatever it takes to either cut back expenses or increase their income. I do not mind compensating you for the extra work we will be requiring you to do. In addition, I will also increase your salary and pay you for the weekend you don't work. You do have a family member here on the island where you can spend your weekend off, correct?" Rosario who had not expected this wonderful turn of events said "But of course, I do. I have a cousin and friends and that will present no problem for me!" Saúl, satisfied with his decision said "Please discuss the details with my wife when she returns and we will figure out the new schedule sometime next week." Rosario had not expected his generosity, but did expect that her scheme would be effective and not only did it prove effective, it was substantially beneficial to her finances. She got up, raised her glass and downed her wine in one gulp, resting her left hand on her hip, another typical Solimar nuance which did not escape Saúl's eyes. She gingerly walked over to where he was seated and sat on the couch, leaving very little space between them and said "I don't think you know how much I appreciate this." Saúl allowed her to lean in as close as she could, as her intent was to kiss him and he wanted to see how far she would take her "appreciation." She must have helped herself to a bottle of his personal air freshener, Solimar's body spray, because she was reeking of it. For a second there, his head became heady with desire, but not for Rosario. The phone rang and Rosario reached for it causing her to lean over Saúl's lap as the phone was stationed on the end table. She answered "Residencia Santana." Solimar simply said "Put my husband on the phone." Rosario's disappointment was obvious as she handed Saúl the receiver and said; "Señor Santana, your wife is on the line and would like to speak with you." Saúl took the phone and spoke with his wife, giddily receiving her call like a sophomore who had just received a phone call from the prom queen. Rosario took her empty wine glass, placed it in the dishwasher and thought it best to go to her bedroom. She was sick and tired already of these two, but today she had won an important battle that would gain ground for her and that would have to suffice. She sat down on her bed and opened the drawer taking out her vibrator and stared long and hard at it. She wanted this to be the night that she would seduce Saúl, but now she not only feared rejection, but worse, she feared losing her job which now paid more than it did before. She tossed it back into the drawer, but the wine kicked in and she retrieved it. This night should not be a total loss. She took her robe and pajama bottom off, slipped under the covers and the hum of the device was soon replaced by her muffled moans. Morning would come soon enough and her plans were coming together very nicely. She reset her alarm clock to rise before Saúl and prepare him a hearty breakfast, a detail he never expected from her as he often left on business at 6:00 a.m. and had his coffee and a cinnamon bun at the airport.

Across the way, Solimar and Lili Anne both woke up early enough to see Carlos Juan off. Instead of going back to bed, they agreed to begin their day early. Lili Anne and Carlos employed a house staff fit to run a ship. The ladies went to the garden where their breakfast would be served. Solimar timidly asked "Should we change our clothing?" Lili Anne waved her off. *"Tranquilita mija.* You change when and if you want to. I'll probably go back to bed after breakfast and then we will plan our day for tomorrow. I think today would be good to stay here. I will give the staff the rest of the day off except for the driver in case we gotta go somewhere or need him to pick something up for us; he has a lot of free time anyway. I always let him roam around when Carlos isn't home, but he has never, ever not answered my call when I needed him."

Solimar, donning pajama bottoms and a loose fitting midriff, showing off her baby bulge, was feeling like she was finally in her own skin. She walked the gardens in the pair of leather flip-flops Saúl had purchased for her, begging her to give up the dollar store ones she always carried in her purse. She inquired about every fruit-bearing tree, every plant and the little leaping lizards she saw. Lili Anne, pleased to have an apprentice, explained all that she could to Solimar. Solimar shyly approached Lili Anne after finishing up their breakfast.

"Lili, may I please have a cigarette. I haven't smoked in days and I really want one." Lili Anne did not hesitate. She slid open her solid gold, semi-precious gem encrusted cigarette case that she had picked up when she went to Brazil for next to nothing, and placed a filter on the cigarette for Solimar. Solimar nodded her gratitude and lighting her cigarette said "I've been meaning to ask you some things." The San Juan sun was already upon them, making their skin tingle, threatening to scorch it and it was only 7:00 a.m. "Solimar, I'm going back to bed after this cigarette. In the event that you haven't realized, I am 67 years old. My husband is 64 and is about ready to retire. We have worked hard and we are very tired. Can we have this conversation later on today? By then we will have a nice snack prepared and we can talk all you like after that."

"Oh, I'm sorry; I thought that you were giving the staff time off."

"Yes, I am. Meet me in the kitchen at noon and we will cook for ourselves. I do like to cook from time to time, and I think you need to learn a thing or two about Puerto Rican cookery." Solimar excitedly said "Oh my God, yeah! I'm going back to bed and will set my alarm for 11:30!" She kissed Lili Anne who said "See you then Bella!" Solimar extinguished her half smoked cigarette and went straight back to the guestroom, immediately falling asleep, even missing Saúl's call to let her know that he had already arrived in New York. Lili Anne walked the gardens for a while longer. She picked up a small basket that she always kept nearby and begun to fill it with nature's bounty; a bounty that she had sowed herself and would now reap its riches.

Solimar promptly woke up at the appointed hour, showered, dressed excitedly and looked forward to spending time with Lili Anne. Solimar had missed bonding with her mother, having lost much of her mother's teachings; her mother having died when Soli was only a teenager. With no father, no real family interested enough to take an interest in taking care of her; she was placed in foster care and lived by the will of God and the charity of others, going from house to house. Thankfully, Solimar was not mistreated nor abused in any way, but every time she got comfortable, she found herself displaced for this reason or the other, reasons that she had no say in or given an explanation as to why. As a direct result, she learned many things. Some were good, some bad, some interesting and a lot sad. For some reason unbeknownst to Solimar, she never made a solid connection with a woman during those years, but always seemed to manage a rapport with the men around her who looked out for her. Looking back, Solimar thanked God and His Mother that nobody ever tried to violate her. Her life could have been so very much worse. She knew that from a little girlfriend of hers, Nichelle, who had randomly been given the nickname "Nice." Nice had suffered greatly during her stay in the foster care system, but had sworn Solimar to secrecy. Solimar promised her that she would not tell, but that someday, she would find Nichelle and help her. Nichelle said "I know you will try to Solimar, but I don't think that will happen for a long, long time. Just lay low, try to get by and not make waves or bring attention to yourself. Maybe if you don't find me first, I promise to try and find you too." These two would meet monthly as their foster mothers reported to the agency that placed them to hand in their accountings and pick up their checks. They were left to wait in the corridors drinking a soda and given over to their own devices while the meetings were conducted. Solimar shook the memory of Nichelle from her head, crossed herself and frantically searched for the little bottle of Holy Water she always kept near to her. She poured out the bottle and washed her face, smoothing back her hair off of her face and said to herself "I am ready for whatever comes my way. God please bless Nichelle, wherever she is and all the people that I love. I think that I am going to be well here and I thank you." In that short statement of gratitude and petition on Nichelle's behalf, Solimar had begun praying again. She walked towards the kitchen in her pretty yellow sun dress and was surprised to find Lili Anne in blue shorts, an orange tank top and a multi-colored apron, the kitchen door wide open. Lili Anne was already working the kitchen and Solimar was more confused than ever. Solimar gingerly approached, trying to ignore all the different vegetables that were placed on the kitchen's island. "Hi Lili." Lili Anne wiped her hands and hugged Solimar and said to her "Mamita, the proper way to address your elders is *"Bendicion."* Solimar vaguely recalling that protocol from her younger years automatically repeated the word *"Bendicion."*

"*Que Dios te Bendiga*, my dear." Solimar found it somewhat strange, somewhat amusing that she would begin her day asking to be blessed. "Come, we are going to have a lot of fun today." Solimar decided that it would be in her best interest to listen and shut up for once in her life. She took on an apron and proceeded to do everything Lili Anne told her to do. Solimar found herself grating *platanos, yucca* and mixing all kinds of green things together. She was not ignorant to what she was doing. She knew that she was learning how to make *pasteles*, but God Almighty, why so much work? Solimar lost herself in the learning of how to be a good Puerto Rican wife. She grated, she sweated, she listened, she simmered and she learned a complicated wrapping technique, which took her a few tries to grasp its concept. Finally, she stopped to drink a cold one and then went back at it. She listened intently to Lili Anne's conversation with her husband when he called. She did not care about their conversation, only about how she could learn from this real diva how to be a diva for sure. Hours passed and Solimar kept to her labor, following every detailed instruction to the letter. Anxiously waiting for Saúl's call that she had missed, she finally asked Lili Anne "why are we doing this? There is nobody here to eat it." Lili Anne, already feeling a bit woozy from all the work said "My dear, this you will take home for Saúl. I will keep some here too. When they come back and we serve them this, they will fall more in love with us than they are already!" Solimar giggled and asked "Are we not having the *pasteles* for dinner tonight?" Lili Anne smiled and wickedly said "Hell no. We are going to get all dolled up, and off to Old San Juan we go for some real food, folks and fun and I ain't talking McDonalds, unless you need me to boil one of these for you right now to hold you over." Solimar slyly said "I think I can wait." She hoped that Lili Anne, who enjoyed gambling, would take her to a casino so she can try out her luck, which seemed to have been taking a turn for the better.

As so it was, so it went. The further education of Solimar Santana broadened in the bountiful arms and intellect of this elegant, selfless woman who fell in love with the story that she herself had once lived. They shopped, spent hours walking the shoreline, collecting seashells for a project Lili Anne had in mind and ate everything from the cheapest empanada at a kiosk located on the beach to lobsters that were just caught moments before. Strangely enough, Saúl did not call during that time and Solimar did not seem to mind, after a while knowing that he would come home soon enough. Little did she know that Lili Anne had agreed with Saúl to give Solimar the space she so desperately needed to acclimate to her new environment, the never-ending sound of the *coqui* who filled the night with their endless song, and the learning process of becoming a proper wife to a diplomat. Saúl understood that Solimar needed to ease into her new role and lot in life; a lesson he had learned from their dear friend, Marisol. Solimar was never to be pressured or she would run and that is the last thing in the world that he wanted.

On their last night together, as they sat drinking coffee heavily laced with an almond flavored liqueur and a small scoop of vanilla ice cream instead of milk, Solimar asked Lili Anne to please recount her story. Lili Anne, set aside her coffee cup, silently walked away and poured herself a double from an unmarked bottle. It was homemade rum, laden with molasses known as *añejo,* fermented in her very backyard, having been buried for a period of no less than a year. She went to her humidor and pulled out a slim, miniature cigar and placed a filter on it. She leaned into her rocker, closed her eyes and said simply "I was only fifteen years old. I came to Puerto Rico on a summer vacation because my mother started to work that year full-time and didn't want to leave me alone in The Bronx while school was out, so she sent me to my grandparents' house, not very far away from here actually, right there in *Carolina.* So many people greeted me because I believe that they thought I was something special because I was from the States. I didn't know who family was and who was not. Carlos Juan and I met during my many excursions into town, liked each other and I, being a couple of years older than him, begun to flirt. He was but a mere boy, but as you can tell, Puerto Rican men mature rather quickly and my grandparents let him take me to parties with his family and escort me around town. Really, I did not know that he was actually my cousin because everyone there was referred to as cousin even when they were not, and the family was very large. Our grandmother watched us, but it escaped her eyes that we were slowing falling in love; I guess she chalked it up to infatuation or really didn't give a damn. On the last week of my trip, our grandmother asked me if I had my period yet because she hadn't found any 'pasteles' in the garbage." Soli choked on a bit of ice cream, learning now that 'pasteles' was the Spanish 'code word' for sanitary napkins. Lili Anne paid her no mind, puffed on her cigar and continued; "I said no that I wasn't sure when was the last time I got it because I had only begun menstruating a couple of months before the trip and it was still irregular." She called our grandfather and without saying a word to me, they put me in the car and took me to a doctor. The doctor did a urine test, told my grandmother I was pregnant and right then and there, they performed an abortion on me. It was …. Awful. No anesthesia, no pain killers, nothing like today. I could swear that doctor took a wire hanger to me, but I cannot say for sure as I was strapped down. It all happened so quickly and to be honest with you, I'm not sure I want to remember. When we got back home, I was hunched over in pain and rapidly losing blood. They should have taken me to a hospital, but they did not want anyone to know what they had done to me. You know how that is!" Soli slowly nodded. She knew full well the power of *'La Gente'* had when it came to gossip. She heard it too many times as a young girl. *"Pero la gente…"* Which meant - 'What would the people think?' Solimar always wanted to ask 'What people' and why should we care what they think?' but never did.

Lili Anne gave Soli a smile knowing that Soli fully understood where she was coming from. "Our grandfather called Carlos Juan and lied to him telling him that he would like him to escort me to a street festival, seeing that I would shortly be returning to New York. I didn't understand. I didn't want to go to anywhere in my condition. I had no idea that it was just a ruse to get Carlos Juan to come over. When he showed up, our grandfather beat us both with a belt." Solimar winced in pain at the thought. Soli knew full well that back in the day, the belt used for "discipline" was called a Garrison belt. It was a thick, two inch wide leather belt that had a big steel buckle. In a street fight it would be used as a weapon and resembled a barber's razor strap! Lili Anne caught Soli's reaction and asked "You okay?" Soli nodded yes. "Do you want me to continue?" Soli whispered "Please do."

"I was an inch away from death and Carlos Juan left there crying like a baby, welts even on his face. Our grandfather hit us with the buckle of the belt which tore into our skin. Our grandmother joined in with a switch, all the while cursing us and screaming at us that we were the devil's children. The welts were unbearable and instead of stopping they continued hitting us creating welt on top of welt. After the beating, she made us shower together. The cold water stung so badly, but still that wasn't enough for them. She made us wash each other with a nasty rag filled with the lather from a bar soap that was used for washing clothes and general cleaning back then. I think they called it Borax, but later on Carlos Juan told me that it was *Jabon de Azufre*, soap primarily made out of sulfur, used to treat acne. It burned like all hell." Soli thought she could handle it, but the vivid images that Lili Anne painted were too much. Horrified Solimar said, "Please *por Dios no puedo mas*, stop!" By then Lili Anne was too far gone into her recounting and said "you wanted to know, now shut up and listen. After they savagely beat us and forced us to bathe and humiliated us, they offered us a bed to see how far we would go. It was almost like they were going on a sado-masochistic feeding frenzy, enjoying our pain. I can't even imagine what their sex life consisted of, if they even still had one. The old bitch, may her soul burn eternally in the flames of hell, pulled out some twine and literally tied me spread eagle to the four-poster bed, cutting deep into my wrists and ankles. *Pobre* Carlos was whimpering, completely terrified. My grandfather yelled to him "If you think you are such a man, fuck her, fuck your *prima* now, she is all yours, see if you can get her pregnant again." Carlos obediently climbed on top of me, shivering and trying to stifle his tears and groans. Mercifully, he collapsed and fainted on top of me. Our grandparents were finally satisfied that we would never touch each other again. They left us in that position and went off to have *un cafecito* and no doubt, a shot or two of rum. We were there for what seemed like hours, but in reality it could have just been minutes. When they came back into the bedroom, they did something, I don't know what for sure, but they got Carlos Juan back on his feet. They made him dress over his bruises and welts and threw a sheet over me, some of which got stuck in my opened wounds as they had not bothered to try to dress or even tend to them. They left me to sleep in that position all night and somehow Carlos Juan made it home, beaten to a pulp, shame and guilt written all over him. When word somehow got out, he became the laughing stock of the town. The fun didn't stop there for me either. My grandmother woke me up the next morning by throwing a bucket of cold water on my face. She untied me, gave me a hideous housecoat and put me to scrub the floors with the very soap she had us bathe in. They worked me like a slave barely giving me enough to eat to sustain my broken body, never mind my soul. I was on my way home two days later, forbidden to return to the island. My mother never said a word or asked me what had happened. I assumed that having been raised by those *animales*, she might have suffered some of the same. A few years later, Carlos came to the States to find me. He had quit school and worked day and night, saving up every penny. I was 18 and he had just turned 16. Somehow, he managed to get an uncle of his on his father's side to sign the marital consent form for a minor, forging his father's signature. We got married in a civil ceremony over there in the courthouse in el Bronx, I believe it was in the Grand Concourse and he promised me that no one will ever hurt or humiliate us ever again. We rented a tiny furnished room and commenced to live our lives. Eventually he joined the Marines, which is how he got his trade and I earned my living working in a factory, assembling cheap plastic dolls. He re-enlisted and made a career of it. By then, I was allowed to travel with him and we traveled the world, never looking back. We took advantage of the benefits and individually entered into therapy, faithfully going to our appointments and from time to time we were asked to present ourselves together to gauge our progress as a couple. Twenty-five, twenty-six years later, he woke up one morning; I think we were stationed in Italy or Germany and simply said *"Negra*, it's time for us to settle back home; by now those bastards have to be dead, but if they aren't I really don't care. I want us to go home." I had no reason to dispute him. He put in his retirement papers and in a month we were back in the States. Shortly after, we relocated to Puerto Rico where Carlos Juan had already received the offer of an interview to start working as a deck hand on the very boat you got married on. He worked his way up and in two years, took the helm." Lili Anne paused, took a long sip from her homemade drink and said "and as they say, 'the rest is history'!" Lili Anne unconsciously rubbed her belly, probably because Solimar was doing the same thing. Lili Anne reached over and lovingly placed her hand on Soli's baby bump and sighed. "We could never have children, but we don't talk about it." Lili Anne retreated and took another puff of her cigar. "We don't know if it was because of the botched abortion, or if I'm sterile or if he's sterile. The reason never really mattered to either one of us. We just do right by each other, every day for the rest of our lives." Solimar moved by her sincerity, pressed on. "What about the rest of your family?" The answer came short and sweet and with no emotion. "There is no family. When they found out that we had married, everyone deserted us, totally abandoned us and denied our very existence, including our parents. Nobody stood up for us, nobody listened to our story. The only one that stood by us was his uncle that signed the marriage consent." Lili Anne blew out a long stream of smoke "but he has long since passed away. May God have that man in his glory, if nothing else but for having saved us".

Solimar's tears were warm, soft and heart wrenching all at once. She had no more questions and much less answers. Lili Anne allowed her tears to flow as well and only said "Do you understand now why my husband so graciously performed your marriage ceremony?"

"Yes, yes I do. I will hold your secret dear to my heart. I think I am sorry that I asked." Lili Anne, now composed reached over and wiped the tear forming in the corner of Solimar's eye and said "No *nena*, don't be sorry. For whatever reason, God placed you and Saúl in our path to help us deal with our demons and help heal us a little bit more. The therapist encouraged us to discuss it from time to time and I am glad I just did. I celebrate your pregnancy and only wish you and your brother the very best in life." They stood up, faced each other holding hands and staring long and hard into each other's eyes and finally they embraced. Lili Anne then whispered in Soli's ear; "and besides… your situation is so much more fucked up than mine!" Solimar's jaw dropped. "Lili Anne!" Solimar exclaimed. "You, you, you bitch!" Lili Anne laughed hard and hugged Solimar tighter and rocked her in her arms. "Yeah, it takes a bitch to know one! I love you too!" Lili Anne kissed her on the forehead, both cheeks and right on her nose, leaving her lips for last – the infamous Saúl type kiss, except in the wrong order. Solimar laughed at the irony, the camaraderie and said "You are ever so right, but at least I didn't get my ass kicked, not yet anyway! Shit, in my case, they'll probably drag me down by the collar to the dungeon in one of those old stone churches, put me in chains, whip me and then try to quarter my ass!" They needed to make fun of their situations to help ease the tension and strengthen them for their continued journey with men that suffered their pain, as well as their own. Lili Anne knew that all too well. "Now c'mon, finish wiping those snots hanging out your nose and call your husband and tell him that you are okay, *vale?*"

"*Vale.*"

Solimar could not remember a time, other than her brief time with Olaya, that she felt so much love, so much compassion and now complete understanding. She walked up to the guest room, called and he answered at the very first ring. "Bello?"

"Si, Bella, I'm right here."

"I love you."

"I love you more. Are you having a good time?" Solimar repressed the tears and said "I'm having the time of my life."

"Good Bella. I will swing by to pick you up tomorrow around 4:00. Have your stuff packed and ready to go. I can't wait to get back home, see my baby girl, sleep with you all cuddled up; these trips are taxing the hell out of me." Saúl never had a problem traveling on business before, but then again he never had someone waiting for him at home that he wanted to get back to. "I will be ready in the morning. I miss you so much, but this time away from each other has proven to be pretty good."

"We are blessed Soli. We have more than what most people can ask for. I know our situation sucks, but you know we have to remember that…"

"We were born to mothers and fathers and we have to behave that way." Saúl kept his peace and so did Solimar. "*Bendicion* Saúl." Saúl said "I think I should be asking you to bless me, not the other way, but either way *Dios te Bendiga*. May God bless you tonight and always *querida.*" They said their goodbyes and Solimar went to bed fully clothed, cuddling up with Hickey who never dared once bite the hand that fed her. Solimar slept without a care in the world. Lili Anne came in to say goodnight, but found her fast asleep. She gently covered her with a lightweight blanket and placed Hickey back into her beautiful cage.

Lili Anne hated to see Solimar go, but she was full of anticipation to greet her husband later that night or bright and early the next morning, depending on the tide of the sea, or more accurately, the administrative work he had to hand in before abandoning ship. The recounting of her story did re-open the welts and the wounds, reawakening her desire for her husband. They hadn't made love in quite some time and not only did she need it, this time around she very much wanted to. She promised herself that no matter what time Carlito arrived, she would make love to him, like they did when they were newly married, even having burned a couple of dinners and leaving destruction in their ravenous wake. She confided this to Solimar over breakfast and they set to the task of creating an environment conducive to Lili Anne's plans. Over the course of a few hours, they turned the master bedroom upside down. Solimar, being a believer in the art of Feng Shui, had the staff move the television out of the bedroom, rearranged the furniture and strategically placed a bowl and pitcher with a balm she prepared on Lili Anne's nightstand, removing her lamp. She draped a scarf over the remaining lamp and lined the top of the chest of drawers with lavender scented candles, in all shapes and sizes, which they purchased when they hurriedly ran to the mall to buy a *"mosquitero"* or rather a delicately knitted canopy that hung from the ceiling and draped over the four posts of their king-sized bed. They gathered, washed and prepared a fruit bowl and set a bottle of champagne to cool by Carlos' bedside. Solimar gave Lili Anne her IPod, promising her that she had another one at home and could download all the music which was saved to their computer. The IPod contained more than five hours worth of romantic boleros, Latin jazz and a variety of classical music and nature sounds and Lili Anne couldn't be more thrilled. They sent out the driver to purchase a docking station and set it up behind the bed to give the illusion that the music was being piped in. They agreed that Carlos should not have the *pasteles* beforehand or he might fall asleep, opting to feed him fruit and cottage cheese and lots of chocolates instead. Lastly, they rummaged through Lili Anne's lingerie drawer. They agreed that everything there had been used at least once and decided to head right back to the mall to buy something absolutely extravagant. They settled on an amber colored, full length chiffon nightgown that would offset Lili Anne's light brown eyes and coppery hair. They also purchased a matching pair of mules with only the slightest heel. They ended their seductive preparations with Lili Anne seated at her vanity, which had now been temporarily moved to the guestroom. Solimar brushed out Lili Anne's hair that had earlier been set in rollers. Solimar reminded Lili Anne that the gardenia they had died to match the nightgown was in the refrigerator and that she was to pin up the left side of her hair with it, making sure to sweep it as far back as she could. Satisfied with their day's work and noting that Saúl had already landed and was on his way to pick up Solimar, they went downstairs to meet him.

When Saúl arrived, Lili Anne thoroughly enjoyed his surprised look when she handed him his bundle of homemade *pasteles* to go. To see those two together, was a reflection of her love for Carlos Juan who would be returning home soon enough. Saúl had appeared with a bouquet of exotic flowers for Lili Anne and ceremoniously handed them to her saying "These are for you madam, for having taken such good care of my wife." Lili Anne looked around at her lavish garden and responded "Does it look like I need fucking flowers around here?" By now, accustomed to Lili Anne's sarcastic sense of humor, Saúl simply said "Well you can take a bath in them or put them in your bedroom while you're preparing a little voo-doo hoochie coo for your *esposo* who should also be arriving today." Lili Anne laughed, hugged the two, sent them on their merry way and wiped the tears from her eyes trying not to smear the make-up that Solimar had so lovingly applied. She accepted the flowers as it was a sweet gesture on Saúl's part and proceeded to put them in a vase and find a place for them upstairs, a detail that both she and Solimar had overlooked.

As she watched them drive away, she hoped that Solimar remembered that she had given Solimar explicit instructions not to eat anything that her housekeeper had prepared "just for her." Lili Anne did not trust Rosario as far as she could throw her and they had somewhat agreed that Rosario probably had the hots for Saúl, but that wasn't what troubled her; Lili Anne was afraid that her girl would fall into the venomous hands of a woman that obviously had evil intentions for Solimar, and if she didn't, it was only because she was still in the planning stages. Lili Anne was not easily fooled by appearances, but confident in Solimar's intuition and natural intelligence, she turned her thoughts back to welcoming her husband home.

    A couple of days later, Solimar wisely using the excuse of Rosario's added responsibilities, alleviated Rosario from all kitchen duties, having hired a cook specifically to work the kitchen exclusively and serve their meals personally. During those two days, while she interviewed cooks for the position, she prepared their meals and Saúl did not mind much, as Rosario's cooking was average at best and it seemed that Solimar knew her way around a kitchen. Rosario did not protest as she was assured that her salary would remain intact although her duties were primarily changed to the cleaning and upkeep of the house and shopping. Solimar also withdrew her responsibility of maintaining the household budget, to which Rosario voiced her unsolicited opinion and resistance to losing this, a key part of her employment that also distinguished her from just being the maid. "Solimar, *yo soy la ama de llaves*, I mean I am the housekeeper. It is my responsibility to do the shopping and accounting of the household expenses!" Solimar simply responded "Rosario, you may be *'la ama de llaves,'* but I am *'la ama de casa'* and as Saúl's unemployed wife, I choose to employ myself as housewife, which is probably a few steps higher than that of housekeeper, don't you think?" Rosario did not expect Solimar's concise bi-lingual response, which left no room for argument. She maintained her composure, but shot back "If you think it is best Solimar, I am sure that your husband will support your decision." She excused herself and left Soli sitting behind her husband's desk, reviewing the household budget of the prior six months.

    About a month later, Solimar asked Saúl over dinner if they could go to Panamá to meet up with Marisol and Roberto. Her closeness with Carlos Juan and his wife was great indeed, but she missed her friends in Panamá dearly. "Bella, you are only in your second trimester. You know that you cannot fly and obviously they cannot come here because of the same reason, plus Mari's deportation situation is complicated. It is going to be a while before we will see them again." Soli understood that she would have to wait, but there was another concern lingering on her mind. "How about our father, does he know that he is going to be a grandfather?" Saúl rubbed his temples, knowing that her question was going to turn into an issue. "Solimar, you are my wife, my sister, my soul mate and my life. Nothing will transpire of that sort until you and I come into agreement. My parents only know that I am back in Puerto Rico, and that is it." Solimar leaned back, resting her hand on her protruding pouch. "I think the bastard ought to know." Saúl took a deep breath and asked "Do you wish to call "the bastard" yourself?" Soli responded rather nonchalantly. "No. I will wait my time until he can see with his own eyes the consequences of his actions."

"Solimar, with all due respect, you are not being fair nor Christian like at all."

"Nor was he when he went fucking around with your witch of a mother, left mine in abject poverty and created a nice cushy life for himself."

"What about forgiveness Solimar Santana?"

"Fuck that. I ain't God or anything near that majesty. Let his God forgive him. As for me, he can well rot in the caverns of hell for all I care!" Solimar excused herself and went to the backyard to have her after dinner smoke, having cut-down from a pack a day to just three, one after each meal. She walked over to the hot tub that she so longed to share with her husband, longing to share the view of the setting sun behind the ocean, as they did not so long ago, but kept focused on the smoke she was enjoying and hoping that things would be less tense tomorrow. That night Saúl slept in the guest room under the pretense of having to work late and not wanting to disturb Soli. Solimar did not venture into the spare room. The atmosphere cooled between them, while the tension mounted. They were cordial, but not demonstrative of their love or concern. Physical contact was limited to a peck on the cheek. Saúl remained in self-exile. Rosario was in heaven; even bending backwards to accommodate Solimar's every whim. After a while, Solimar decided it was time to call her friend. The phone rang and rang, but nobody answered her cry. She looked up Olaya's telephone number, but was met with an answering machine instead of a friendly voice. She slammed down the phone then opted to call Lili Anne, but halfway through dialing remembered that Lili Anne went on board with her husband for yet another excursion.

Rosario, who had taken to lurking daily in every corner of the house, took advantage of the situation and appeared in Saúl's guest room under the guise that she was ventilating it. When Saúl stepped into the guestroom to find Rosario changing the bed sheets, he fell prey to her ploy. Rosario explained that she was airing it out and maintaining it dust-free in the event that the Ramirezes would come to spend the night. She aired out the room and immediately changed the scent of the guest room, spraying a light musk instead of Solimar's scent and simply said "*Buenas noche Señor Santana.*" Saúl having been sucker punched answered. "Good night Rosita."

Mar Y Sol

Marisol was happily preparing for her child's birth. Having no girlfriends in Panamá that would throw her a baby shower, she copied another expectant mother's registry and purchased a good ninety percent of the items, having them delivered and stored in her new home. She also occupied herself with the resurrection of Roberto's law practice while he was still in rehab, albeit on an outpatient basis, and made contact with a couple of his former clients with Lydia's help. She had a good business strategy set up for his comeback. Upon his discharge, Marisol Espinoza-Betancourt became his very first client and retained him to draw up her divorce papers. With Ricardo still in the States, the divorce would be granted by default in no time, and so it was. It was only a simple matter of placing a public announcement in the local newspaper, which would obviously go unanswered. Marisol had still not communicated with her parents, only to send them a postcard to say that she was well and would be in touch. She loved her life with Roberto and Lydia and they worked day and night rebuilding Roberto's clientele list, attending Alcoholics Anonymous meetings at night and anxiously expecting the birth of their child. Marisol accepted Roberto's second marriage proposal the very day she was declared legally divorced, but they later agreed to be married through the church after the baby was born. Roberto planned to place his deceased mother's engagement ring on Marisol's finger with Lydia as their witness, but before doing so, he called his future wife into his study and had her seated. "Marisol. You know that I am in love with you, am planning on marrying you and make you a part of my life forever." Marisol, a bit nervous said "Sure, Rober, you know that I feel the same way about you."

"Then why don't you ever talk to me about this dude, your ex-husband?" Marisol lowered her eyes. Although she was never physically abused, the pain and heartache was more than she could deal with. "Rober, I already said what I was going to say. I just can't; it was just such an awful experience that I choose to leave it behind and not re-live it by recounting it. May I have that privacy?" Roberto shook his head no. There were things he needed to know before they could move on. "No; not if you're going to be my wife. I need to know as much as I can about him because I need to know if he's gonna come barreling through the door one day on some machismo trip. Married people are entitled to some privacy, but not all this mystery, and certainly not if not knowing the truth is going to negatively affect me or have a negative impact on our relationship."

Marisol sat back, breathed deeply and recalled the day she met Solimar at the Marriage and Singles seminar they both unsuccessfully attended. She said "Look, Rober, like I said before, the man used me okay? I'm not proud of having been such a fool. I met him at the embassy the day they approved my Student Visa and he had gotten turned down. I guess he overheard me talking on the cell or whatever and followed me, telling me that he needed my advice on how to successfully get one. We went to an outdoor Café, and I started to tell him how to go about getting his own Student Visa. I didn't know that he already had connections in the States because he was looking to deal drugs. How could I have known? We exchanged numbers and he started courting me, if you can call it that. A month before I was scheduled to leave, he asked me to marry him. Yes, by then I was in love with him, but I was more scared to go to the States all by myself, so I figured it to be a win-win situation; he got an entry into the States and I got a legitimate companion out of the arrangement." A lot more than that happened, but please don't put me through it now in a moment when I'm making a right decision based on feelings instead of insecurity." Roberto softened and said "Do you know that Saúl and I have already discussed hunting this motherfucker down and giving him the beating of his life?" Marisol said "Please don't do that. Not for him, but for us. We are starting a beautiful, promising brand new life. This guy will get what is coming to him in due time; let karma handle it! I just want us to be the way we are whether or not you marry me."

Roberto called Lydia in who knew it was time. She handed Roberto an elaborate, egg-shaped box and stood back quietly. Roberto opened the box, presented it to Marisol and simply asked her "Will you be my wife and I mean like forever?" Marisol extended her left hand and said "Yes, and this time, I mean it from the bottom of my heart. I'm not scared of anything, and Roberto, *mi amor,* please do not ever doubt my love for you." With that affirmation having been made, they went to an exclusive restaurant for an intimate celebratory dinner, Lydia included, and they peacefully went on with their lives, committed to their future together.

Marisol missed Solimar, but she was content to know that Saúl was looking for her and was more than confident that he would someday find her. She never bothered calling for fear of interfering or upsetting Saúl. Roberto did the same. Lydia never breathed a word to either one of them that she had already told Saúl where to find Solimar for fear that she would be chastised for her intrusion in the event that things did not go well. Panamanian life suited Marisol. She was, after all, back home. Roberto promised her to get her back to the University once the baby was born and Lydia was more than willing to help raise yet another child. All was well in Panamá. Praise be to God.

Sadly, the panorama in Puerto Rico was rapidly changing. Saúl and Solimar found themselves sleeping in separate quarters more often than not. They had their share of pretenses, cordial excuses galore, but the truth of the matter was that as Solimar's baby grew within her, her resentment towards their father continued to fester and started consuming her. As much as she loved her husband, she needed to express her disdain for the man who set all this pain and heartache in motion. She took to both sun and sea on a daily basis, mostly to avoid Rosario who seemed to be gaining ground with her employer. Nor sea nor sun fulfilled Solimar. Saúl watched his wife retreat deeper and deeper into a depression and he often cried himself to sleep at night, but was determined to wait for her invitation back into their marital bed. He had moved mountains to get them back together, and although Solimar sealed the deal by arranging their marriage, Saúl was beginning to feel that Solimar did not understand that he was also in a compromising position. He loved and respected his father very much. Just as much as "the bastard" had abandoned Solimar, he had always been there for him. His father had pushed him to earn his law degree and through his affluence, helped him to become a diplomat. Solimar hated their father, but she needed to come to the understanding that they were one in the same. Saúl kept away from his family to avoid revealing his marriage to his sister, and Solimar instinctively knew this. 'Hell,' she thought. 'I'd be ashamed of myself too.' Soli remembered how Lili Anne had jokingly remarked about how fucked up her situation was. Lili Anne had said out loud what everyone dared not utter, not even in private, but indeed, no truer words had been said.

 Their home was beautiful, yet had grown cold and regimented. Nobody laughed anymore. Gone were the pillow fights and the lullaby, which Solimar now hummed in her head as she rocked herself to sleep. Nobody did anything more than what they were supposed to do. Saúl woke up one Saturday morning to find that his now seven-month pregnant wife was not home. He knew where to find her and strolled down to the ocean. He saw Solimar, knee deep in water, wading around aimlessly, unaware that a huge wave was rapidly gaining in on her. Saúl recalling his own near death experience ran as hard as he could. Solimar lost her balance in the undertow and then the wave came upon her, spun her around and pulled her under.

Saúl was horrified, but kept running driven by what seemed like supernatural adrenalin. "God, please don't hurt me anymore than you already have" came Saúl's open prayer as he watched his wife struggle with the massive wave of ocean water. Saúl ran towards the area where he saw his *sirena* fall captive to the ocean's treacherous grip, knowing that it would only take seconds for him to lose his wife, his sister and his child and then he would have no recourse but to drown himself along with them. By the time he got to her, Solimar was on her feet, throwing up salt water, snots and tears covering her face. When she saw Saúl, she found the power to wade the short distance towards him. When she reached him, Saúl took off his tee shirt and wiped her nose. "We're going to the hospital right now!" Solimar laughed and choked at once .... "What are you fucking nuts?!"

"Solimar Santana, you almost just drowned and you are carrying our child! How much salt water do you think you drank?"

"*Puta! Me llamo Sol y Mar,* duh, Sun and Sea, remember? I dominate this, not the other way around!" Saúl stepped back and finally saw his sister in all of her ugly, raw radiance. "You just got knocked on your ass, after getting hit by a giant wave, with your big belly and you're telling me that you dominate this?" Solimar continued in her defiance. "Yeah, man, Yemaya got my back, what you think?" Saúl was speechless, but then nervously laughed at the arrogance of his woman or was it her faith in forces that she knew little or nothing about that perplexed him. He struggled to find words and finally gave up, throwing his hands up. "Solimar, you just mess with me in ways that I can't even begin to describe." Solimar placed her hand on her hip and said "Maybe you should stop thinking I'm messing with you and understand that I'm just being me."

"Can we just go get some lunch then?"

"Lunch, brunch, who cares? I don't even know what time it is. I've lost track, Bello, of both life and time."

"Solimar Santana, you are my wife and in case you don't know what that means, it means that you are mine and I am yours. I love you. I cannot keep sleeping in the room next door.

My heart and soul belongs to you and when I saw you drowning, I thought that suicide would be my only alternative."

Soli took her husband by the hand and led him to shore. They walked without speaking, cried without tears and within them both a revolution was born, yet Saúl had but one more question to ask. "Bella, I gotta ask you something and don't be offended please."

"What already?!"

"I noticed that you inscribed in my wedding band LOL. Do you think our marriage is a laughing matter?" Solimar smiled, placed both hands on his cheeks and tenderly said "I'm glad you finally noticed; I've been waiting for the moment when you would question my humor." She pulled off hers and showed him that she had inscribed the same in hers. Saúl was confused, he didn't understand. Solimar S. Santana de Santana simply said … "I made up my own acronym … it means Love Over Lust." Saúl plunked down, sat on the sand with his head in his hands and said, "I can't believe that you understand our love so well. I do love you Soli and desire you more than a thirsty man desires a glass of water, but I respect you even more. You are my sister and I know that I can't always be all over you like an octopus because I also want to have a relationship with you as my sibling. I missed growing up with you, learning your ways, fighting with you, protecting you from guys around the block. This is why I've stayed away, slept in the guest room and waited for you to invite me back to our bed. I come to you sometimes, when I know that you are sleeping, just to watch over you, care for you, but it is not all about the desire at all. I am double blessed to have you, and I have to treat you as both wife and sister. I accepted that a long time ago, but I never thought you would ever get it."

"Saúl?"

"Que es mi amor?"

"I get it. I always did. Forgive me for hating our father. Maybe I am jealous that he loved you more than me….it could be."

"Hush Solimar." Saúl placed his index finger on her speaking lips and then kissed them.

"The man was an ass or maybe just a man. I don't deny you that he was a piece of shit for having abandoned you and your mother, but how about forgiveness? Can you try to find it in your heart? I just want us to have a family life, raise our child with no animosity towards his grandparents because if not, we are going to be raising our child in a war zone with him or her in the middle. Not to mention, you are our father's firstborn, claim your inheritance and take it all and be done with it. Please. Do it for me! My inheritance is yours anyway, I don't care about all of that; I am the luckiest man in the world because I inherited you!" The anguish on his face made Solimar decide that she better lighten up the conversation and she said "Saúl, you know that you ain't shit." Saúl raised his eyebrow and shot back "and I'm not ever gonna be shit."

They leisurely strolled hand in hand, taking the long way home, walking along the shore, trying to dry off a bit, the sun high above their heads. Solimar asked if they could stop by Beba's kiosk for a snack; Saúl, knowing his wife quite well realized why she wanted to walk along the shore instead of going straight home. "You're in the mood for a cold one aren't you?" Solimar nodded and Saúl was just as radiant as she was, falling in love with her all over again. "You mind, Papi?" Saúl would be capable of making a treaty with hell itself if his blue-eyed enchantress wanted the unreachable. Fortunately for him, he was very well set and could probably give her things she never imagined she could ask for. "You're a cheap date Solimar. C'mon lets get that brewsky, but no more Coronas. I was reading that the dark beers are helpful with lactation in case you want to breast feed our baby."

"Saúl, where did you read that?"

"Well, I really didn't read it, but I overhead some women talking about it once at a baby shower."

"You know, Saúl, I'm not even going to bother asking you what your ass was doing in some heifer's baby shower."

Saúl laughed and said, "I was about 12 or 13; Esmeralda dragged me along, so I had no choice but to make myself useful so I volunteered to help serve the ladies there, but what I was really doing was eavesdropping and checking out the heifers, as you would call them."

Solimar "obeyed" her husband, and instead of ordering a Corona ordered a Guinness Extra Stout. Beba, so happy to see her favorite customers again, piled on the empanadas filled with crab meat, Solimar's favorite, put down a bucket of ice cold beers and joined them for a friendly chat. Business would not pick up for yet another half hour or so, and for the moment, the threesome enjoyed the beauty of their surroundings while Beba's much younger lover decided to take a break himself and played his congas beachside; music for the soul. Beba commented that she had not seen Lili Anne since the last time they visited together. Saúl explained that Lili Anne was yet again traveling with her husband and wouldn't be back this time for a month or so as the cruise was making five stops before heading to South America. As was customary, Saúl tried to pay Beba double the bill and they fought over the difference between $12.00 and $25.00 pesos. Saúl won this time around, Beba adamantly stating that the next time would be on the house. They hugged and said their good-byes. Solimar now tired, flagged down a *guaguita*, a mini bus that served as local transport for the cost of a dollar, much to Saúl's chagrin and subsequent laughter at himself that his wife could so easily convince him, a diplomat, to ride, knowing in his heart that he would walk through hell in gasoline-drenched drawers so long as he could follow his *brujita* into eternity.

When they got home, Solimar decided it was time to take care of something that had been on her mind. Having already made a decision that would enhance their lives; she decided to effectuate it immediately. Solimar bathed, changed into one of Saúl's V-neck tee shirts that accommodated her bulge just fine and pulled on a pair of white maternity capris. She sat behind Saúl's desk and proceeded to write out a handsome check payable to their housekeeper, Rosario, which amounted to three month's salary. As the lady of the house, she called in Rosario, who hated to be summoned by Solimar. When Rosario appeared, Solimar coldly handed her the check and asked her to please pack up and leave. Saúl was not aware of Solimar's plans, but did not interfere in his wife's decision. The pleas were simple, but adamant. "Please, *por favor*, Señor, I have worked with you for five years now. Your wife has no reason to dismiss me!" Solimar simply said "It is not Saúl's decision anymore. I am *La Señora de esta casa* and there is no room for us both. You have been relieved of all of your duties effective immediately and I have my reasons for making this decision." The housekeeper pressed on and continued to ask why. Her incessant pleas forced Solimar to lose her diplomacy. "*Mira, mujer*, do you want me to tell it to you in Spanish, English or Spanglish? I do not like you and I trust you even less. You have been on the phone with Panamá talking to my in-laws constantly. I may speak imperfect Spanish, but Spanish I do speak and worse for you, I understand it perfectly. You never thought that because I always converse with Saúl in English, but I have heard you refer to me as *la gringa* more than once. Well, get ready, pack up and leave because this *gringa* is full-blooded *Boricua* and knows more about this island's history than you. Now, I'm saying it nicely for the last time. Please pack up and get the hell out of *mi casa*, and if you don't get it, I will be more than happy to tell it to you in one Spanish word. *Fuera!*" Saúl finally intervened gently stating "Rosario, if it is true what my wife has just said, you must leave immediately." Rosario, digging her own grave and throwing the dirt on Saúl's feet said "She is making false accusations against me; there is no way she can prove that!" Saúl said "We are not in a court of law and my wife needs to prove nothing other than the fact that she doesn't trust you and I can clearly see why." Saúl picked up the phone and begun to dial Panamá as the housekeeper cringed, but continued pleading. "No! Your wife *esta loca!* I have done no such thing!" He kept his eyes fixed on Rosario and with the phone to his ear said "We will see." Saúl patiently waited while the phone rang. His mother answered and without a hello he said "Mami, by any chance are you aware of the fact that Solimar and I are married and expecting a child?" His mother, fearing more repercussions, quietly answered "*Si, hijo*. Rosario advised us and since you hadn't called to inform us directly, it was our only way of knowing what was going on."

"Gracias Mami, I will talk to you about this later." Saúl hung up. Solimar did absolutely nothing other than cross her legs and recline in her husband's chair. Rosario, profoundly embarrassed, excused herself and left the room to go pack up her belongings. Saúl took the check that Solimar wrote out and deposited it in the shredder, instructing his wife to void it from the checkbook register. When Rosario had finished packing her belongings, she returned to the study and humbly asked if she could please have her pay. Saúl gave her a week's wage from the cash in his pocket. She then asked about the check Solimar had written out, which would have constituted a severance package. Saúl simply said "That you can get from my parents since you were obviously working for them and not for me." Rosario broke down in tears and begged for her job back, but her plea fell on deaf ears. In her desperation, she cried to Saúl "but you know that I love you and would do anything for you, where am I going to go now, you know my situation?!" Solimar calmly stepped around the desk and took Rosario by the arm. "Saúl, I'm putting out the garbage, I'll be right back!" She escorted Rosario out the door, came back and wheeled out her suitcase and hurled it to the curbside causing it to partially break open. Rosario was uncontrollable and Solimar acidly said to her in crystal clear Spanish *"Si te atreves a volver, te voy a dar una golpiza, la pela de moza que tu madre nunca te dio! Estamos de acuerdo o necesitas que te lo escriba para que te acuerdes?"* (If you dare come around here ever again, the beating that you will get will be the one your mother should have given to you. Do I make myself clear or should I write it down so you don't forget?)

"Si Señora, yo entiendo."

"You're a joke; now I'm *Señora* and now you understand? You had it good here, but you wanted to be a sneaky, down low dirty ass bitch. Don't count on my reference. Should someone call here for it they are only going to get a verification of the length of your employment and a confirmation of your hourly wage, so try not to lie, if only to help yourself." The displaced housekeeper picked up her suitcase, and frightened by Solimar's threat, slowly walked to the corner to wait in the scorching sun to be picked up by the cab she had called who informed her that her car would be there in about an hour. Saúl had been watching the scene through the window. When he saw his wife open the gate, he opened the door. "Come upstairs with me Solimar and I mean I need you to come right now!"

"*Si mi amor*, I am with you every step of the way."

The Santanas spent the afternoon making love, trying to find one another once again. They chatted for hours and began to fall back into their comfort zone, one with the other. "Babe, have you been in touch with Roberto and Marisol?"

"Actually, no, I haven't spoken to them. I called a couple of times, left messages, but they never called back. The last time I spoke to them was right before you showed up in the States. They don't know anything that has transpired in our lives since."

"Well honey girl, let's call them and see what's cooking."

"I feel bad not having stayed in touch with them this long."

"Don't. They needed their space adjusting to their new life and between the four of us it was just too much damn drama. Now we have two pregnant women. That's a lot to digest Solimar. We needed our space too. I'm sure they feel the same way."

"Why don't we just go see them?"

"We cannot do that Solimar. You are six or seven weeks away from giving birth. Your medical treatments are here, and with our bad ass luck, the child will be born in Panamá; not very smart, huh?" Soli wrinkled up her nose. "I'm not so sure I like it that you are calling me Solimar."

"Would you prefer that I keep calling you Bella?" Solimar contemplated deeply, all the while burying herself deeper into her husband's chest. *"No se.* I don't know who or what I am anymore."

"Bella, Sol, Soli, Solita, Solimar, Mamita, Sirena, my Blue-eyed Bruja, you are my wife and I am your husband. What more can I say to make you get over our tragedy and move onto our blessing? Don't you think that I hurt like you, feel like you, cry like you. Puta, men aren't made out of stone! Especially not me! Men are probably weaker than women when it comes to the affairs of the heart, but when you came into my life, I said to myself 'Hell no. She is mine, and I don't care. Love Over Lust!' If you had never slept with me, I'd be okay because I still have you with me, under my roof and if you want to change up and be brother and sister, your wish is my command. Damn it woman, I just want you around me because you make me happy!" Solimar let out a sigh and said "Babe, I thought we were talking about our friends. How do we always get back to this point?"

Saúl got out of bed, took both of Solimar's hands and gently raised her to a seating position. He kissed her forehead, kissed her nose and did what he dared not do before; he unbuttoned her top and suckled her breasts filled with milk, licking a small bit that through his cautious manipulation released itself. Just as Solimar was losing her control, Saúl came to his senses, not sure if his sucking was causing Solimar discomfort, yet wanting to suck more. Saúl buried his head between her breasts and said "Come Mamita, let's give them a ring," the delicate taste of freshly drawn milk still on his lips.

They both went on to Saúl's study, never even bothering to throw on a robe, enjoying one of the many benefits of not having Rosario around. They reveled in their nudity because they adored one another. Saúl dialed and handed the phone to his wife.

"Residencia Robles."

"Hola Lydia."

"Solimar!" Lydia squealed and immediately put them on speaker phone and Marisol and Roberto came running when they heard Lydia utter Solimar's name. "Where in the hell are you Sol?" Mari asked. "I'm in Puerto Rico, here in the land of the coquis and bad ass bitches."

"Did he find you?"

"Did who find me?" Solimar asked playfully. "Don't play with me Solimar Santana!" Saúl laughed "Of course I found her!"

Roberto yelled out "Oh shit. Is he there with you right now?"

"Didn't you just hear him? My husband is sitting right next to me, patiently waiting to speak to you Roberto." Lydia broke out first. "I knew it! I knew it! Thank you God, Thank you Jesus and all you other people that make dreams come true!" Marisol asked "Soli, you and Saúl are really like married? How did that happen, *amiga*?"

"Well, I guess it was a shot gun wedding. When he found out that I was pregnant, he forced me to come back to Puerto Rico with him so I forced him to marry me in return. We took a cruise to Puerto Rico because we didn't want to endanger the baby by flying, so we had our honeymoon first and got married in el Mar, *Marisol*. The captain of the ship married us." Everyone began talking at once. One hundred and one questions filled the air. The Santanas promised to visit as soon as the baby was born, which was only a short time away. They figured that they both must have gotten knocked up that very same night Saúl carried Mari to Roberto's bed or at any rate, right around the same time. They laughed, cried and told one another how much they missed each other. Seizing the moment, Lydia confessed that she had been the one to tell all to Saúl, and Solimar chided that she had just fired a nosy housekeeper for blowing the whistle on them. Roberto suggested that the men call each other from another line and let the women speak; after all they were dominating the conversation. Following Roberto's suggestion, Saúl went to the home office phone and dialed Roberto's cell phone, which was immediately answered. A couple of hours went by before they all ended their conversations happy and content.

For the next several weeks, they talked daily and emailed each other pictures and words of encouragement. The friendship was back, which was a good thing because Saúl had to travel to Panamá on embassy business and Solimar felt better that he would stay with their friends instead of with their family.

It was two weeks before her due date and Soli was missing everybody, most of all her husband. Once again, tanning on the beach, her now giant belly exposed to the sun, she patted her stomach and said "Well, kid, it's you and me again; I hope you are a boy, but if you are a girl, you will be just as awesome." Solimar rested the headphones to her IPod on her belly, believing strongly that music is a good influence for babies still in vitro. She had begun to doze off when she heard the distant cry of her name. She was too tired, too spent to even get up. It wasn't that easy these days with an extra 49 pounds on her ass, that actually now looked like one. She ignored the voice inside of her head, but the voices grew closer. Solimar pulled her weight, got up and turned around. Soli squinted and shielded her eyes. Her eyes must had been deceiving her, but no they weren't ... There was Saúl, Roberto, Marisol and Lydia slowly approaching her. Soli begun to cry and Marisol was already bawling. They tried to hug, but their bellies were too big. Lydia was a puddle of tears and Roberto just smiled as did Saúl. Soli asked "What are you guys doing here?"

"I wanted our child to be born on American soil even if we are forced to stay in Panamá because of me. I don't want what happened to me to someday happen to my child so Saúl and Roberto worked something out with the embassy through Saúl's connections. Once he is born, the child will have dual citizenship."

"You guys are freaking amazing."

"No" said Roberto. "You women are something else. You changed our lives."

The five joined hands in no particular fashion and walked towards the sun and sea or could just be the sea and sun. Solimar and Marisol realized their womanhood, babies about ready to make their appearances, men that adored them by their side and they all enjoyed a bit of a swim, the two girls splashing water, never leaving each other's side. The paradox of Sol y Mar/Mar y Sol unfolded before them on the edge of forever. Back at the house, Lydia yelled "Hey Soli, need a housekeeper?" Soli hadn't lifted a finger since firing "the informant." Soli grinned. "Wanna job?" Mari and Roberto balked. "No Mamita, I got a good one with benefits." The check that Soli had written out as severance pay, Saúl had already reissued payable to Lydia and the stash was safe in her purse. When the four woke up the following morning, the house shined, was filled with flowers in just about every corner, an assortment of fine scented candles strategically stationed for future use and the aroma of a home cooked breakfast banquet left warming in silver chafing platters. Lydia slept, as she had worked diligently throughout the night, leaving the bedrooms for today. The four friends sat down to breakfast and they all served one another. As they enjoyed their meal and each other once again, Solimar came up with a brilliant idea. "Hey, I just got a great idea!"

"Oh boy, here we go" said Roberto.

"Papi?"

"Oh shit, here it comes. She never calls me that."

"Papito. Can we go to Panamá when the baby comes? We can live there and go back and forth."

"Yeahhhhh" chimed in Mari, excited by the idea. "Maybe you can get dual citizenship too!" Soli and Mari high-fived each other and Roberto shook his head enjoying their antics. Saúl raked his hair and said "Bella, you are the wife of a diplomat. That means that we can go anywhere, anytime and stay as long as we want. Yes, we can go to Panamá and live there and come back and forth." Solimar looked at her man with pride and love. "You go Papi, you blue-eyed devil!" Marisol, supremely at peace and happy to be among the people she most loved said "Hey Soli, we are in our last trimester, we can drink! Want a Mimosita?"

"Hell to the 19th power! Hell yeah!" Marisol happily prepared the Mimosa and the three drank a full pitcher. Roberto declined, but had a *malta* instead. Lydia walked in, rollers in hair, declaring to Soli and Mari that they weren't worth much with their pregnant drinking asses and threatening them with her 'hangover remedy.'

They spent the next week and a half loving each other in different ways, baby shopping, sightseeing, taking in the beauty that is Puerto Rico, its riches, its warmth, the rain forest, as well as the cobblestone streets of Old San Juan, but mostly hanging out by the beach, frequenting Beba's kiosk. Beba loved to feed the pregnant ladies, always heaping more on their plate and never failing to say to Solimar "you remind me of a friend I had many years ago when I lived in the States. She always laughed like you and drank a glass of beer with sugar in it." Roberto fell in love with Beba and took it upon himself to purchase beautiful plants and flowers to adorn her plain little hut.

One balmy Caribbean night, Soli got a light knock on her bedroom door as she was taking inventory of what, if anything, she still needed to purchase for the baby. "Come in." Marisol opened the door and stood there with a pained look on her face. Solimar immediately knew. "Are you in labor?"

"Soli, I don't know yet. I just feel funny."

"Funny ha, ha or funny oh-oh?" Mari let out a small moan. Solimar sounded the alarm at the top of her lungs. "Let's go everybody, Marisol is in labor!"

"Soli! What are you doing?! It could just be something I ate!" Soli looked at her like she was crazy. "That's not the end I'm worried about." While Solimar pulled her hair back in a pony tail she said "Mari, we are too old to be taking chances here. Now get moving before I punch you in your head!" She escorted her back to her room to pick up her "hospital suitcase." Within minutes, everybody was in Saúl's limo on their way to Auxilio Mutuo Hospital. Solimar's doctor was already there when they arrived.

After she was admitted, the doctor appeared and gave the others his prognosis with a broad smile on his face. "Yep. The little woman is in labor, but it is going to be a long wait. She is only three centimeters dilated. You can take her home and come back tomorrow or you can sit around and wait."

"We're staying." Lydia said defiantly. Roberto and Saúl knew that there would be no arguing with Lydia's decision. The long wait commenced with the ticking of the clock in the waiting room and the sweep of the never ending minute hand. Saúl managed to get a bed for his pregnant wife, Lydia fell asleep on a chair and the men stayed up, visibly ill. The nurse came and asked for Mari's birthing coach. Roberto ran down the hall with the nurse and Saúl went to Solimar to awaken her. He found Solimar pacing back and forth reciting her rosary for her friend's life and that of the child. "Mamacita?" Solimar held her hand up to silence him. "Wait, I'm on the Mystery of the Nativity." She finished her decade and Saúl pulled out a black string of beads. "Come on; let's finish the whole thing....together." They went back and forth, finished the remaining two decades and joined hands. They walked to the waiting room to find Roberto dumbfounded. "What's up bro; what are you doing here, *que paso?*" Roberto threw up his hands, shaking his head, but unresponsive. "What?" Saúl demanded. "Marisol doesn't want me in there. She wants Solimar!" Lydia understood perfectly what was going on, but there was no time to explain the dynamics of a woman in labor to these two knuckleheads. She pulled out a little video camera from her large handbag and offered it to Roberto. "Listen. Let Soli coach her and that way you can videotape the whole thing." Saúl nodded in agreement and Roberto, mumbling something under his breath snatched the video recorder from Lydia. Solimar and Roberto both took to the room, to find their girl perspiring and panting like a dog. Roberto stood back and begun to film the birth of his child. A contraction took hold of Marisol and she let loose a string of profanity that would make a longshoreman blush, screaming *chucha madre* as if it was the only word in her vocabulary! She begun to vomit, soaking Solimar's hospital gown and Roberto thought to himself; 'If her head starts to spin, fuck this, I'm out of here!' Marisol focused on the prism created by Solimar's engagement ring reflecting off of the metal lamp as Solimar wiped her brow. Ever so tenderly, Soli instructed her to focus on her face and breathe. As Marisol begun to push, she bit down on Solimar's hand. Soli never felt the pain. She only felt the connection between her and this woman she considered to be a sister. Their son, Roberto Saúl Robles, weighed in at eight pounds even. Within minutes of his birth, Saúl and Lydia were right at Marisol's bedside, once again laughing and crying. Marisol was scheduled to be sent home within 24 hours and they all agreed to wait for her at home, except for Roberto who, of course, was already feeding his son in the nursery.

Solimar's due date was days away. She was too excited with the new baby and her friends living all under one roof to even notice that her time was quickly approaching. They all took turns feeding the baby. Marisol slept well and was recuperating rather nicely, her newborn sleeping peacefully in the nursery that Solimar had set up for her own child.

When Robertito was all of three days old and in his future godmother's arms for his morning feeding, Solimar yelled for help. She felt this awful need to throw up and when she looked down, she realized that she was drenched from the waist down. Her water bag broke with no warning. Roberto came running, took his son and the bottle from her hand as the others followed. Solimar was sweating profusely and started pushing and pushing hard. Lydia said "Oh shit, we aren't going to make it to the hospital!" She ran to get clean linens and put on a pot of water to boil. There was no time to even get Solimar back to her bedroom as she couldn't climb the stairs. Saúl was frantic calling for the doctor as her due date was still a week away. Mari and Roberto were frozen, but somehow they all managed to lay down a few pillows and a quilt. Saúl tore Solimar's clothes off and there once again, laid this creature before this man's eyes in naked splendor, this time giving birth to his child. He stood there and marveled at her beauty. Soli tried to make light of the situation by saying to Saúl; "What are you staring at you blue-eyed beast; can't you see I'm giving birth?" Saúl nervously tried hard to stifle his laughter. Roberto turned his head and started to walk away, embarrassed. Solimar cried "Don't go Roberto. Stay with us please." Lydia carefully draped Solimar with a white sheet that ended up something of a crimson red and Saúl got down on the floor, his face in between his woman's legs. There he saw the baby's head crowning. "Where the fuck is that fucking motherfucking *hijo de puta, maricon* fucking doctor?!" Lydia said "Saúl, *calmate*, okay? Even if the doctor shows up right now, there is no way an ambulance is going to take her. She is going to give birth right here, so please, do what you can. Nothing bad is going to happen. Do I make myself clear?" Solimar was strangely calm and even laughed at Saúl's outburst causing Marisol to start laughing too. "Babe, don't worry about it; the baby will get here soon. Just try to help guide the baby out if you see him or her stuck." Saúl pulled the sheet from off his head and said "What the hell do you mean stuck?" Solimar said "Don't tell me that you didn't read the birthing manual I gave you!" Roberto took that as a signal and went for the trusted video camera, and quietly started filming the absolute delicious madness. Even Robertito had quieted down and was on the floor, keeping Solimar good company, waiting for his 'play cousin' to hurry up and show up. His mother had placed him by Soli's face to coach her. Hickey crawled by and hid under the sofa, sticking her neck out, watching. Solimar was too overwhelmed with pain to scream, but she bore down and pushed forth some more. Saúl Omar Roberto Santana was born. The total labor took all of fifty minutes. "It's a boy!" Saúl screamed, tears falling from his eyes. "Marisol! Solimar! we have another son!"

"Leave him attached to the cord until the doctor comes." Solimar weakly whispered.

"I can cut it." Lydia offered. "No, Ma. I don't want the kid to have an outie. He already got a bunch of shit against him."

"Solimar Santana! Our son is perfect and he has our eyes!"

"Duh!" she responded. "Now will somebody light me a damn cigarette?" Roberto went running and came back with a lit cigarette, puffing hard on it, although he had given up smoking.

She reached for it with her trembling hand and brought it to her mouth. After a puff, she said "A drink would be nice and since it is morning Lydia please make us a pitcher of your fabulous peach champagne cocktail and leave out the peach nectar in mine! My pussy and ass are on fire!"

"Solimar Santana! The baby is still attached to you!"

"He'll be fine, I promise." Lydia shook her head because she knew what was coming next. Soli took another drag of her cigarette when she felt another contraction. "What the fuck!" she exclaimed. "Am I having twins?" Lydia shook her head. *"No loca...* It's the afterbirth!" Lydia cleaned Soli up and remarked "Maybe you should have read the birth manual!"

The doctor walked in shortly to find the motley crew, one laid out, naked baby hanging out of her "private," resting atop of a pillow, the others drinking, taking turns filming each other and Robertito fast asleep on the sofa. They did have "some" common sense. "What the...?" Saúl immediately cut him off. "Doctor, don't breathe a word. *Ni una palabra.* Just cut the motherfucking cord and don't bother sending me the bill. I'll pay you cash. How much is it for an umbilical cord cut?" The doctor, a bit taken by Saúl's irritation said *"Nada."* He went to work right away and as soon as the baby was separated from his mother, the doctor ignored Saúl's rather crass and erroneous implication that he was there only to perform an 'umbilical cut.' He gave the baby a thorough checkup, checking his lungs and his heartbeat before cutting the cord. He knew better than to argue about the time it took to get there or the fact that he had just performed a C-section on a fourteen year girl whose vaginal canal was too narrow to deliver a nine pound baby, deciding wisely that discretion was the better part of valor, but he wasn't about to leave either. It was his responsibility to make sure that mother and child were fine.

Marisol protectively snatched the crying baby from the doctor and started wiping him down with baby wipes, warmer and all. Lydia, who had been pacing up and down, exploded at Marisol. "What in the hell are you doing?" Marisol replied "I'm wiping the baby down, can't you see?" Lydia said "Give me that baby before I slap the tan off of you!" Marisol, a bit confused asked "What do you mean?" Lydia said "Either you hand over the baby or take his newborn ass to the kitchen sink and give him a proper bath!" Marisol bathed her soon to be godson under Lydia's supervision, using a brand new bar of good old fashioned Ivory soap. She quickly diapered, wrapped and swaddled him and gave him to his mother. Lydia placed one of her many knitted caps on his head giving Marisol a nasty look. By then, Solimar had been moved to a rocking chair; Saúl had long since managed to get her into one of his summer robes. "Saúl. The ambulance is outside waiting."

"Go to hell doctor. Women have been drinking, smoking, fucking and having babies at home from since the beginning of time. My son is perfect and we aren't going anywhere." Everyone was a bit shocked that Solimar spoke to the respected doctor in this fashion. She pulled out her left tit, the one with the beauty mark on it, and shoved it into the newborn's mouth. Instinctively, he suckled and Soli rocked back and forth and cried painful tears of joy. The doctor pulled Saúl to the side and said "Saúl, I realize that you are a bit put off right now, but I must insist. You know we have to do tests and we need to see if the baby tore Solimar's vagina so we can stitch her up. If you want, I will wait until Solimar feeds the baby and I can examine her." Solimar, elated, disgusted and pissed off at the doctor for no good reason crassly stated "My vagina done been torn up, doctor, so for my son to have done it is a pleasure for me. What you can do is prescribe some damn painkillers and don't make it the cheapy kind either. I need some damn morphine or something!"

Saul reasoned. "Doctor, *que sera*, already is. My wife is not ready. We will go tomorrow."

"*Bien.*" With that the doctor, took out his prescription pad and wrote out a prescription for a mild sedative that would help Solimar sleep through the night, having observed that she opted to breast feed. He handed the prescription to Saúl, offered his congratulations and unobtrusively let himself out, realizing that there was no way he could examine her in her current emotional state. He would have to wait until after her hormonal rage subsided and hope for the best.

Saúl momentarily slipped into his study and made a phone call the minute the dust settled. "The *Ibeyis* are here; Victor will pick you up the day after tomorrow, just follow his lead."

Dedication

Saúl Omar Roberto lay comfortably on his mother's chest, as did Roberto Saúl on Marisol's lap. The women were having quiet time on the porch, twin rocking chairs, a gift from Roberto, and cherubs in diapers; not just any diapers, but the real diapers made out of the finest blend of linen and cotton, safety pins on each side. Lydia insisted that disposable diapers were only to be used right after the kids were fed and when they went out for the day. She had a theory that in twenty years or so, a report was going to come out that disposable diapers would be the cause of male sterility and she didn't want the boys to be part of a class action suit. She called Victor early one morning and went into town with him to purchase an unglazed giant barrel that she filled with water and bleach and set up a clothes line in the backyard. She did not mind the washing of the diapers and did so by hand on a wash board in a tin tub that she had also purchased on her private excursion. Nobody dared to challenge her, although when she was setting up this whole project, the four commented amongst themselves that she was going overboard, but they loved that she loved their babies to this degree and said nothing to the contrary. While Solimar and Marisol chatted about the wonders of Lydia, the limo pulled up and Solimar arose to greet Victor expecting that he would be bringing her husband home for lunch. Saúl could not spend one moment away from the newborn if he didn't have to, and always came home for lunch and even breaks when his days were longer than expected. He did all he could to adhere to the children's feeding schedule. Victor opened the door to the car and Olaya appeared looking as regal as ever in a white pantsuit and a Panamanian hat.

"Olaya?"

"Yes." Marisol looked at Olaya and then at Soli. "Is this the Olaya you told me about?" Solimar was steadfast and rooted, having forgotten their deal. Olaya cautiously walked over, keeping her eye on Solimar's reaction. When she reached the porch she turned to Marisol and said "Yes, I am that Olaya. You must be Marisol, the mirror of my friend."

"Well, I don't know about all that, she has a real mirror, but yes, I am Marisol." Marisol's wit did not escape Olaya's comprehension causing her to smile broadly. "May I come in?" Solimar handed the baby to Mari, leaving Mari with her hands full. She ran to Olaya squealing loudly as Roberto and Lydia came to see what was causing all of the commotion. The women hugged long enough for Saúl to show up with a grin on his face and joined the women in their hug. Lydia yelled out "C'mon guys and stop eating shit, we have work to do!"

That night, they ate al fresco, in the backyard, which was once a haven for Saúl's lady friends, away from the hustle and bustle of Isla Verde. Saúl was able to relate more and more with each passing day to Roberto, remembering how pleased Roberto felt to have all of these people in his house. Saúl didn't say much because he had the greatest gift of all: Peace and the most beautiful wife in the world. Marisol and Roberto, who were just as intrigued by Olaya as Solimar was when she first met her, asked thousands of questions.

Lydia blurted out and said "I knew it. I knew it, I knew it. I knew the minute these two blue-eyed devils walked into our lives, that there would be more people following. Roberto and I have been alone for so long, we have forgotten about everything except each other. Now, we have a family and it keeps growing." Olaya touched by Lydia asked her "May I ask, where are you from?"

"Oh, I'm from Panamá; this is my first trip ever, I have never been anywhere except for now." Olaya patiently repeated the question "Where are you from?" Lydia nervously said "I really don't know. They tried to tell me a story that my family comes from a place like in Africa – oh man, what's the name - it sort of sounds like shrimp in Spanish!

Olaya asked "Could it be Cameroon?"

"Yes, yes, that's it, but all I know was that I was born in Panamá, that is what my birth certificate says even though I do not know how to read, only a little bit and my father's mother raised me with what she calls the Silver People, but I had to go to work when I was eleven as Roberto's babysitter, so I didn't have time to go to school. His parents picked me because they did not plan on having more children and wanted Roberto to have someone old enough to care for him, but young enough to play with. When I was fourteen, his parents died. They were drunk and fighting together, you know, so I just stayed with him right there in the house we still live in today. He was three years old. A letter came with money for him, but nobody else came to tell me what to do, so I got the idea to go to the Silver People Place where they read to me the letter and they made sure I went to the office where the lawyer was. Oh my God, I was so nervous. That day, I remember, I had not too much nice things to wear so I said "God, please don't strike me dead, but I'm going to take a piece of clothes from Señora Robles even though she is now in heaven. I found the most beautiful pollera. Come and think about it, it was probably too fancy to go to a meeting, but I really didn't think about it like that back then. I still have it; only thing I kept about her. She must have worn it when she was my age at the time because it fit like it was made just for me. Oh, I tell you, I felt divine and fine as wine. I fixed my hair like they do and put flowers and everything into it. And you know since I have kinky hair, a lady from the foundation came to show me how to straighten it out and looking back now, she did a pretty good job. I still have the hot comb, but haven't used it much now that they have the products." Nobody said a word. Lydia was gushing out her story and they were all enthralled. "I did not know anything about making up the face, I still don't know, but I found some lipstick and put that on too. I took my little boy, dressed him in black shorts and a red top and turned his collar up. I scrubbed his face until it was all shiny. I made sure his hair was combed real nice too. I don't know how I knew, but I fixed his hair in finger wave style, until I found out later that the hairstyle was for girls, but he was cute as a button. I got there with the help of the many good, nice people from the Silver Place and the lawyer explained everything to me and told me that if I took responsibility for Roberto, I would be fine, so I agreed. The Silver People helped me to understand how to count money and do the shopping. They came to the house to teach me how to read and write and help me, so I learned to go to the schools when it was time for Roberto to go and how to pay the taxes for the house and Roberto, if you want, I can show you all the papers when we get back home, everything from the receipts from the grocery store to your tuition payments dating back to when you were three years old. But wait! Here, let me show you, I have the paper from the tribunal place they took me to because they told me that I always had to keep it in my pocketbook just in case anything happened that nobody would think I kidnapped Roberto and to prove in the school and to the doctors that I had authority to make decisions."

  Roberto got up from his chair and watched her run to the guest room assigned to her. Anticipating already what she was about to deliver, he walked to the breakfront and poured himself a stiff drink. Saúl walked over and said "Put that shit down, man. Save it for later. This is no reason to fall off the wagon." The two of them, having law degrees knew what was about to come. Solimar joined the trio, also anticipating what was coming up, but said "Listen you two, I don't think it's going to be that bad. Relax and let her come back with whatever she wants to show. Don't jump to conclusions, okay?" The trio went back to the table. Marisol not knowing what to expect became angsty and Olaya held her peace. Lydia returned with a parchment document that she had long since laminated because it was falling apart. The document bore a gold seal and stated that she had legally adopted Roberto. She handed the document to Olaya, who immediately, without a glance, passed it to Roberto.

"Nana, do you understand this paper?"

"No, I can't read too much, but they explained to me that I can take care of you and that I am ... *como se dice* ... your legal guardian." Roberto said "No, that is not what it says. It means that you are my legal mother. You adopted me officially and I am your son and Robertito is your grandson by law." Lydia stunned by this revelation stated "Well how can that be? I was a minor!"

"If what I'm surmising here is correct, my parents must have willed me to you; I'll look over the legalities when we get back home. So it seems to me that the courts had no choice but to honor their Will because it went unchallenged! That is why the Silver People helped you until you reached the majority of age; they appointed the foundation as your legal guardian until you reached your majority, which is when you officially became my mother. Oh my God! This judge was a fucking genius! He applied every loophole in order to protect and honor my parents' dying wishes! Lydia again stunned said "Well, I guess that means, it means that I cannot be the godmother to Robertito if I am legally his grandmother." Roberto started crying openly. "Mami, Robertito has a godmother already and you know that tomorrow when we go to the sea, it will be Olaya and when we do the Catholic baptism, it will be Solimar, but you are his grandmother and you will never, ever again clean, cook or do housework here. You're not hired help, you are my mother!" Lydia rubbed her head as if this gesture would stay the impending headache, and said "Son, do not take my work away from me; it is all I have to live for." Olaya cautiously stepped in and said, "This is not your job; it is your calling. If your son wants to spoil you, let him. You got him through law school and God only knows what else. You never did anything that did not revolve around him. It is time to enjoy the fruits of your labor. Your freedom has come and God has seen it fit to reward you richly with a son." Roberto hugged his mom and cried in her arms. Lydia was confused by all of this, but rocked Roberto back and forth, soothingly saying *"Nene,* it's alright, I've only been like your mom anyway so please calm yourself." When Roberto simmered down and Marisol put out a fresh pitcher of Sangria on the table, Solimar gently asked "Lydia, have you ever been married? Had a boyfriend?"

"What do you mean?" The women looked at each other, figuring that Lydia was still a virgin, having dedicated her life to Roberto. Mari cut in and asked "Can we go shopping tomorrow?"

"For what?" asked Lydia obviously nervous and irritated by Mari's stupidity. "For starters, we can shop for a new housekeeper; clothing; toys, anything." Solimar raised an eyebrow, Saúl walked outside to smoke a cigar, but turned right back around before even lighting it. He just kept playing with it in his mouth. Olaya said "Well, I have been planning the trip of my dreams all of my life, and frankly, this is as good a time as any. After leaving you guys, I firmly decided that I will not put off my dream a moment longer; I'm going straight to Africa from here." She turned to Lydia. "How about if I take you with me on this trip and we can explore our roots together?" Lydia, for the first time in forever was speechless. She turned to Roberto for a sign of approval. "No problem" Roberto said. "You guys can go as soon as we get these two kids dipped in water." Saúl timidly asked Olaya "Can we baptize the twins the day after tomorrow at sunrise?"

"Of course we will." Saúl gratefully said "Don't worry ladies, I will call my office and have you booked on the next flight to Nigeria and get accommodations for you, which could be as soon as Monday."

"Macho. Get on that right away; I appreciate that. We will take care of the financial matter later. The sooner they go, the sooner they will be back." Saúl said "Sure, man, let me just get in a couple of questions." Turning his attention to Olaya he asked "Are you financially able to make this trip?"

"I've saved up all of my life for it and I left everything back home squared away for the next four months. The minute I got your call, I knew that once I was on that plane, I may not want to go back just yet, but rather keep on going, for a while anyway." Saúl asked his final question. "Do you ladies want to have private rooms or would you rather share?"

"Share" they simultaneously answered. Saúl smiled and said "Let me call Jessica, she'll handle all of the arrangements" and left the room to attend to the business at hand. Roberto, turning his attention back to his mother, a million and one questions running through his mind asked "Mami, why did you keep this to yourself all of these years?" Lydia shrugged and said "Son, what was there to tell? I didn't know that I am your mother, like you say the paper says and I was waiting for you to come of age so I can give you the papers and the bank accounts, but you never asked and then got too busy with the drinking, so I waited for the right time. I was also very selfish Roberto, I didn't want to leave your side and figured once you got all of your bank records, you'd dismiss me, yet you never asked, never questioned about your parents or their Will, so I just kept on living with you, doing what I was told to do because I loved doing it. I love you with all of my heart, *hijo*. Did I do something wrong?" Lydia was petrified, thinking she had messed up. Roberto hung his head, nodded and said "Yes Mom, but your wrong could never feel so right." They stared at each other from across the table, neither one knowing how to step into that definitive hug that bonded them since always. The roundtable meeting ended in silent awe.

The following day, at Marisol's suggestion, they went on a shopping frenzy. While the women looked at christening clothing, Olaya kept telling them no, no, no ... that the kids were to be offered naked. They went to all of the spiritual shops known as *botanicas* they could find in Isla Verde, and Olaya even suggested Loiza Aldea, but that idea got vetoed. Olaya purchased every oil, incense, prayer book and flower imaginable. Satisfied with her stock, she then took off with Lydia into a boutique that specialized in plus sizes. After the frantic shopping spree, Lydia and Olaya went to get their hair done along with manicures and pedicures for their impending trip, piling their purchases into the trunk of the limousine, dismissing the rest having decided that they would take a cab back home when done. When they arrived to the house, they were met with a stream of "ooohhhhs," "ahhhhhhs" and "oolalas."

The meeting of the roundtable settled into the business of the dedication/baptism matter, and Olaya handed them each a list of African names to dedicate the children with. Marisol toiling with the piece of paper asked "Why do we have to do this?" Olaya raised an eyebrow and said "Girl you starting to work an angle and one of my nerves. You're Catholic aren't you?" Before Mari could answer she said "Even Catholics take on names in the ceremony they call the Confirmation. What is your Confirmation name?"

"Milagros."

"Okay Miracle, see the connection? Pick a godly name for your son." Saúl raked his hair; this was starting to get hot. He went for the cigar he did not smoke the night before. Soli got up for a glass of water and Roberto said, "*Mi amor*, we don't have to do this if you feel uncomfortable about it. We can just go to the Stone Church over there and baptize our son in the traditional way." Marisol picked up her son and said "I have to excuse myself. I know nothing of what I am doing here and would prefer to not agitate anyone anymore, so I'm going to rest with my child." Roberto excused himself and followed his fiancée up to their bedroom. Saúl whispered into Solimar's ear and she nodded in agreement. He turned to Lydia and Olaya and said, "Listen, we are going upstairs too to finish our project. I think it might be better if we order in tonight and everybody keep to themselves, what do you think?" Olaya said "If it is alright with Lydia, I will handle the kitchen. I'll bring you guys something to eat when it is ready. You are wise beyond your years Saúl. Spiritual matters are very delicate and raise doubt, fear and confusion, among the ignorant or should I say the unlearned." Saúl lit his cigar and thought to himself; 'Spiritual matters my ass! There are way too many 'Alpha Females' in this house!'

Lydia said "Come on Oli, let's see what we can do in the kitchen. These two mommies are starting to get a little bitchy and they need some food to calm their nerves down." Saúl kissed them both and within the hour they were all taken up a serving tray with a mountain of grilled vegetables, brown rice and steamed codfish together with a handwritten invitation to meet out front at 5:00 a.m. No RSVP required. Lydia took her meal with Olaya out back. They stayed up well into the night doing what mothers do, watching vigil and fantasizing a bit about their dream trip, imagining what Africa could feel and sound like, picturing muscular men built like thoroughbreds, black skin offset by clothing as white as snow and otherwise thanking God for this chance to go see for themselves. Hickey had come out of hiding and grazed Olaya's foot taking a playful bite out of her heel. Olaya picked up Hickey and Lydia said "Oh shoot! I forgot all about Solimar's pet!"

"Well it seems like Solimar's pet hasn't forgotten me!"

Confused Lydia asked "You know Hickey?"

"Girl, Hickey or whatever you wanna call her, kept me company since my husband's death until the pregnant blue-eyed one showed up and fell in love with the darn turtle. I'll tell you all about it on the plane, girl, we've got loads to keep us busy on that long haul we are about to take."

Sunday morning arrived and the crew found themselves walking caravan style to the beach at sunrise, Marisol, Roberto and baby in tow. When they got to Piñones, the beach of Isla Verde, Marisol approached Olaya and apologized for her outburst. Olaya, in kind, responded "All that anybody does in the world is by faith. Truth of the matter is we should have done this …. Hmmm, let's see, I think it is seven days after the girls are born, nine days after the boys and eight days for twins. But in my heart, I know God really does accept the sacrifices of simpletons like us. I really am not sure myself exactly how to do this. I have no children of my own, but we try to please God, however, you think you can do it. There is no right or wrong way to thank God for his blessings. So, do you wanna thank Him?

"Yes, I most certainly do."

"Did you pick a name?" Mari kissed her son on his forehead and he giggled and cooed.

"Taiwo" Marisol said proudly.

"Why did you pick that name?"

"He was the first of the Divine Twins, the Ibeyis to be born and although our children are not technically twins; they practically are." Saúl stepped in and said "Wow Mari, I'm impressed! Great minds think alike. We chose Kehinde, the second of the cosmic twins to be born." Lydia shyly stepped in quietly and asked "May I dedicate my son too?"

"Well, I don't think you can hold him up, but we can improvise and dip him in water. Have you chosen a name?"

"Yes, I have a name for him." They all patiently stared while Lydia composed herself and said, "I would like to give my son the name Tokunbo. It means "parents overseas when child is born."

"Why did you choose that name?"

"I chose it because his parents were over the seas, in heaven, when I became his mother."

Olaya took each child in turn from his mother and handed him to their respective fathers. The men were shirtless wearing simple white shorts and donning white caps. They waded into the living waters as she walked behind each man waist deep into the ocean. Olaya watching, praying as the father lifted the child onto the heavens thanking God, the Saints and Angels and making a lifetime commitment to instruct the children in the faith of believing that God does, in fact, exist, commending them to their unknown Guardian Angel and thanking that Angel for their safe delivery from the spiritual realm into the material realm.

"Heavenly Father, we approach your throne with thanksgiving in our hearts and praises upon our lips to offer these gifts that you have given us back to you. We pray your blessings upon Taiwo and Kehinde and upon each and every person that will be instrumental in their lives. In gratitude and humility we ask that you never forsake us, but give us the clarity of mind and tenderness of heart needed to raise these children in accordance with your perfect will and divine providence. We pray their Guardian Angels guide them and take control of their lives, for the length of their lives that you have already pre-determined. I, Olaya, daughter of Yemaya, commend these children onto you so that you may be glorified by the Work of Your Hands as You knitted them in their mothers' wombs and know what their path in life is. I pray this with faith, conviction and sincerity in my heart, soul and mind believing that Your Will be done over their lives, together with my witness who trusts that I believe that you are the Most High God and no harm will befall these families that come so humbly before Your Glorious Presence for a blessing that is to last a lifetime, so be it." Slowly, but surely, the "Amens" started to roll off of each tongue. Solimar and Marisol hovered together. Neither said a word of value other than Amen, but stood in admiration of what they had just witnessed, their matching white floor length cover ups flapping in the breeze; their heads wrapped in white turbans. The men, touched by the simple ceremony, waded back and handed over their children to their mothers who had been solemnly waiting, holding hands. Lydia contemplated this marvelous sight and inspiring moment, but kept her emotions to herself knowing that there was still one child left to be offered. She turned to her son, Roberto, and asked "Are you ready?" He nodded simply with tears forming around his dark eyes and with him in the middle, Lydia and Olaya walked hand in hand back into the water, looking towards the heavens. Lydia said "Wait! Let me slip off these little shorts here, so he could be naked like the babies." Roberto yelled "Ma!" looking back where the others stood, but then said "What the hell, I've already seen Solimar giving birth, Saúl caught a glimpse of Mari's ass when he bought her to the bed for me. Go ahead, just do it!" Lydia slipped down his shorts to his knees and together they held his frame, closed off his nostrils and dipped him into the water three times ... one for each face of God. When they had finished, everybody took turns dipping themselves into the ocean, basking in the soft, warm waves and caring even less that the sky was growing darker instead of lighter. As they laughed and enjoyed themselves, bolts of lighting flashed across the sky and they ran for safety. Olaya simply said "Chango and Oya are happy. They are playing now, but we must run for cover because they play hard!"

"Is Yemaya happy?" asked Solimar.

"Don't you see child that even in the storm the ocean is tranquil? This was not an offering to Yemaya, but to God himself, whatever name you choose to call him, to me he is Olofi." The others just responded in kind by keeping quiet.

At home, they were met with a delicious fare that Marisol had secretly ordered to be catered the night before. She ordered a variety of delicacies from the French restaurant she had noticed while shopping near el Hotel Miramar, and she had arranged for it to be delivered and set up while they were all at the beach. They ate quietly, feeding each other, even eating with their hands. They ate while sitting on the floor on *esteras*, prayer mats that Olaya purchased the day before. The children peacefully slept wherever they were laid to rest. Saúl broke silence. "Señora Lydia, Miss Olaya, there is a private plane waiting for you to take you tomorrow to the Ivory Coast."

"Why private?" Lydia inquired.

"For your comfort; it is an excruciatingly long flight and I wanted you to have better amenities than could be provided in a first class cabin on a commercial flight. A tour guide that will never leave your side except at night will be waiting for you when you arrive and another will replace him when night falls." Lydia beamed as did Olaya. "C'mon Lydia, let's get it together because miracles like this don't happen every day." Roberto took his mother's hand in his and gently said "Nana. Take as long as you need. A plane has been reserved to bring you home whenever you're ready. I will be counting the days until you get back, but I know you need to know things and learn things and if you want to go to school, I will make sure you get the education you deserve, like you made sure that I got educated." Lydia simply said "I am going to take time, but I will be home in time for you guys." Marisol just couldn't take it anymore. She was bawling like a baby and literally screaming "How the hell are we gonna live without each other? I mean, you guys are going to Africa, we have to go back to Panamá, the kids will be separated, this is a mess, a bloody, bloody damn mess I tell you and I ain't happy at all. I'm sorry if I sound selfish, but I don't like it. As a matter of fact, I hate it!" Roberto took his woman in his arms, surrounded by Soli and Saúl and said "Ñeca, we got this. Saúl and I came up with a plan. We got us an architect who is working on the specifications as we speak. We are going to build identical houses here and back home. Soli and Saúl will have their own space, you and I will have our own space, Lydia will have her own space and the twins will share a room until they get older. We will also have three guest rooms, one for Olaya if she agrees to come along and the two for whomever of our families or friends decides they want to stop by for a while. We gonna have identical dining rooms, kitchens and family rooms. We even got a landscaper to do our backyards and porches just the same that way when we move from place to place, we don't feel the difference. If things work out right, we won't even have to travel with nothing but the clothes on our backs. It is only in the beginning stages, may take several years, but it can work if we all cooperate and we will all be co-owners of both properties."

"Soli, did you know about all this?"

"Not really."

"Really Soli, you're giving up life in the States to be with us? You're not going to convince Saúl to move to New York?"

"Yes, I'm giving up life in the States to be with us, but now that I know that mansions are being built for us, I'm gonna have to take a long look at the blueprints because I love my house as it is and I don't know how we are going to merge Santa Fe and Victorian ... hello?" Saúl corrected Soli. "Um honey? It's not going to be a mansion..." Soli held up her finger to quiet Saúl. "Mari and I will decide that." Soli shook her head. "If you're going to make plans without telling us, we get to choose what kind of home you're building!" Saúl pinched the bridge of his nose and shook his head. Roberto sighed and put his hand on Saúl's shoulder and looked to the ceiling. "This is going to cost us dearly, isn't it?" Saúl just held onto his friend's hand that rested on his shoulder and said; "We knew the job was dangerous when we took it, but let's look at the bright side, we all know Solimar is a piece of cake when she's happy, right Bella?" Solimar winked at him and said "Sure, Bello, we will see just how sweet that cake is!" Mari sighed profoundly and said "Okay. So be it. Sol, you do the blueprint thing, I'll watch the twins." Olaya graciously added "Thank you for including me like family."

Marisol, in her infinite wisdom and swept up in the exuberance of the moment said "You know I bet if I get more information, we can make a recording of today and get certificates!" Olaya looked at Solimar while holding and shaking her head said "I can't, you deal with her." They all burst out laughing and Lydia said, "I will record this day and maybe I can go to some counsel in Africa somewhere where they will believe what happened today over here." Solimar said "Don't waste your time Ly, *no te apures,* I'm going to the Photoshop thingy on the Internet and I will make our own damn certificates and hang them on the walls myself just to shut this one up!" Mari put her hand on her hip, picked up little Robertito and said; "I think it's time to feed my baby!" She then walked off muttering in Spanish to herself as she put her tit in her baby's mouth.

Lydia was aglow. She never did know that she had a dream to realize, but now that her dream was about to come true, she was excited and hopeful, but still something ate away at her. Timidly she asked "Can the Ibeyis sleep by me tonight? I'll do their night feeding. It will be my last turn for a long time and by the time I get back, who knows, they probably will be feeding themselves." Deeply moved and having fallen in love with the "twins" Olaya said "I'll help, if that's not an imposition on my part." Roberto said "Mom, I don't think anyone here would deny you that, nor you Olaya." Saúl chimed in "not me." Marisol, still breast feeding and rocking her child said "what do you think, Mom?" Solimar said "you two can take over like right now because I ain't waiting no forty damn days to get my groove on. Come Bello, let's go!" Surprisingly enough Lydia turned to Marisol and asked "are you going to wait the forty days?" Mari said "I hadn't given it much thought, but" Roberto said "Don't think Mari, let's do this!" Soli was half way up the stairs and yelled out "you know where *la leche* is!" Saúl was right on her tail, eager and ready to please his wife.

"Wait guys, wait!" Solimar turned and impatiently asked "What now Mari, *que, que, que*?" Saúl gave Mari a dirty look all the while thinking that she better not interfere with him and Solimar's plans. "Why don't we all do the hot tub thing first?"

"Awww shit, you getting freaky on me now?" Roberto asked. Olaya nudged Roberto and said "Run with it and shut up. The girl needs to relax" came Olaya's unsolicited input. Olaya was pro anything that would take the edge off Marisol. Saúl said "let's do the hot tub thing then, I'm game."

"Like how, what are you proposing Marisol? We only use the hot tub individually or as a couple." Solimar was rather taken aback at Mari's suggestion and was very curious to hear her answer. "Well, I don't mean to sound like a *fresca*, but these guys have already seen our tits, our you know whats and our asses, and nobody hides when we are breast-feeding or pumping the milk in the bottles; we have no secrets from each other so, can we just go topless; they do it in Europe don't they?" Roberto and Saúl simultaneously doubled over laughing. Solimar was completely shocked, but mildly intrigued, but mostly happy to see her girlfriend coming out of her shell. Soli put her hand on her hip and looked at Saúl. "You've done this before?" Saúl looked at his wife and brazenly said; "Yeah, but not with you..." Olaya turned to Lydia and said "Grab a baby; I'll get the other one." Lydia, not missing a beat said "Damn right, I hate to see what that Jacuzzi is going to look like in the morning with those jet streams beating on them milk jugs." Olaya laughed and said "Well, you won't have to see it, we are out first thing in the morning, and somebody else gotta clean up that mess." Roberto and

Saúl silently nodded their consent to one another and the foursome went upstairs to change into their best swim suit bottoms.

As they shared the jet streams, the Latin jazz music accentuated by the never ending sound of *el coqui*, imbibing their icy beers, each begun to cry happy tears and congratulate themselves on their accomplishments; telling each other how much they loved each other. Their children were in the best hands ever: God's Hands. The boys were sleeping their angelic sleep and Olaya and Lydia watched them from their shared bedroom window. Even Roberto had one Corona, a Corona that he appreciated, savored and nursed watching the others go Corona and Tequila crazy. Marisol started complaining that the jet streams hurt her breasts and Solimar sent her packing upstairs to fetch two bikini tops and a couple of tee-shirts. They moved their party to the swimming pool, splashing water, dunking each other, playing volleyball with two beach balls, one that bore the Puerto Rican Flag and the other bearing the Panamanian flag. They even went as far as having a good old fashioned chicken fight where the guys put their girls atop their shoulders and the girls wrestled to knock the other off. Sol y Mar knew, they would go down together. Olaya laughing her head off turned to Lydia that was staring obviously stunned at this behavior. "What's up woman, what is it with the look?" Lydia simply said "I never seen my boy, I mean my son have so much fun."

"I don't think any of them has had this much fun. Seems to me like they are just getting loose, you know?"

"Do you think that ..." Olaya, sensing Lydia's thoughts said "Hush your mouth! These kids are just being kids, got it?"

"But they are not kids." Olaya took her new friend's hand in hers and placed it over her heart. "Do you feel the beat of your own heart?" Lydia silently nodded. "What is it saying to you?" Lydia closed her eyes, opened them and said "My heart tells me that, except for Saúl, they were all lonely kids."

"Keep going, what else?"

"That they are more than friends, they are brothers and sisters."

Olaya said "You are advancing very quickly Lydia. The minute I walked through the front door I perceived exactly everything that you just said." Lydia kept Olaya's hand of wisdom over her heart and said "I am not confused, I do understand, but you and I are going away tomorrow and I need to know a little bit more about you. I mean, you're taking me far away, far away from my people, from those fools out there having fun, they are my life!" Olaya breathed profoundly and said "Look woman, I am just as vulnerable as you. I'm investing trust here just like you are and it is hard, but I am going with or without you! It is something that I have to do for me." Lydia asked "Why did you ask me if I was ever married or had a boyfriend? I mean like I was just a girl taking care of a kid; there was no time for monkey business. I don't know what it is like to be with a man, I just don't, how about you?"

"Yes" said Olaya "I was blessed to have a husband of thirty-nine years. I met him when a friend took me for a spiritual reading. I had just arrived from London and came to the States trying to find my way and I was seeking guidance. At the time, the reading was three dollars and I had a little money in my pocket to spare. My friend, God bless her soul, met me and we took the bus cross-town. Could you imagine my surprise when I saw this Spanish guy, a few years older, but not old at all, really attractive, well groomed, but in a damn forsaken wheelchair! I was sick! I wanted to run, but he did not allow me to. He greeted us and without even knowing my name said "You don't need a reading, you need a man and your money is not welcomed here." He was right, you know, and I knew it, so I asked "What do I do, I don't know anyone here, I'm a stranger to this place; I'm looking for a job, not a man!" My Marcelo never hesitated; he said "you're coming here with me. I have been waiting a very long time for you to make an entrance through my door and into my life, but I do not have the right to ask you what took you this long. Eventually you will be my wife, but for now we are going to be good friends and I will teach you all that you need to know so that life does not mistreat you.

Well, if that is what you want; after all, we have free will, which is a gift from God." Olaya reflecting, continued her recounting and said "Those were his very words and that is the only reading I ever had in my entire life. The following day, I became his apprentice, visiting him on a daily basis, literally sitting on the floor on a prayer mat, leaning against legs that couldn't move, but absorbing the information like a sponge, taking in everything that gushed forward from a never ending waterfall; from a beautiful mind and brilliant spirit. I would wake up each morning, excited to call him to find out exactly what I needed to prepare for. Because of his disability, it would take him four seconds after he picked up the phone to respond to me; he was not like us that could just put the phone right away to his ear. Those four seconds meant the world to me because I knew he was struggling to answer my call. I can't describe the feeling ... it was like he was receiving me, as an audience and I called him often just to hear the pause before hearing his soft and sexy voice. He taught me how to dress, he introduced me to a world of herbs and plants and above all, he instilled in me the lesson of reading a person, not through cards or shells, but by looking deep into their eyes. He taught me how to climb into a person's mouth through their laughter and how to dry their tears without lifting a tissue. He taught me how to walk by faith in God and not by sight. He never tired of teaching me. He did it day, noon and night and so with time we became inseparable and I learned not only what he taught, but also how to take care of his physical needs with the help of a beautiful Haitian lady named Wilomena. This woman picked up immediately on our connection, and secretly begun to share with me his secrets, his anxieties and all that I needed to do to assuage them and properly care for him. He had apparently told her that I was the one, so somewhere behind the scenes, in the kitchen, anywhere along the way; she was turning over her duties to me. Eventually he asked me to marry him and I did. All of this we did without knowing, but trusting in the Great Spirit, and naming Wilomena as our Maid of Honor. She stayed with us until she felt it safe for her to move on to another job, but she is my best friend and still checks in from time to time."

That was too much information for Lydia, who had never had a man, but she pressed on for more of Olaya's recollections, believing, hoping and praying that she too could one day know what it would feel like to be intimately cared for by one. "Olaya? Do you have a picture of him, can I see it?" Olaya opened her suitcase and unwrapped two pictures, both professionally framed, one in onyx, the other in silver, but still enclosed in bubble wrap. She ceremoniously removed the scotch tape and unveiled them to her new-found friend. "This is a professional head shot of him." Lydia took the photo in her hands and stared for some time, trying to understand the influence of this beautiful creature with defiant hazel eyes, brown leather gloves with the tips cut off and a mischievous smile that playfully spoke to the world saying "Too bad what you think of me." She reached for the other and it was a picture of Olaya's wedding photograph. Olaya dressed in a simple white dress with a small pillbox hat on her head, Marcelo holding her bouquet of flowers on his lap while Olaya wrapped her arms from behind his wheelchair, her chin resting atop his head, bearing the broadest smile upon her radiant face. Lydia enthralled and confused all at once asked "But were you ever able to have, you know, sex with him?" Olaya bowed her head and smiled with tears in her eyes again responded "Yes. We made our own sex and found our own love. He touched my body with his eyes, his hands and whatever else he could find. From time to time, we took the time to do the necessary work that would allow him to penetrate my body, but that was a little more difficult so instead ... "Lydia had to interrupt; "But, if he was... a... how do you...?" Olaya smiled; "A man's penis... is not a muscle, it doesn't get paralyzed. If a man's mind is aroused, so is his manhood!" Lydia understood and also felt a little embarrassed that she was so ignorant about the anatomy of a male. Olaya continued. "He gave his nights and days over to pleasing me and he was so considerate of me that when he was in pain, he would just ask me to please sleep away from him and come back after he fell asleep. He was born like that, a natural birth defect, but I never dared to ask more than what I needed to know, so we found our own way of relating, our own way of existing and you know what Lydia? Although I never got pregnant, we did have children; not biological but children nevertheless. I developed my faculties as he taught me how to read, write, pray and ask. I took it upon myself to alleviate my husband's burden and I did it all. I did all the readings, all the consultations, all the works and I as I became empowered, I only came to ask him when I had a doubt or a concern for one of our godchildren and their enlightment. He gave me wings, never once questioning my decisions, knowing that in the process he was transferring onto me secrets that are older than time. As a priestess, I have my limits, but he never treated me like a priestess, but as a goddess. Like in all religions, women are not allowed to engage further because we reveal too much information, but a man knows how to hold pain longer and stronger. It is what I call the Libra Balance …. We hurt in childbirth, but the real men hurt through life. My marriage was spent making love, reading, learning and cooking food for the godchildren who paraded in and out of my house. He took me as far as I could go and crowned me Saint himself. It took us almost twenty years to put together my abilities and the monies to travel to Cuba and we deliberately broke all of the rules of our religion. We really never had a fight, only a challenge of the minds, which is a vast difference and he encouraged it in order to sharpen my senses. My husband died, not because anything was wrong with him, but because everything was finally right and he was now able to put down his sword and give it to me. He died peacefully in his sleep right next to me, knowing that he had developed me into the woman, the priestess and the servant that I am today. He was nine years older than me and actually we were born a day apart, but really it was the same day because we were separated by minutes, so we celebrated everything together. Then, it was his time, but by then he had already forbidden me to cry, so I did not nor ever will."

Dedication

"Lord in Heaven, what on earth did you do when you found a corpse sleeping next to you?"

"Lydia, I did not find a corpse. I found my husband in eternal rest; a sleep that he had earned for all of his humanitarian work and his passion for life. I got out from bed, kissed him like I always did each morning and went to the kitchen, found his bottle of rum and drank the whole thing straight out of the bottle while I planned his cremation. Although it is against the faith of our people to be burned, it was his wish, so I did not call any of our godchildren, I didn't even dial 911, which I think probably was against the law. The following day I had him cremated with no ceremony only my faith that God, the Angels and the Saints would take charge over him. I followed his instructions to the letter and I contacted our godchildren after it was over. They each came in one by one, and I gave them what he had left them - something in a little box that I never opened. I have no idea whatsoever what my Marcelo left as his legacy because he kept that to himself. His ashes are with me and that is why I must go to the motherland. I must dispose of them and spread his love on the land of my people. This man knew more about the religion of my ancestors than what anyone had ever bothered to teach me. We helped people live and now I must go help my husband die, but my husband will never ever die because he lives in me; everything that you see in my person is him. My name is Olaya, but really I am the female version of Marcelo. Now tell me, do you want to go have a beer with the kids or what?" Lydia giggled, hugged her newfound mentor and said "yeah, I really do, but can I ask one more question? Olaya patiently said "Of course my friend."

"Was there anything particular in him that provoked your allegiance?" Olaya reflecting on all the wonders of Marcelo said "He made me wear high-heeled shoes until the end. He always wanted me to appear strong and tall, even when I felt down and out. Now again I ask, you wanna go with the kids?"

"Olaya I'm going to miss them so much and thank you for sharing Marcelo with me; I think I will change your name to

Marcelita because I have fallen in love with him!" Olaya laughed her thunderous laugh and said "Don't you dare. As much as I want to be him, I have to be me, so now go, I'll watch the babies, c'mon now let's go, go on, go to your children." Lydia opened her suitcase and said "you know that two-piece bathing suit you talked me into buying yesterday?"

"Yes, the one you didn't want the 'kids' to see?"

"I'm gonna wear it right now!" Olaya looked at her friend and said one of the few words she remembered in Spanish; *"Puta!"* Lydia laughed and left the room. Olaya rocked the bassinet making sure that the children were alright.

Appearing in the pool in her white satin robe, Roberto yelled out "Ma is everything okay?" Lydia did not answer him, but disrobed without saying a word, leaving the four with their eyes and mouths wide opened as she turned around modeling her new "look," which included the braided hairdo filled with multi-colored beads and extensions and a neon yellow swimsuit. She then took a dive into the swimming pool. The cheers and praises went up and the blessings came down. Olaya watched the Angels in flight, her third eye wide open as she kept thanking God for the blessing of witnessing a captive set free; having been set free herself. She let the flow of joyful tears wash her face as she witnessed her sister enjoying the fruits of her laborious life.

Saúl climbed out of the pool first and said "Ma, what you want - a beer or a shot?" Lydia said "I'll take both please." Saúl laughed and said "Okay Miss Hotstuff, but don't complain tomorrow about a hangover, your flight is very early, but don't worry about it, I got the recipe!" Lydia threw back the shot and chased it with a long sip of her beer. "Well. You can't fly on one wing, gimme another!" The party sat around the pool and Lydia said "I'm sorry if I crashed in on your fun, but I just had to tell you guys how much I'm going to miss you."

"Mom stop! Really, again?" Roberto asked. "Yes, really again and don't make me box them ears in. You know kids, I'm going to a strange land with a stranger, but nothing ever felt so divine, like, I don't know; God or somebody up there arranged for all of this just for me. Even the disappearance of Solimar played a big part in this day happening. She wouldn't have ever met Olaya otherwise and I wouldn't have had a reason to find the information to give to Saúl to bring her back. It's all a little mystical to me right now, but if you put it together, what were the chances that this all would be a coincidence?" They all nodded in unanimous agreement. Lydia kept talking, revealing information. "Olaya bought me a Notebook so we can stay in contact. I'll be learning how to write better, but I do alright for now."

"Mom, a letter from Africa to here will take days to arrive; we can just talk on the phone."

"Oh no, she got me one of those little portable computers, you know the lap top kind, but smaller? That way I can practice everyday and what better way, don't you think?" Saúl started giggling as he handed Lydia her fresh round of drinks. Marisol and Roberto were trying to keep a straight face and Solimar, now two sheets to the wind, said "Two piece bathing suit, lap top, new hair, what else you got upstairs condoms?" Lydia nodded seriously. "We have. You never know what could happen and it is better to be prepared, right? They say it all the time in the TV commercials." Her innocence and sincerity was so endearing that not a one would dare to question or comment further. After all, Lydia was still a virgin, pure, untouched, but hopeful that perhaps one day she could experience the exchange of security, friendliness and companionship that her children were feeling.

Olaya, who was now holding the 'twins' in her arms, both who were giggling and cooing, looked down at the play that unfolded before her eyes and said to the boys "Oh dear! What have I unleashed on the world?" and she laughed and kissed and nuzzled both the babies placing them back into the bassinet. Roberto smiled, hugged his mom and said "Don't let me find out that you are dating on the internet." Solimar, with her bad ass self hugged Lydia and whispered into her ear "Are the condoms lamb skin and magnum sized?" Lydia hugged Solimar tightly and whispered back "I'm not sure, girl, but pray that I find out." Marisol was drunk out of her mind and blurted out "I think that, I think, I think that, I think that they gonna come back with one or two Congos." That signaled the end of the festivities.

Amidst laughter, the family walked up the stairs, Roberto practically carrying Marisol. They stopped in to kiss the kids and said their good nights and thank yous to Olaya. Marisol went straight to bed, wet bathing suit bottom and all having ripped off her top along with her tee-shirt. Roberto gently pulled it off of her, knowing that even nude, tonight would not be the night. Marisol was wasted and snoring like a broken chainsaw. He slapped her bare ass and the only response he got was a burp and a hiccup. Roberto went back outside, picked up another cold one and sat to enjoy the vivid sound of the enchanted island. He didn't need sex; he was blessed to be content and he didn't mind to wait out the forty days, if necessary. Roberto grabbed the beer and was about to open it, but he stopped, looked at the bottle and put it down on the floor next to him. He reclined on the lounge chair, crossed his fingers on his chest and began to sing to himself. Unbeknownst to him, Marisol had gotten up, wondering where her man had gone off to and was watching him through the window. She placed her hand over her heart and a tear formed in her eye. She quietly went downstairs, naked as she was and walked out onto the gardens. Roberto sensing that someone was behind him, turned to see his wife standing there nude. "Mari? Is there something wrong?" Mari shook her head no. "Would you care for some company?" Roberto got up, wrapped the mother of his child, soon to be wife in an oversized beach towel and they decided to go to the hammock Saúl had set up between two palm trees. Mari shimmied and shifted until they were both under the makeshift blanket and in each others arms. She reached down between Roberto's legs and seductively moaned "There are other ways I can show you how much I love you..." She disappeared under the towel, eager to satiate her soon to be husband and reward him for all he had done.

Solimar and Saúl took their time this time. After much time playing in the pool they were both very aroused, and having

had their 'playtime' interrupted by Marisol's idea of having an impromptu pool party, it all only served to intensify their desire. After much foreplay in the pool, they quietly set up their bedroom with candles, incense and continued to listen to their Latin jazz at a very low volume. They stepped into their bathroom and showered together, tenderly taking turns lathering a lavender scented gel on each other's bodies. There wasn't much left to be said and for once, it felt good not to converse. As Saúl was rubbing his woman's body with baby oil, his favorite method of relaxation, she out of nowhere said "You know something Bello?
"What?"
"Tonight is going to be the very first night we make love with no guilt and no shame."
"I've never felt guilt or shame Soli, only respect and concern."
"Well, give me a minute; we are throwing those bitches out the window too."
Solimar opened, then locked herself within their walk-in closet and searched high and low until she found a plain hat box. Saúl leaned back, having stacked all pillows, anticipating that his woman was up to something wonderful. She had to come out of that closet sooner or later, and he was prepared to pounce on her the moment she did. The "hat" box contained the simplest outfit, an outfit she purchased while spending time with Lili Anne. She opened the box and there it was. A pair of silver-heeled stilettos, a white baby doll with matching thong made practically from onion skin and a matching feathered and sequined mask that only covered her eyes. When she stepped out of the walk-in closet, Saúl said not one word, but gently laid his woman onto their bed and pleasured her in ways that Solimar had never imagined. She concentrated and shivered with every lick of his tongue and begged him for more. He gently drew milk from her; the milk of a mother, the milk of his wife. Solimar was hungry to return his favor. She feasted on the banquet that had been prepared just for her, using methods that she had only read about, causing Saúl moans of ecstasy. When they finally laid spent,

baby doll ripped to shreds, one shoe on either side of their king size bed, Saúl removed Soli's mask and asked "Are you mine now?" Solimar breathed into his ear. "I always was. I just needed to make sure we could do this, like this." Solimar gently pushed her husband off of her and straddled him. "Sis, I'm tired, give me some time here to replenish." Solimar stared blankly at him for what seemed like an eternity, realizing that with that one word, he had just defined their relationship, their existence and the enormous extent of their love. "You know what little brother, thank God for the family because if I had to feed our son right now, he'd be assed out knocking on Mari's door to fix him a bottle and you know that won't work either with her stank drunken ass." Saúl reached, softly tumbling her down from him and placed her in her cradle, his body. Stroking her hair, they started to hum, but barely made it to the first bar.

Morning came too soon, but when the alarm rang, each soldier obeyed their call. Wrapped in robes and/or shorts, each went to reclaim their child and see Lydia and Olaya off. Roberto, who had not slept at all, having spent the night reading a cookbook while out back enjoying his newfound freedom from alcohol, ventured into the kitchen and made pancakes and sausages, his mom's favorite, and this time, he had managed to keep the kitchen impeccable as his mother always did while she was cooking. Instead of a sparkling pitcher of Mimosa, he had made a pitcher of Alka Seltzer and poured out fresh pineapple juice that he had blended through the juicer. The family convened in the dining room. Roberto served everyone a heaping plate full of silver dollar pancakes, sausages and some fruit he sliced up and drenched in ginger ale; his own concoction. He served his mother her favorite cup of coffee, placing the Anis on the table. The women ate while feeding their newborns, Saúl reflecting on the fact that he had to face one more good-bye. It took everything inside of him not to cry when it was time to say goodbye, but he had to stay strong for Roberto and Marisol. Lydia, feeling like a brand new mom broke their comfortable silence, openly saying "Son, if you need me to stay, you know for the kids and everything, I can cancel the trip and leave it for another time." Olaya nodded quietly in agreement. She too had fallen in love with the babies, and even more so with the crazy bunch that had robbed her heart and given her hope of not spending her latter years alone. Her trip to the homeland could wait. "Mami. Lord knows, I want you to stay, but I need you to go, just like you felt when I went to Hogar Crea." Lydia stood up and said "Saúl, how can I ever repay you?"

"Why do women always reverse things? Lydia, the question is how can I ever repay you for bringing my family together?" Lydia kissed Saúl on his lips and kissed Solimar on her forehead and hugged her for what seemed like forever, but she broke down crying when she said her goodbye to Marisol, the daughter she never had. Olaya made her rounds of good-byes as well, but couldn't quite get herself to say good-bye to the Santanas, who stood holding hands. Solimar said "Olaya, this isn't good-bye, it is an Adios. We leave everything in His hands until we meet again." Saúl keenly noting that Olaya was feeling weak from excitement and sadness, took her in his arms and said "Ssshhhh. You can come back and stay with us anytime you want. I won't let anything happen to you, ever. Think about moving here with us while you're away. We can talk about it whenever you like. All of our doors are opened to you." She hugged him tight, clinging to him as if he was her Marcelo. Saúl, receiving the magnitude of her love, but realizing that she was leaving here and now, gently pulled her away saying "Oli, Victor is waiting in the car and so is Nigeria." She kissed the babies and looked at Solimar profoundly before saying "You do know that you are responsible for all of this, don't you?" Solimar put her hands together as if in prayer, bowed down and said "I read somewhere, I don't know where, but that if you bow down like this it means that the divinity in me is acknowledging the divinity in you." With no questions or answers required, each got up and took turns bowing down each to the other. This moment was followed by a group family hug, the sound of kisses that drowned out the sound of the songbirds and Victor who had waited patiently at the door to bring them to the airport announced "Let's go folks. That's all she wrote. The Puerto Rican good-bye is officially over. I got to get these ladies home!"

Nurturing

A week to the day, Roberto and Mari returned to Panamá along with Solimar and Saúl. The boys were in perfect health and the team had worked out a routine to alleviate the stress on both mothers. Solimar constantly pumped milk from her breasts into bottles, inspiring Marisol to do the same as she was becoming weary of breast-feeding. Nobody knew whose breast milk they picked up from the fridge and nobody cared, especially not the babies. Their trip to Panamá went smoothly and they settled into Roberto and Mari's house. They were inseparable. A safe contained unit also known as a family. It was time, however, to choose whether or not to further extend that family. Saúl had already phoned ahead and advised his parents that they were officially grandparents. Solimar agreed that it would only be fair to do so and Saúl breathed a bit easier having received her consent with no resistance. They planned to go see the family before traveling back home.

"Solimar?"

"*Si*, Marisol."

"Are you going to start some stuff when you get over to your family's house?"

"*Puede ser*, I don't know yet. I suppose that it depends on what kind of reception I get."

"That's what I thought. Why don't you just give it up, make peace and be better than them. Be the sensible Christian woman that you are, and if you can't be that, do it for Saúl and the baby."

"I may. I may not. We will see how the wind blows on my ass that morning if I even wake up." Marisol made a face and Solimar stuck her tongue out. They were having their evening chamomile iced tea, having decided to cut back on their drinking as the men fed one another's babies according to the rotation schedule they had set up when it had just been Robertito that needed feeding.

Solimar woke up at the break of dawn, checked on her son, glanced at their schedule, which was prominently posted on the refrigerator, and was quite happy that it was Roberto's turn to feed her son and Mari's turn to feed her own child. Saúl would sleep peacefully for at least another hour. Solimar quietly crept into the bathroom, showered and then soaked in white gardenias, a little something her husband had taught her. She was ever so careful to apply her make-up and even took scissors to hair and cut off a good amount, pulling it off of her face with a broad white headband. By the time she was finished, she looked school girlish, more than womanish. She headed for the breakfast table and drank a full glass of Sangria with an extra shot of brandy before beginning to prepare breakfast for all. She played Europa, by Carlos Santana, however softly and swayed to the music that always spoke to her tender heart. Lydia's duties had long been divided among everyone in the house until she got back or Roberto hired a new maid, although Marisol was not too keen on the idea of having another woman in her house, especially after having heard Solimar's explanation as to why she fired Rosario. They had all become accustomed to the idea that whoever got up first would have kitchen duties. By the time they all came downstairs; the breakfront was filled with French toast, bacon, coffee, Mimosas and Anisette in honor of Lydia. They had all agreed that leaving the food warming on chafing dishes would be the most logical thing to do to accommodate their schedules. Again, nobody said a word. Thank you was no longer a necessity. They were family, but as they appeared, each gave Solimar a good morning kiss, as they did to whoever got up in time to prepare their

Nurturing

morning meal, which became an unspoken ritual. Sometimes, two got up simultaneously and helped one another; Saúl and Mari got to catch up on things while they cooked together, much like Solimar and Roberto when they ran into each other in the kitchen. The ladies made appointments to make breakfast a couple of times a week and let the guys sleep in, and occasionally, so did the men. There was no schedule etched in stone, but the one sacred schedule they adhered to was the feeding of the boys. Nobody ever broke that rhythm; they stayed true to the fulfillment of the needs of their children, which was only seconded by their care for one another.

After their leisurely breakfast, they each readied themselves to go to Saúl's parent's house, including the extended family. Solimar kissed her husband and said "Bello, let's just do this and get it over with." Saúl went into Roberto's study for a cigarette and paced nervously. Roberto paced with him, while the ladies packed up the kids and their provisions for the day. Solimar had already overruled the idea of spending the night.

"Roberto?"

"Yeah Macho, what's up?

"I'm fucking terrified."Roberto looked at his friend long and hard and said "Bro, you should be. I'm not even going to pretend otherwise and fill your head with some bullshit."

"It's just that Solimar…" Roberto, fully understanding his partner said "Dude, your woman is no joke and if she doesn't get that fragrance up her ass, there's going to be a jump off, so hope for the best and expect the worse. She's definitely going in!" Saul punched a pillow and said "But, I…" Again, Roberto did not allow him to finish the sentence. "Listen, you know I have an enormous amount of love and respect for you, but, with all due respect my man, you don't come from where Soli comes from, or where Mari comes from or even where I come from for that matter. The world as you know it is being blown apart at what? 43, 44? Our world was destroyed even before we had a chance to form an opinion. I got lucky with Lydia, but it didn't go so well for Solimar and I still don't know why Marisol doesn't want to visit the family that adopted her. Saúl, head bowed down, hands clasped together said "But what am I supposed to do here?"

"Macho you're on your own with that one, but if I was in your shoes I'd man up, stand firm behind my female and that's it. Do you have any idea what Solimar is planning for today, did you talk with her?"

"She said she will go according to how the wind blows on her ass." Roberto chuckled. "Isn't that what I just said? I love that crazy ass witch of yours; she keeps the shit on the real. Did you hear her going at Mari yesterday when Marisol came in with size 0 to 3 pacifiers for the kids? She was like "Mar, get the fuck out of my face with some dumb ass shit like size 0 to 3 *bobos*! Let them little niggers suck on their thumbs like we did!" Roberto, enjoying the recounting of the story continued "and Mari was like, why do they gotta be little niggers?" I died laughing when I heard Solimar say "Mari, do either one of these kids look like crackers to you?! Robertito is already growing an afro!" Marisol got heated and caught me outside the door listening and laughing my ass off. She didn't say anything to me, but knocked me right upside my head." Roberto was really trying to assuage Saúl's concerns with a bit of humor and a lot of truth. Saúl faintly smiled and said "I missed that one, but you know, brother, Solimar stays on 24/7. Dude, I am shitting bricks here." Roberto tried to distract his best friend who was looking rather pale and on the verge of a *"patatun"* – also known as a heart attack or nervous breakdown. He walked over to his desk, sat and pointed to the chair inviting Saúl to do the same. "Listen, man I was thinking that when the babies get a little older and a bit stronger, I would like Solimar to come work for me, I mean she sees things in three dimensions and I know she will be dynamite for the practice."

"Roberto we don't need the money and Soli has to stay home with the baby for a good long while."

"What if I offer you a fifty-fifty proposition? Robles and Santana, Attorneys-at-Law."

"Are you serious?"

"Yeah I am. Mari already enrolled to take online courses to finish her degree and said that she could watch the babies while Solimar and I work; you're an attorney, so what's the problem?"

"Well, hell, there is no problem other than running this by Sol, but how can we make it work, you here and we living in Puerto Rico?"

"Man that's the easy part. When you guys are here, Marisol will take care of the kids, and when you guys go back to Puerto Rico, I'll just email the research information and stuff to Soli and she can work on it while Machito is sleeping and keep her busy you know, especially when you go away. Should I need her here for the day, it's only a two hour flight. She can be right back home in time for dinner or spend the night. You know that Soli be starting shit in her head, so why not give her a job, keep her mind occupied and productive. If not man, I can see her rolling up to your offices every day, baby carriage and all and there isn't a motherfucker out there that's gonna stop her." Saúl remarked more to himself than to Roberto "An idle mind is the Devil's workshop."

"Trust me bro... the last thing you need is the Devil setting up shop in that head!" Saúl, extremely impressed said "Damn, bro, you really got down and planned this one out. I like it. I like it a lot. Besides, I've been thinking about resigning my post, or at least scaling back. Traveling is becoming harder for me and let's get real about it, shit out there isn't getting any nicer. Let's get through today and when we come back tonight, unless we're bailing my wife out of jail or going to the hospital with my parents, we will all sit together and talk about establishing our legal practice.

"No doubt." With that they clasped hands, hugged and patted each other strongly on the back. Roberto asked "Macho, you still scared?" Saúl answered "Worse than when I saw Solimar giving birth and that fucking doctor no where in sight." Roberto, still trying to take some of the burden off of his friend's shoulders said "*Con tu permiso*, can I make a point here?" Saúl nodded. "Solimar was a Santana, before you were even born man!"

"I don't understand…"

"She was your father's daughter before all this happened and this shit was going to go down whether you two got involved or not!"

"And?"

"Saúl, it's not your problem what happens with the drama that your folks put into motion. Your family members, not you, are the ones that have to deal with the repercussions of their actions. *Tu eres inocente!*"

"And that is supposed to make things easier on me?" Roberto went to the bar, filled a brandy glass to the rim, handed it to Saúl and said "Hell no, but this sure will!" Saúl wanted so hard to laugh but he couldn't; instead he took the drink and polished off half the glass in one gulp.

"Did you notice that your wife cut off a good chunk of her hair?"

"Like I have the *cojones* to question what that was all about. I left that one alone!" Roberto nodded in agreement and stated "I noticed that Mari didn't mention it either. Saúl, Macho, come on man be strong, Solimar is gonna be alright." At this Saúl laughed and said "Yes she will be. I'm just worried about my ass, but you are right, we all gonna be alright, somehow. I wouldn't trade that woman for all of the wonders in the world." Roberto smiled and said to him "Now you see; that's what I'm talking about."

The ladies came downstairs and wordlessly piled into the limo, strollers, diaper bags, playpen and all. It was an eerily quiet day, and even when they arrived at the Santana household, nobody seemed to be around. The streets were quiet; the sky was gray, threatening rain again and the skies had begun to rumble a bit of thunder. Solimar S. Santana de Santana was, baby in arms, in full battle array, her gold rosary delicately dangling around her neck, her white outfit - impeccable. It was a Friday, the day when Catholics recite and acknowledge the mystery of death, not birth, as far as the rosary goes anyway.

Saúl nervously checked with her every now and again, but the peace that radiated from her body and soul surpassed his comprehension. She had not slept, but prayed all night, while resting next to her husband, and those demons that lurked waiting to torment her .... Well they were on their way to fucking hell, or about to be.

The soon to be Robleses opted to stay on the well-appointed porch that seemed more like a living room than an outdoor seating area. They settled in quite comfortably watching the storm approach. They looked at the sky and each other and commented to one another how ironic it all was. Solimar, son in arms, opened the door without announcement. The family was already gathered in the parlor when the new generation of Santanas made their way in. The twins, Soledad and Omar, both in their early thirties came to welcome their brother and sister. Mom and Pop hung back, allowing the siblings to meet and greet. Soledad instantly went for the baby, cooing and kissing his forehead; Omar stood at his brother's side. The mother spoke first. "Saúl, *mi hijo*, what a pleasure it is to see you and your family, but we would have happily traveled to Puerto Rico if you had called us to tell us that Solimar had given birth." Saúl graciously kissed his mother's cheek. Their father approached and greeted his son with a handshake and quick hug. He was cautious and did not know how to approach his daughter. Solimar took back her child from her sister's arms. Thrusting him forward she said "We came so that you can meet your grandson." The parents eagerly went to Solimar and when they reached, Solimar stepped back. "Look, but do not touch him, he is way too little to become contaminated, don't you think?" Raul pleaded "Solimar don't be that way. We accept everything and I take blame for all of my mistakes. What more can you ask of me?" Solimar purposely allowed the air to fill with silent questions and the proverbial pregnant pause. She asked in an acidic tone "May I ask you if you know that my mother, your former wife is dead for starters?" Raul bowed his head and barely audible said "I did not know that."

"Well then, can I ask you if you know that I spent my teen-aged years in foster care?" Raul, starting to get desperate, looked around for support, but none was there to be had, even Esmeralda bowed her head in shame. "Can I also ask you why did you just walk away and ended up in Panamá?" Raul lowered his gaze, focusing it on his first grandchild. He said simply "My grandson is beautiful; he looks so healthy, so strong, he looks like you." Solimar moved in on him. "Who the fuck did you expect him to look like? You or Esmeralda, whom incidentally Cubans refer to her skin tone as dirty white, *una blanca sucia*, isn't that correct Esmeralda?" Esmeralda rarely admitted to her ethnicity, preferring to have people believe that she was a Spaniard whenever she could get away with it. "*Nuestro hijo es color canela* and thanks to your mother, blue eyes too, just to complete the inherited ensemble. I remember my grandmother far clearer than ever remembering you."

Esmeralda stepped in, noticing that her husband was waning, not feeling so well. Solimar ignored Esmeralda's attempt to steady her husband. "Raul, I am here to claim my inheritance right now." She handed the baby over to Soledad who was anxiously waiting to receive him. "I am your first born after all."

"Solimar that is ridiculous and unreasonable! You inherit after a person dies, I haven't even drawn up a Will yet that must now include your son." Solimar calmly turned to her husband and said "Notice that when it comes to the Will, the child is referred to as 'your son,' not "my grandson." Saúl kept quiet, diligently noting that Solimar's temperature was rising. He quickly remembered the advice that Roberto had given him that this wasn't his problem and to let Solimar resolve all her issues with her family, but he wanted to stop her from attacking his mother. Esmeralda was the one person in the room that they did not have in common and Saúl, as any good son would, wanted to protect his mother. Marisol turned to Roberto, as they were hearing everything through the door that was left ajar and the open bay window. She whispered "Rober, I think we might have to step in or call the police." Roberto comforted his wife. "Mari, stay put.

Solimar is crazy, but I think she's on to something here. Don't worry; Saúl is not going to let her go buck wild like the last time."

Back inside of the Santana household, Solimar turned to her siblings and said "Would you guys be interested in coming to live with me and your brother in Puerto Rico? We are leaving the day after tomorrow. If you have passports, you can come and check it out." Omar was the first to react to the announcement. "Puta yes, that's what's up! I have been asking my brother for that for a while, but he has been too busy working!"

"Soledad, are you with us?" Soledad looked at her nephew whom she rocked in her arms, having longed for so long to be a mother herself. She nodded and said "I would like to go, but can I come back?" Solimar, completely understanding Soledad's concern tenderly said "Of course you can *mi hermana*. Your brother and I are working on a plan that will allow us to live here and keep our residence there, but we do have a temporary residence here already." Soledad turned slightly to face her mother. "Mama?" Esmeralda mortified yet afraid to incite Solimar further said "You are a grown woman! Do as you wish *hija*. You need to spend time with your nephew and your, your sister and maybe that will be good!"

"What about school and work?" Saúl stepped in and said "Soledad, we have fine academies in Puerto Rico. Remember and start to learn about your heritage. You are not Panamanian. You are Puerto Rican and Cuban and you are certainly not a Spaniard living in Panamá. Our mother refuses to accept her direct heritage, and as the liar she has been revealed to be, fooled us into believing that our ancestry is linked to Spanish nobility, but I did some research some time ago and we are not." Esmeralda turned her eyes away in shame. "Eventually, we will visit Cuba, but we cannot right now, and you can always finish your degree with online courses as an option. As for Omar, I can find him a job at the embassy; I think they are looking for interpreters." Soledad, still undecided turned to her father. "Papi?" Raul, with tears in his eyes said "It is well with me; it hurts and I will miss you but, it is time you left the nest and found your own way in the world!" Esmeralda approached Soledad, the closest child to her heart and tried to plead her case using Soledad's on again, off again romance against her "But honey, what are you going to do about Diego, you know that he has been leading up to ask you to marry him; that proposal can come any day now." Soledad, embracing her true Santana spirit said "Diego can kiss my *culito* and go to *el infierno*. He had his chance a long time ago and blew it. I've moved off Diego's Dominican ass since then and I just kept him around for amusement purposes. *Yo me voy!*" Esmeralda looked at her daughter in shock and dismay. She glared at her mother. "Mami please… like you really waited for your wedding night as you would have the world believe!" Solimar looked at her sister with a newfound respect, having had erroneously come to the conclusion that Soledad was weak and subject to her parents' wishes. Soledad turned to Solimar, handed back the child and studied the expression on Solimar's face. With a slight smile, she raised an eyebrow and said "Excuse me. Did you actually think that you were the only bitch in this house? I got a little something for you too hermana!" Solimar winked at her sister, hugged her with her free arm and said "Go pack your things, but pack lightly. We will go shopping back home."

Once Soledad and Omar cleared the room, Raul started to sob loudly, realizing that he was losing his family. Solimar simply stated "That, right there, is my inheritance. The family that you robbed from me, kept far from me, I now take from you with absolutely no remorse. Now, that I have taken care of personal business; we have financial matters to discuss. I need money…" Raul looked directly at Saúl. "Don't look at him… he's perfectly capable of taking care of his responsibilities, this is about what you owe me! Solimar handed the baby over to her husband and pulled out a ledger that she had tucked in her baby bag and handed it to Raul. "Here are my calculations based on what the child support rate was around the time you left. I went to the lowest end of the scale assuming that you made little money at the time since you had us living in the projects. I'm collecting

Nurturing

this on behalf of my mother and will donate it to a third world country or set up some type of foundation with it. Additionally, you owe me tuition. As you can see, the names of my creditors are listed, as well as the name of the college I attended. You owe me a lifetime of affection and guidance, but since there is no price tag on that, you will see I valued it at zero. You owe me the funeral expenses for my mother's death, which incidentally you never divorced, so that responsibility would have fallen on you, if you had been around. I have provided you a copy of the cemetery's business card, as well as your wife's death certificate for your file. Therefore, my friend, I think you can hand over your bank account to me and let Saúl handle your assets." Raul, outraged, stopped his crocodile tears and yelled "Are you out of you mind, *estas loca*?" Solimar answered "Yes, Papi, I am very *loca* thanks to you. Besides being crazy, which thanks for reminding me, I'll need to pay for therapy for being in an incestuous relationship with my brother. Your children will need the best of everything, like continued piano lessons for Soledad, golf lessons for Omar, not to mention new wardrobes to introduce them into Puerto Rican society or do you think I'm going to let Soledad run around in a pollera all day long and Omar in a guayabera seven days a week? Or better yet, do you honestly think we are going to support them?" Saúl said "Please be reasonable Baby."

"Oh no brother, you are sadly mistaken. The time for reason is right now! What if our child winds up fucked up because of this old bastard here? He won't be there day in and day out enduring our pain and suffering. He must pay and pay he will." Esmeralda said "Raul, write her a check and let us have peace." Solimar laughed. "No Elsie, I don't want a check. I want your ATM card; you know the one giving you access to the family account? Trembling, the woman did not resist, recalling that Elsie was the name she used while in the States. She readily reached for her purse and handed Solimar her entire wallet. "Elsie. Just the ATM card and the PIN number please. I'm an heiress not a purse snatcher!"" Mrs. Santana fumbled, got out the ATM card and gave Solimar the PIN number. Solimar handed Saúl his child, reached for her husband's cell phone, took it off of his hip, flipped the card and made the call. She changed the PIN number. "Thank you Elsie. You are gracious and wise although you were a former slut that broke up my parent's marriage." Saúl intervened and said "Solimar, her name is Esmeralda, not Elsie. You're out of control! Bella sit down, you are on a roll." Solimar, frustrated and desperately wanting to make violent contact with Esmeralda slightly pushed Saúl, being careful that he would not drop or upset their son and said; "You think I was out of control before? I suggest you sit down and strap yourself in because I haven't even gotten started! You don't even know who your own bitch in heat of a mother really is! She is Elsie. Elsie the cow! Elsie who lived in the projects across the hall from my mother, married to some fucking Italiano that used to beat the shit out of her ass every other day. My mother, Titina, would take her in and care for her bruises and black eyes and broken bones. My mother took your crying bitch ass mother to the hospital when that motherfucker broke her nose, but you know what my mother didn't know? She didn't know that the fucker that was beating her ass knew that his wife was fucking his neighbor … yeah, that's right; your mother was fucking our piece of shit father in her apartment while her husband was at work. And if you want to know more, I'll fucking tell you more. Your fucking mother stabbed her husband, supposedly in self-defense and fucking Raulin here stepped in and rather than bringing all of this shit to the justice system, he ran off with her. That's how they fucking winded up in motherfucking Panamá, not because they made 'an investment with their friends.' Look up the records, these motherfuckers are fugitives, but the statute of limitations for murder has expired because at the time it ran for twenty years and it's been way longer than that, but who knows, the law could have changed and they may still be held liable!" Raul, obviously shaken by her revelation demanded to know "How on earth can you know all this; you were but a toddler unless you are making this up to ruin my

Nurturing

family and my good name!" Soli was more than glad to reveal her sources. "You know what, Raulin, the internet *es un hijo de puta* and what I couldn't find out while taking my paralegal studies and learning how to conduct legal research, I found out when I went to the projects looking to find you to tell you that my mother had died. I went there with the purpose of finding out if anyone knew where I could get in touch with my father. One of your neighbors recognized me and invited me into her home and told me every single detail. I won't give you her name, but she is a witness, and whether or not you believe it, she has some evidence. They took her in to make a statement and I have a copy of it, and what I couldn't find out in the States, opened itself up to me once I suspected who you were. It wasn't hard to put together this puzzle!" Raul grabbed his chest and Saúl stepped back, sick to his stomach, feeling that he had been punched, slapped and kicked. He handed Solimar their child and went to the porch for air to find Marisol openly crying her heart out and Robertito crying loudly. He walked right past her and fell into Roberto's arms. They said nothing. Roberto gently wiped his friend's tears and urged him to go back inside and not leave Solimar alone. Saúl attempted to compose himself to no avail. Solimar was relentless, unstoppable and the rage in her filled the room.

"Raulin, since I am taking your children with me, I suggest you immediately put up this house for sale and the proceeds of the sale wired directly to my husband. Again, I will be overseeing. Liquidate whatever assets you have and, that too, is to go to Saúl for management. Believe and trust that the monies will be equally divided among five, now that you have a grandchild, and will be used wisely. None of your children, including me, will want for nothing. My brother and sister, my brother and husband, my child and nephew shall only want what they cannot obtain on their own, and I will never again eat from a stranger's table." Esmeralda foolishly interrupted Soli's tirade. "But where will we live?" Soli, without missing a beat flatly stated "Fortunately for you, you're too old to live in foster care homes like I had to.

Once you settle into a moderate two bedroom flat, I will be more than generous to make certain that you receive a monthly stipend to cover all of your expenses, within reason of course, and a little extra so that you can drink yourself into oblivion and hopefully die a peaceful death. Same goes for you Santa Esmer-fucking-alda." Saúl stood at the doorway, shocked and appalled, but mostly in awe at this demon from hell that stood there holding his son. "Solimar!" As if on queue, Soli calmly walked over to him and handed over their son. "Saúl. Hold your son, respect your older sister, and don't speak while I'm conducting business, please." Saúl took the baby in his arms, but screamed at her, anger raging within him, wanting to defuse this horrific situation. "But Soli *no mas*... let it go already, *basta!*"

"But my ass. Saúl, did you forget that it was you that advised me to claim my inheritance?" My inheritance is not money, maybe in this Santana household it constitutes *dinero*, but not in mine. Now, with your permission, allow me to finish this transaction and we can talk privately if you need further explanation at home, and give me back my son, you're obviously in no condition to hold him right now." Saúl handed Solimar their son, visibly nervous, but knowing that he had better. No one dared enter the house; they knew that the storm that was brewing outside was a sun shower compared to the Tsunami that raged inside.

Omar and Soledad, having clung to one another upstairs while Solimar ripped into their parents, sobbed quietly. Omar, very tenderly wiped his sister's tears. "Soledad, you have to believe that you and I are legitimate siblings, after all we are twins and I will take care of you. Not like Saúl and Solimar take care of each other, but I got your back just the same, sis. Let's just get away from these two miserable fucks that have made our lives hell and kept us prisoners for the past thirty three years." Soledad, wanting to trust her brother asked "Do you think we can trust Solimar? She seems a bit unstable, don't you think?" Omar did not miss a beat. He hugged his sister and whispered into her ear "Listen, she told the truth and anyone that does that can be trusted, whether we like the truth or not. She is more stable than our parents are that's for sure." Soledad said "C'mon then. *Vamonos.* I'm tired of Mami's ridiculous expectations and Papi bowing down to her every whim. They make me sick and now I know why." They descended the stairs, each hauling two small suitcases. They hurriedly said their goodbyes, promising their parents to come visit soon. Esmeralda tried one last time to take control of the situation and calm down who clearly was her nemesis. "Mrs. Santana, I mean, Solimar, may I offer you something before you go, we have gifts for our grandson." Solimar wickedly smiled and said "I have everything I came for, but thank you anyway, but just so you are clear, Mrs. Santana was my mother's name. **Yo me llamo Solimar Soledad Santana de Santana.**"

Roberto closed his eyes and said "Oh shit, Mari, here comes *la bomba.*" Marisol went pale and said "I had once asked her what it stood for and she said it stood for shit. Fuck! That's her sister's name!"

Soledad and Saúl looked incredulously at each other and then at Solimar. Solimar had finally revealed the secret 'S'. "And just to clarify it for you, your husband, my biological father, was so pathetic that he even named all of your children after me, but also after his real wife, my mother." Solimar who was now riding the crest of the wave started playing the name game. "Solimar ... Omar! Soledad, my middle name is Soledad after my mother whose actual name was Soledad Celestina, but everybody only knew her as "Titina," follow? You want me to draw you a diagram? Your son Saúl, named after your 'husband' Raul, but for some reason could not forget the bloody 'S', but you Esmeralda must have been so happy to take him from my mother and destroy a marriage, that you never even questioned him what was my true name; never bothered to care that you were leaving behind a little girl named "Solitita." You could care less, but frankly, if I had been in your shoes, my kids would have far different names." Solimar turned to leave and Raul ran to her. He placed his hand on her shoulder and dropping her shoulder she immediately said "*No me toques.* When God fills my heart with forgiveness, I might forgive you, but that day surely ain't today."

"Solimar, I need my children, my only grandchild!"

"And I needed you, but you were too busy. Now I will be busy multiplying my inheritance. And by the way, your marriage is not valid old man, if you even married that old bitch at all. You served my mother with divorce papers and then took off to Puerto Rico, but the divorce was never finalized because you never followed through and my mom never signed them. I looked it up in the County Clerk's office after your legitimate wife died. You played your cards all wrong. Who would have "thunk it" that I'd be your son's wife and a paralegal that stayed on your ass behind the scenes throughout the years. So, in the end who are the real *bastardos* here? Not me, I was born within the scope of a legitimate marriage! You destroy everything you touch, and if you want to put this into litigation, you can start right now; my lawyer is outside ready to serve you with divorce papers based on abandonment. Obviously, Solimar was posturing as Raul was now legally a widower and Roberto had drawn up no such document, but she continued to threaten him profusely stating that she could make a case against him for bigamy. Saúl, now somewhat composed and ever the diplomat said "Look people, all of this can be resolved. Let cooler heads prevail and we will call you when we settle back home. Nobody is going to sue, nobody is going to fight anymore, but I do agree with my sister who just so happens to be my wife and who comes first. When you get a call from Roberto Robles, answer it. He is our attorney and my partner and he will figure out a way to set up the trust funds and all that stuff, okay?" Raulin was desperate. "Saúl, *hijo*, do something, this makes no sense." Saúl coldly responded "Papi, I just told you everything that is going to be done. I will spend my life making restitution for your mistake and that is fine by me because I adore and worship the ground my wife, your first-born daughter, walks on, unlike you that left her to die in New York City when she was but a toddler." He put his arms around Solimar's shoulders, their child joining Robertito's cries. Addressing his mother he said "Mami, I love you, but you disgust me totally and the two of you kept all of this hidden from the three of us; the fact that we had a sister out there somewhere that we could have met way before I met her and unknowingly fell in love. You kept from us the fact that your marriage is not valid. Of course, nobody would have suspected that you were criminals on the run; you both even changed your names! You raised us to live a lie and there is no reversing that. Raulin, I suggest you have a drink and a cigar and carefully listen to Solimar's demands because I am completely behind her, and if it is true that you are not legally divorced from Soli's mother and that you aided Esmeralda, who killed a man, I don't care under what circumstances, I may have to have you both extradited from this country and return you to where you began. As a diplomat of the U.S. embassy and an attorney, I am also an officer of the Courts and I may just have to research your position if you keep pushing us, or take it further if you don't comply with our demands. What you both have done, I believe, is a crime, but even if it can no longer be classified as one, it is despicable, immoral and I can't begin to believe that the three of us were born to and raised by human garbage that lived with no conscience and less remorse. Now, have I made myself clear?" Raul and Esmeralda slowly nodded, but Solimar still had to have the last word. "But you know Raulin, I'm going to cut you a sweet deal here. I'm going to allow you to try and see if you can bless me." Solimar lowered her head. Raul made the sign of the cross over her and told them all to go with God. She smiled and said "Your blessing didn't work. You, of all people, can't penetrate through this white scarf on my head, but yes God did this and he's coming with us and that is all that counts. Don't worry Papi Chulo, I will take care of the family. I learned that important lesson from my mom." Raul tried one last plea. "Solimar *perdoname*, please do not take out your anger at me out on my children." Saúl instinctively reached for his son, knowing that his father had foolishly rekindled the fire that consumed Solimar after the embers were about to be extinguished. Solimar surprised Saúl with her somewhat gentle response. "At another time Raul, I would have spit you, slapped you, and beaten you to a pulp with my own hands, but today I see what a cynic you are and by the look on my husband's face and your children's faces, which still seems to exclude me, they can tell as well. Rest assured that the two of you will never set foot in our homes, nor will I ever again set foot in yours, but your children are just as innocent as this newborn child and they are free to come and go, free to feel whatever they want to feel with no influence from me. In the event that you haven't noticed, your children are adults that can reach their own conclusions, but they will have facts, full-facts, not lies upon which to build them. I only came by to claim my long over due inheritance, but even if I would have walked out that door without one red cent... I leave richly blessed."

Soledad took the baby from Saúl and Solimar gratefully said "Thank you Solitita." With that they walked out the door, leaving the remorse-filled "Santanas" to their miserable existence in their shattered glass house. When they reached the porch, Omar asked; "Hey Soli who are these guys?" as he started playing with little Robertito who smiled at meeting his new uncle Omar. Saúl simply replied "They are family, and there are four more where they came from... plus a turtle." Soledad looked a Saúl. "A turtle, really?" Solimar wrapped her arm around her sister's neck tightly and kissed her cheek. "It's a long story, but we have time..." They all got into the limo and drove off leaving the storm behind them as it was not raining in the humble town of Rio Abajo. The sun was brilliantly shining, waiting to warmly embrace them, all but two or three kilometers away.

The demons that were left waiting to prove their ability to successfully torment and ultimately destroy the Santanas and the Robleses lingered behind...impatiently awaiting approval to continue their mission. Confirmation appeared shortly. Prior to their demise, they were informed that their mission had been aborted. The modified mission had been reassigned to a principality that would assume full responsibility for the soulless souls that walked within the cold mansion walls located in a breathtakingly beautiful, yet tranquil town known as Cerra Azul.

Author's Note: The story you have read is fictitious in nature, yet a compilation of true life happenings to women, men, children and humanity in general. If you are a victim of incest, abandonment, betrayal and the like, there is help to be obtained. Spiritual void usually follows the defilement of a human being. The first step is to identify what is causing your emotional pain. My greatest source of unloading my fears, doubts and concerns is of course, my hand-picked friends, certain family members and the depth of my faith in the Supreme Being. Others find solace and acceptance through therapy; others still yet lose themselves in the creator of their minds. Churches of all denominations are a safe haven, both for spiritual and emotional counseling. For those that abuse alcohol or drugs, the danger of addiction lies as a trap just waiting to maim you. Alcoholics Anonymous is a world-wide organization easily accessed, as is Celebrate Recovery found in many evangelical churches, and both sources can be accessed electronically on the internet. Our hurts are irreversible, but not insurmountable; the healing process begins with finding yourself and then finding God, whatever name you should call him. Divine Providence is at our disposal. His Angels and Saints are real, as is everything that oppresses us although we cannot see into the spiritual realm with the human eye. Trust in yourself and above all, trust that no matter what mistake, mishap or tragedy has happened, you are Divinely Made.

Ana Eli Yansa was inspired to share these stories by the biographical novels written by C.J. Cassidy

Glossary

Adiós	Good-bye
Adiós amiga, hasta mañana	Good-bye my friend, until tomorrow
Adobo	Seasoning
Agua	Water
Alcohólico	Alcoholic
Amigo(a)	Friend
Añejo	Aged rum
Animales	Animals
Arepas	Flat bread made of corn meal or flour
Basta	Enough
Basta ya carajo	Hell, enough already
Bastardos	Bastards
Bendición	Blessing; customarily asked of elders
Bery mucho	Slang (spanish accent) very much
Besito	Small kiss, beso being a kiss
Bienvenidos a Panamá	Welcome to Panama
Bobos	Pacifiers
Bochinche	Gossip
Boricua	Puerto Rican
Botanica	Spiritual shop
Brinca	Jump
Bruja(s)	Witch(es)

Brujita Boricua	Puerto Rican Witch
Buena gente	Good people
Bueno	Well
Cabeza	Head
Cabron	A man that accepts a woman's infidelity
Café	Coffee
Café con Anis	Coffee with Anisette
Cálmate	Calm down
Caminando	Walking (on our way)
Cariño	Affection; term of endearment as in dear or beloved
Casita	Little house
Chinelas	Slippers
Chiquitas	Little ones
Chucha madre	Motherfucker
Cocina	Kitchen
Como	What
Como se dice	How do you say
Compadre	Comrade, Godfather
Comprendes	Understand
Con mucho gusto, es un placer	With much pleasure
Con tu permiso	With your permission
Coqui	Coqui (miniature frog indigenous to Puerto Rico)
Cuchifritos	Assortment of fried foods, including blood sausages, etc.
Cuchitril	Bar, pub, watering hole
Culito	Small ass
De nada	For nothing – you're welcome
De veras	For real
Deseas algo más	Do you desire something more
Desgraciado	Unfortunate wretch
Dinero	Money

Glossary

Diplomático	Diplomat
Discoteca	Discotheque, Disco
El capitán	The captain
El Espíritu Santo	The Holy Spirit
El grito de las sirenas	The cry of the sirens
El hombre es mi hermano	The man is my brother
El infierno	Hell
El pastor	The pastor
El placer es todo mío	The pleasure is all mine
El show es gratis	The show is free
Embajada	Embassy
En mi corazón	In my heart
Entiendes	Understand
Eres bruja	Are you a witch
Eres tú	Is it you
Es un paraíso	It is a Paradise
Eschucha mi pregon que dice	Listen to my proclamation that states
Escúchame bien	Listen to me carefully
Esposo(a)	Husband, Wife
Esta bien	It is fine
Estas loca	Are you crazy (feminine)
Estas loco o que	Are you crazy or what (masculine)
Este tipo	This dude
Estúpido(a)	Stupid
Estúpido(a) de mierda	Stupid piece of shit
Familia	Family
Fresca	Fresh; fresh face
Fuera	Out
Gracias	Thank you
Gracias Dios mío	Thank you my God
Gringa(o)	A female/male foreigner, especially from United States

Guaguita	mini van
Guajiro	Countryman of Cuba
Guerra	War
Guerreros	Warriors
Hermanito(a)	Little brother, Little sister
Hermano(a)	Brother, sister
Hija(o) de puta	Son of a whore, Daughter of a whore
Hijo(a)	Son, daughter
Hola	Hello
Hombre	Man
Hoy	Today
Ibeyis	Twins
Idiota	Idiot
Jabón de azufre	Sulfur soap
Jibaro	Countryman of Puerto Rico
Jicotea	Turtle
La bomba	The bomb
La dama	The dame
La gente	The people
La Iglesia de Piedras	The Stone Church
La isla	The island
La leche	The milk
La playa	The beach
La Santísima Virgen María	The Most Holiest Virgen Mary
La vida	The life
Levántate	Get up
Licenciado	Attorney
Linda	Pretty
Llámala	Call her
Loco(a)	Crazy, masculine and feminine
Machista	male chauvinist
Madrina	Godmother, Maid of Honor
Malta	Dark beer, non-alcoholic

Mano a mano	Man to man; hand to hand
Maricona	Lesbian
Me entiendes	Do you understand me
Me explico	Do I explain myself
Me explico claramente	Do I make myself clear
Me muero	I die
Mi amor	My love
Mi casa es tu casa	My home is your home
Mi cielo, mi fucking puta vida	My sky, my fucking bitch of a life (ahem, term of endearment)
Mi sirena malcriada	My spoiled mermaid
Mía	Mine
Mierda	Shit
Mi cojones	My balls
Mijo(a)	Composite of My son or My daughter
Mil gracias	A thousand thanks
Mira	Look
Mírame	Look at me
Morcilla	Blood sausage
Mosquitero	Mosquito net; draping bed canopy
Mujer	Woman
Muñeca	Doll
Nada	Nothing
Negra(o)(ita)(ito)	Term of endearment used freely despite skin color or ethnicity
Nena(e)	Girl, boy
Ni cojones	No balls
Ni una palabra	Not one Word
No empiezes conmigo	Don't start with me
No me metas en esto	Do not involve me in this
No puedo	I can't
No puedo más	I can't any longer

No se lo que esta pasando	I don't know what is happening
No se	Don't know
No te apures	Don't worry
No te vayas	Don't go
Novela(s)	Novel, soap operas
Nuestro hijo es color canela	Our son is the color of cinnamon
Ñeca	Short versión of Muñeca – Doll
Oye Chica	Listen girl
Oye mira	Listen, look
Padrino	Godfather, Best Man
Para que lo sepas	Just so you know
Pasteles	Puerto Rican food specialty
Patatun	Slang for heart attack, nervous breakdown
Payaso	Clown
Pecas	Freckles
Perdón	Excuse me
Perdóname	Forgive me
Pero	But
Pero no, gracias	But no, thank you
Pero que bella	But how beautiful
Pero tengo una idea	But I have an idea
Pesos	Dollars
Plancha	Iron
platanos, yucca	plantains, cassava
Pobre	Poor
Policía	Police
Pon una botella del Duque	Bring a bottle of Duque de Alba
Por Dios	For God's sake
Por favor	Please
Porque no	Why not
Preciosa	Precious

Glossary

Primo(a)	Male cousin/female cousin
Princesa	Princess
Príncipe Azul	Prince Charming
Puede ser	Could be
Pues	Well
Pura mierda	Pure shit
Puta	Whore (ahem, another term of endearment)
Puta es tu madre you fucking maricon	Whore is your mother, you fucking faggot
Que	What
Que Dios te Bendiga	May God bless you
Que es	What is it
Que es mi Bella	What is it beautiful
Que más quieres	What more do you want
Que pasa mi vida	What is wrong, my life
Que paso	What happened
Que sera	What will be
Que sorpresa	What a surprise
Que te pasa	What is wrong with you
Querido(a)	Beloved, masculine, feminine
Quieres	You want
Ratonera	Rat trap, hole in the wall
Reina	Queen
Salud	Cheers
Santa Ana	Saint Anne
Santa María Madre de Dios	Holy Mary Mother of God
Señor(a)	Mr. Mrs.
Si	Yes
Si por las moscas	Precautionary adage: "in event that the flies show up"
Sirenas	Sirens, mermaids
Siete meses	Seven months
Sinceramente no puedo	Sincerely, I can't

Sirena(ita)	Mermaid
Te amo	I love you
Te quiero mucho	I love you alot
Tranquilo(a)	Be tranquil
Trato hecho	Done deal
Tremenda borrachera	tremendous drunkenness
Tu eres inocente	You are innocent
Tu estas loca(o) o que	Are you crazy or what (feminine, masculine)
Tuya	Yours
un banquete	a banquet
Un bebe	A baby
Un cafecito	A coffee
Un minutito	A minute (second)
Un poquito loca	A Little crazy (feminine)
Un problema	A problema
Una blanca sucia	Dirty white
Vale	Okay
Vámonos	Let's go
Vamos	Let's go
Vamos a ver	Let's see
Ven	Come
Vino tinto	Red wine
Y ahí estamos	And here we are
Y que	And what
Yo estoy aquí	I am here
Yo me llamo	My name is
Yo me voy	I am going
Yo no se	I don't know
Yo soy la ama de llaves	I am the housekeeper
Yo tengo vergüenza	I have shame
Yo vivo en	I live in

www.ingramcontent.com/pod-product-compliance
Lightning Source LLC
Chambersburg PA
CBHW032034150426
43194CB00006B/272